The October Revolution

Отъ Военно-Революціоннаго Комитета при Петроградскомъ Совѣтѣ Рабочихъ и Солдатскихъ Депутатовъ.

Къ Гражданамъ Россіи.

Временное Правительство низложено. Государственная власть перешла въ руки органа Петроградскаго Совѣта Рабочихъ и Солдатскихъ Депутатовъ Военно-Революціоннаго Комитета, стоящаго во главѣ Петроградскаго пролетаріата и гарнизона.

Дѣло, за которое боролся народъ: немедленное предложеніе демократическаго мира, отмѣна помѣщичьей собственности на землю, рабочій контроль надъ производствомъ, созданіе Совѣтскаго Правительства — это дѣло обезпечено.

ДА ЗДРАВСТВУЕТЪ РЕВОЛЮЦІЯ РАБОЧИХЪ, СОЛДАТЪ И КРЕСТЬЯНЪ!

Военно-Революціонный Комитетъ
при Петроградскомъ Совѣтѣ
Рабочихъ и Солдатскихъ Депутатовъ.

25 октября 1917 г. 10 ч. утра.

Proclamation of October 25, 1917, announcing that power has passed from the Provisional Government into the hands of the Military Revolutionary Committee of the Petrograd Soviet, whose aims are democratic peace, abolition of landlord property rights, workers' control over production, and creation of a Soviet government.

THE OCTOBER REVOLUTION

Roy A. Medvedev

Translated by George Saunders
Foreword by Harrison E. Salisbury

New York   Columbia University Press   1979

Library of Congress Cataloging in Publication Data

Medvedev, Roï Aleksandrovich.
  The October Revolution.

  Includes bibliographical references.
  I. Russia—History—Revolution, 1917–1921.
I. Title.
DK265.M375   947.084   79–9854
ISBN 0–231–04590–5

Columbia University Press
New York   Guildford, Surrey

Contents

CONTENTS

PART FOUR. The Difficult Spring of 1918

Photos appear as a group following page 136

Foreword

Harrison E. Salisbury

Nearly six decades have passed since the death of Vladimir Ilyich Lenin and a year does not pass without new efforts to evaluate, to comprehend, and to generalize his great creation, the Bolshevik Revolution.

I do not use the term "creation" accidentally. And I deliberately distinguish between the Bolshevik Revolution—which aprang from his broad brow and nervous mind as surely as Minerva sprang from that of Jupiter—and that tidal movement of the *narod,* the black people, the peasants, the frozen and starving women, the deserting soldiers which we know as the February Revolution.

The February Revolution was Russia's; the Bolshevik or October Revolution was Lenin's.

The two events, taken together (they are, of course, inseparable), constitute in the opinion of Roy Medvedev the biggest event of the twentieth century, a judgment with which it was difficult to disagree until the 1940s—the time of nuclear breakthrough, China's Revolution, and the flowering of a kind of capitalist-socialism or socialist-capitalism not anticipated by Karl Marx (in fact, it seems to constitute a synthesis between nineteenth-century industrialism against which he inveighed and twentieth-century "communism" which he hardly envisaged).

Whatever the case, Medvedev's effort to come to grips with the reality of Leninism, the February and October Revolutions, and the hybrid society which has emerged in Lenin's wake represents a breakthrough not so much in terms of western thought, where many of his ideas are familiar, but in terms of *Russian* thought. Regardless of his dissenting and divergent views Medvedev is and remains a Soviet citizen, living in his homeland and dedicated, as he has been throughout his life, to the pure and idealistic social model which he believes could have been created in Russia.

We can argue as we wish over Medvedev's concept of a Leninism fatefully distorted by his successors, Stalin in particular, but we cannot fail to applaud the vigor and insight he brings to his examination of the Russian Revolution more than 60 years after the event. This is a task particularly difficult for a citizen of the Soviet Union, exposed as he has been to generations of myth and the lacquering over of the reality of 1917 (and post-1917); his extraordinary difficulty in gaining access to source materials; the warping of perceptions by decades of falsification—which influences even an independent mind like Medvedev's (as for example in his suggestion that the July uprising of 1917 was "spontaneous"); his acceptance of the notion that the peasants obtained their long-awaited land thanks to the Bolsheviks (actually they took it on their own); and his presentation of Lenin as an enemy of terror at the moment he was creating the Cheka and raging against abolition of the death penalty.

But no matter. None of this should obscure our view of the role Medvedev is playing in illuminating *from within Russia* the true nature of the Revolution; of beginning the extraordinary task of blasting away the plaster images, the craven idols, the boilerplate which has for so long been substituted within the Soviet Union for the blood and toil, the error and chaos of the Revolution; the heroism and the horror; the planned and the accidental—and, above all, the dominating role of the people themselves, taking history into their hands without leadership, without design, without even knowing the word Revolution and destroying in a few days the intolerable autocracy which had reigned for 300 years.

Medvedev may be the only person in Russia today who is capable of this kind of broad-focus examination of the Revolution, even though there is now growing up a generation of young and not-so-young Soviet historians, social scientists, and students competent to tackle revisionist history.

Indeed, some have actually begun this endeavor, chipping away in small areas, in quiet byways, examining with scientific skill individual patches of the pre-history of 1917 and even daring to assault segments of the main theme; cutting down to size, for example, the role of the so-called Red Guards in Petrograd; illuminating the total weakness of the Bolsheviks in February 1917, their lack of either Party cells or Party program, their remoteness from the reality of the Petrograd streets and conditions in the workshops, their failure to understand that February *was* the Revolution and not merely one more of the wrangles which boiled up and frothed away in wartime Russia.

But none of these brilliant young scholars and social scientists can tackle the Revolution as a whole. This is still *verboten*, still off-limits, reserved for the priests of the Institute of Marxism-Leninism, as loath to touch sacred doctrine as an acolyte would be in the Vatican library. Even to question openly obvious discrepancies in the stereotype into which the events of 1917 have long been cast is to bring a nest of stinging dialectical hornets down upon the head of the unwary scholar.

There is, for example, one enormous, glaring, and obvious hole in the legend of Lenin's spotless leadership of the October coup—the question of when he returned to Petrograd in the weeks just before the plot was hatched (not to mention the even more tricky question of *why* he did not return until two or three weeks before the event). This is a legitimate question of historiography. The records are confused. The witnesses disagree. Lenin had been underground in Finland since the July events. Did he come back in late September, say the 26th or 29th? Or did he return only on October 7 or 8, or 9 or 10? Did he come secretly on his own or did he come at the invitation of his Central Committee colleagues?

It is obvious that these questions bear heavily on the planning and carrying out of the Bolshevik coup on October 25. Yet, 62 years after the event this question has not yet been resolved. In fact from 1930 until the early 1960s—that is, for some 30 years—it could not even be *mentioned* without the danger that the individual who asked the question would lose his academic standing, his party card, or even his head—obvious testimony to the sensitivity of the problem. Now nearly 20 years more have passed since the first scholars and surviving colleagues of Lenin raised the question publicly after Stalin's demise and it is still not resolved despite one stormy meeting of historians and Party theorists after the other.

This issue may seem to the unwitting a trivial matter akin to an argument over the number of angels which might dance on the head of a pin. But the attitude of the historiographers tells us that it is not trivial even if we did not ourselves perceive why Lenin's presence or absence in Petrograd bears so heavily on a host of related issues: the depth of the split in tactics between himself and many of his colleagues (who did not believe a coup was warranted); the respective roles of these colleagues (for example, suspicion strongly hints that Stalin, for one, was opposed to Lenin's plans and that it was he who imposed the total ban on discussion of the question); the falsity of the legend that the coup was both inevitable and planned with military skill and timing (it was not—the chaos and muddling were beyond belief); and even the penultimate question of whether previous to the moment of Lenin's arrival at Smolny Institute on the evening of October 24 the Bolsheviks actually were planning to carry out a coup at all rather than simply to protect themselves against a countercoup by Kerensky.

These, it can quickly be seen, are no minor questions. They are, to be certain, practical historical matters that should be resolvable by examination of the records of Party meetings, discussions, orders, instructions, plans, etc. They are matters which were known in part or in the whole to many individuals. They were discussed with no great heat in the early years of the Bolshevik regime when Lenin was alive and briefly after his death in 1924. Then the iron hand of Stalin came down. Stalin's hand did not move lightly. If it came down it came down for a reason. With that action by Stalin the myth which had been born in the dramatic October days quickly was turned into a cardboard legend, the cardboard legend which it has remained ever since.

This is the kind of papier-mâché dogma against which Soviet historians struggle today and no member of the academic community in good standing can move too far or push too hard without risking political reprisal. Not until the ruling oligarchy is willing to decree a change in the legend or open the whole subject to honest scientific inquiry will it be either safe or possible to fully illuminate the question.

It is true that in the permissive atmosphere of Khrushchev's 20th and 22nd Party conferences some old-Bolshevik survivors were able to raise questions as to where Lenin was and when he came to Petrograd and when he went to Smolny. Some of them were actually witnesses and participants in the events. But this did not get very far. There have been at least four important "scientific" conferences of historians to discuss these questions but they have not been resolved, and important "establishment" historians and academicians like I. I. Mints and V. V. Startsev have taken their stand firmly on the line upheld through the long Stalin years that Lenin came back to Petrograd only about October 9 and only at the call of his comrades and not by any means secretly and much earlier and in opposition to their views.

This, it should be said at once, is not a question which is illuminated by Medvedev. The sources are no more available to him than they are to anyone else. Without intimate access to the still sealed records of the Institute of Marxism-Leninism and the other storehouses of revolutionary memorabilia in Russia the truth cannot be determined.

But Medvedev, operating outside the establishment as a dissident, can address himself fully to what is, in fact, a more important basic question: would the October Revolution have occurred without Lenin? His answer is a resounding NO! He quotes with approval the unquestionably accurate assessment of Nikolai Sukhanov, the supreme diarist of the Revolution, that the main role in 1917 was Lenin's.

"To be left without Lenin," Sukhanov wrote, "would that be the same as tearing the heart out of the organism or cutting off the head? . . . In the party next to Lenin, there was no one . . . without Lenin [it] amounted to nothing, as would several huge planets without the sun."

And Medvedev repeats the question asked by N. V. Valentinov, an associate of Lenin's early days in exile: would October have happened if Lenin had drowned (as he nearly did) when ice gave way under him as he was illegally crossing the Gulf of Bothnia on December 15, 1907? Medvedev's answer is that the fate of the revolution might well have come out differently, for "the fate of the October revolution was not inevitable although it was not accidental either."

It is not unimportant to emphasize here the philosophical viewpoint which Medvedev brings to the Revolution and Lenin's role. He and his brother Zhores are a unique pair and they have made a unique contribution to our understanding of the Soviet system, Roy, the historian, still living somehow in Moscow, and Zhores, the biologist, living in exile in England. Despite their separation the twin brothers work in an extraordinary kind of collaboration and it is not possible to imagine one without the other. They are a genuinely remarkable pair, artifacts themselves of the Revolution, sons of what is now called in Moscow a "romantic" revolutionary father—that is, a father who really believed in the idealism and sacrifice of the Leninist period. The two men carry in their names evidence of this romanticism. Roy's name should properly be transliterated *roi*, the imperative form of the Russian verb "to dig," and Zhores was originally called *reis*, a word meaning "trip" or "route," both words favorites in the early vocabulary of the Revolution. Such made-up names were given to hundreds of thousands of children in the dawn of the Red era in protest against the saint names of Ivan and Igor and Vladimir and the others in the calendar of the Russian Orthodox church. No priest, of course, would baptize a Russian baby with the name of Roi or Reis. If you visit the Novodevichy or Vvedenie cemeteries in Moscow you will see names on many graves, evidence of this romantic tendency, and instead of crosses the headstones may be great gears, airplane propellers, hammers-and-sickles.

The "romantic" names of the Medvedev brothers are not their only survivals from the revolutionary era. Roy describes himself as a "socialist" in the pure Marxist sense—Marx as interpreted by Lenin. In an age in which belief in and knowledge of Lenin's genuine philosophy has almost disappeared under the lavish distortions of Stalin, the pragmatic necessities of a geriatric bureaucracy, the polemics of anti-Leninists, anti-Stalinists, anti-Russianists and pro-Maoists Roy Medvedev sometimes seems—although he profoundly disagrees with this—a true believer and keeper of the Leninist shrine. It is hardly too much to say that Medvedev genuinely believes that the ills of Russia and of the Soviet Union, to say nothing of those of the world, can be traced in almost a direct line to the movement in the Soviet away from the founding father's faith and the outer world's continuing failure to understand Lenin's teaching.

This extraordinary dedication to what must be described as Medvedev's own idealization of the early Revolutionary doctrine leads him occasionally to what seems to this writer an overstatement of Lenin's wisdom and underevaluation of Lenin's often shifty tactics. Medvedev is willing to concede the obvious—that Lenin was unable to prophesy the Russian revolution (this is not accepted by the standard Soviet historians) but, he emphasizes, "I continue to believe in the power of Marxism and the abilities of our native historical scholarship"; and he is convinced that only Soviet historians can understand and construct a theory which corresponds to what actually happened in 1917.

It is important to note that a fundamental difference exists between Medvedev and Aleksandr Solzhenitsyn in respect to Lenin and the Revolution. The two men have differed before—how could they not in view of Medvedev's continued belief in Marxism? It is natural that they differ on the key question discussed by Medvedev. Medvedev attacks with great bitterness the portrait of Lenin painted by Solzhenitsyn in his *Lenin in Zurich,* calling it "the weakest, most malicious and most dishonest" of Solzhenitsyn's pen and he challenges Solzhenitsyn's view that it was not Russia which abandoned the Romanovs but the Romanovs who abandoned Russia.

But Medvedev's picture of Lenin and the Bolsheviks on the eve of February is not too convincing nor, in the light of the best contemporary Soviet scholarship, entirely accurate. He contends that only the Bolsheviks in 1916 and early 1917 were able to maintain a widespread underground organization in Petrograd, Moscow, and other industrial centers; that Bolshevik prospects were "splendid" in January 1917; that the Bolsheviks "coordinated" the strikes and demonstrations which led to February; and that the uprising did not catch the Bolsheviks by surprise.

Contemporary accounts by the handful of Bolsheviks on the spot and still active in Russia contradict this rosy panorama. They had been almost wiped out by the tsar's Okhrana; they had almost no contact with Lenin; they were too weak to mount a leafleted demonstration in early February; Lenin did not even know for several days that the February uprising had started; the three or four low-level Bolsheviks still active in Petrograd had no idea of what to do, outside of issuing leaflets, and did not even have the wit to take a hand in the organization of the Soviet.

Far more important than Medvedev's treatment of Lenin is his careful marshalling of evidence suggesting that the October uprising was considered by many revolutionaries, including a powerful faction of Lenin's Bolsheviks, unnecessary and premature. He quotes Plekhanov's words about the Bolshevik coup:

"It would seem that the peasants are a highly unreliable ally for the workers in organizing the socialist mode of production. . . . Having seized political power prematurely, the Russian proletariat will not carry out a social revolution but will only provoke a civil war which will ultimately force it to retreat far back from the positions which were won in February and March of this year."

Medvedev calls these words "too dogmatic and unconvincing"; others might find them remarkably far-sighted and accurate.

The most original and effective contribution which Medvedev makes here is his analysis of the postrevolutionary situation and, specifically, the heavy-handed and provocative methods employed by the Bolsheviks to cope with the food crisis and agriculture. He has traced with great clarity Lenin's land policy to its origins (conceded by Lenin himself) in the program of the Socialist Revolutionary (SR) Party and he reveals the terrifying weakness of the Bolsheviks in the countryside—only 203 rural party cells with a total of 4,122 members in a country in which 80 or 90 percent of the population was still concentrated in the villages. In many areas of Russia, including much of the Don region and the grain-producing provinces of Siberia, the peasants had never even heard of the Bolsheviks.

Faced as he was by starving cities and collapsed industry, the armed forces (almost entirely peasant in origin) simply melted by desertion, Lenin formed a "Food Army" and sent armed detachments of workers into the countryside to seize food and supplies. The result of this and of the formation of "poor peasants" committees in the villages produced civil war. The peasants rose all over Russia, sometimes with the instigation of enemies of the Bolsheviks, the SR and Menshevik parties, the Czech legionaires, the White generals, but more often simply on their own. Medvedev correctly puts the blame for this on Lenin and the Bolsheviks.

"The Bolsheviks," he concludes, "went too far and tried to solve tasks for which neither the objective nor the subjective conditions existed. The consequences were painful for our country—especially the resumption of civil war and the end of the 'peaceful breathing spell.' "

Medvedev concludes that much of Lenin's success in October was owing to his willingness to co-opt the SR land program. His failure in Spring 1918 was due to his inability to understand that if the peasants were to supply food to the cities they must have freedom to buy and to sell, to trade.

He attributes the major Bolshevik problems from 1918 onward to this failure, recognizing that the terribe crises of 1921, the Kronstadt revolt and the rest, stemmed from the Party's lack of comprehension of the countryside.

There was, Medvedev feels certain, nothing malicious in Bolshevik policy. It came not from antipathy to the peasants as a class but simply to a lack of understanding which prevented the Bolsheviks from arriving "at the more correct solution to the economic problems of the postrevolutionary period."

He is quick to defend this failure, saying, in essence, that mistakes are human and that the only fault which can be attributed is failure to learn from mistakes. He cites Lenin's justification for the New Economic Policy of 1921 as an example of his ability to analyze failure and draw the appropriate conclusions.

Unfortunately, as he recognizes, this is not a quality which necessarily is in abundant supply today, particularly in attempting to analyze the cause of "all the political and economic crises" of Russia during the past 50 years. All of these, without exception: the crisis of 1928–32 connected with collectivization and the five-year-plans for industrialization, the severe agricultural crises of 1953–54 and of 1963–64, as well as what he calls "certain recent indications" of crisis, he attributes to errors of agricultural policy—errors of precisely the type which were made in the first months of Lenin's Revolution. What Medvedev suggests is that after 60 years Lenin's heirs have not yet learned that first difficult lesson which Lenin himself found so hard to absorb—that the foundation for prosperity and plenty in a magnificent agricultural state such as the Soviet Union must be laid in the farmlands, in the peasant households, in abundant production and imaginative incentives and techniques; and that without this no amount of industrialization can really succeed since a continental state which is unable to feed itself must remain an economic-political-sociological anomaly.

To the western reader there may be as much to question as to accept in Medvedev's study, but never mind. It is a start. It is an outline for a reexamination of the Revolution, the first of a comprehensive and serious nature to come from inside Soviet Russia in many decades. If Medvedev is right, it will not be the last.

Preface

The bourgeois-democratic revolution of February 1917 and the October socialist revolution differed fundamentally in respect both to the historical forces that produced them and to their results. However, in the retrospective consciousness of humanity these revolutions are most often perceived as two stages in a single revolutionary explosion, which in Russia was the hallmark of the year 1917. It is not surprising that almost every historical study dealing with October begins with an account of the events of February, if not of the events preceding the first world war.

Historians, politicians, and public figures of all shades of opinion have differed in their attitudes toward the events of 1917. Despite all the diversity of appraisals and theories, however, it is generally recognized, even by the most outspoken anti-Communists, that the Russian revolution of 1917 was the most important event of the twentieth century. For example, the American professor James H. Billington wrote in 1966:

> If a central problem for any nineteenth-century thinker was that of defining his attitude toward the French Revolution, a central one for contemporary man is his appraisal of the Russian Revolution. The latter problem is even more critical, for nearly one billion people explicitly claim to be heirs and defenders of the Russian Revolution. Forces called into being by the upheaval of 1917 are even more forcefully mobilized and tangibly powerful than those called into being by the French Revolution of 1789 and the "age of democratic revolution." [1]

This undoubtedly explains why there has been no decline in the interest shown in everything that happened in Russia in that year seemingly so remote from our times; on the contrary, there continues to be a vast amount of literature treating the most varied aspects of those revolutionary events.

History as a social science deals not only with events of various kinds but also with theories based on them. And we would probably not be guilty of exaggeration if we said that no other major event of the past has produced such a great variety of theories as the Russian revolution.

The process of gradual accumulation of factual information and reconsideration of previously established theories and evaluations is also going on in the USSR, official Soviet historiography included. To be sure, this process follows complex and contradictory paths in the Soviet Union, where shameless and crude falsification of history and the suppression of many extremely important historical facts exist side by side with an agonizing search for the truth. And this search has by no means been unsuccessful, though even the most honest Soviet historian, advancing slowly, must tack and veer cautiously amid artificial obstacles and prohibitions. There continue to be many of these, although they are fewer than before the Twentieth and Twenty-Second congresses of the CPSU. Even in the case of historians who have long refused to follow the "official" line, the influence of pseudo-historical stereotypes inculcated since childhood continues to hold sway, often unnoticed by the historians themselves.

In my book *Let History Judge* I expressed considerable skepticism as to whether Western Sovietologists were capable of clarifying many of the difficult problems of Soviet history. I see now that I was wrong; there are quite a few historians in the West who are sincerely seeking the truth and who have made significant contributions to that worthy effort. Nevertheless, I am as confident as before that only Soviet historians can carry out the main work of putting together a picture and constructing a theory that will correspond most closely to the truth of what happened in 1917. I continue to believe in the power of Marxism and the abilities of our native historical scholarship.

It should be noted that any author who writes today about the problems of 1917 and 1918 is by no means obliged to focus primarily on the gathering of previously unknown facts bit by bit. On the contrary, an author almost immediately begins to drown in the vast sea of what is known. Virtually every surviving participant in the revolution and civil war left memoirs behind, and extensive collections of the documents of all the political parties have been, and continue to be, published. Therefore, the difficulty lies not in tracking down the necessary facts or describing the events, but in properly selecting and evaluating the most significant ones to substantiate the view being advanced. That observation also applies, of course, to this book.

At one time Marx wrote:

> Bourgeois revolutions, like those of the eighteenth century, storm swiftly from success to success; their dramatic effects outdo each other; men and things seem set in sparkling brilliants; ecstasy is the everyday spirit; but they are short-lived; soon they have attained their zenith, and a long crapulent depression lays hold of society before it learns soberly to assimilate the results of its storm-and-stress period. On the other hand, proletarian revolutions . . . criticize themselves constantly, interrupt themselves continually in their own course, come back to the apparently accomplished in order to begin it afresh, deride with unmerciful thoroughness the inadequacies, weaknesses, and paltrinesses of their first attempts, seem to throw down their adversary only in order that he may draw new strength from the earth and rise again, more gigantic before them, recoil ever and anon from the indefinite prodigiousness of their own aims, until a situation has been created which makes all turning back impossible, and the conditions themselves cry out:
>
> *Hic Rhodus, hic salta!*
> *Here is the rose, here dance!* [2]

To those who know how lacking in self-criticism the first proletarian revolutions of the twentieth century have actually been, Marx's words might seem quite naive. But I am convinced they contain an important element of truth. For only by stopping and looking back critically over the path we have traveled, without being afraid to condemn forthrightly our own oversights, mistakes, even crimes, can we Marxist revolutionaries achieve success both in our practical and our theoretical aims. It was in the spirit of these words of Marx's that I undertook the present study of some of the key problems of the 1917 revolution in Russia.

ROY A. MEDVEDEV
April 1977

Translator's Notes

ON TRANSLITERATION. In the author's notes I have followed the Library of Congress system of transliteration for most Russian-language bibliographical information. Russian names in the text are transliterated by the same system with some modifications for readability, or in deference to the more familiar spellings of some of these names in English (e.g., Krupskaya and Mayakovsky rather than Krupskaia and Maiakovskii). Names that appear in both the text and notes are transliterated in the more readable or familiar form.

ON DATES. Dates of events in Russia before February 1918 are given according to the Russian calendar of that time (thirteen days behind the Western calendar in 1917). For dates in and after February 1918, when the Soviet government adopted what is now the international calendar, this discrepancy no longer exists.

GLOSSARY. I have provided a glossary which lists many of the personalities, events, and terms that appear in the book.

The October Revolution

PART ONE

Was the October Revolution Inevitable?

one

The Various Points of View: Social Revolution and the Role of the Individual

One of the propositions most frequently repeated by Western historians is that, unlike the February revolution, the October socialist revolution in Russia was not a normal or lawful result of the social, economic, and political processes then going on in our country. Still less do they accept the view that this revolution was a logical consequence of events in the early twentieth century in Europe and the world as a whole. To them, this revolution was the result of an unforeseen convergence of circumstances cleverly seized upon by Lenin and the Bolsheviks. The British Sovietologist David Lane, for example, has written in one of his books, "with the abdication of the Tsar, a political vacuum arose" which was filled by the Bolsheviks, but "the Bolshevik revolution was not an inevitable event in history." [1]

The American historian Robert Daniels argued in one of his articles:

> From any rational contemporary standpoint the Bolshevik Revolution was a desperate gamble, unlikely to succeed and still less likely to hold out. . . . Chance put Lenin in power, and chance kept him there during the dizzying days that followed. . . . It was a series of such unpredictable events that diverted Russia from the customary course of modern revolutions and paved the way for the unique phenomenon of twentieth-century Communism.

Daniels also contended that the October revolution won out against all rational expectations only because of "a series of lucky developments that no one could have counted on." "The accession and sur-

vival of the Soviet regime in its early days were little short of a historical miracle." [2]

James Billington in his article "Six Views of the Russian Revolution"
reports that some Western historians continue to view the October revolution as the accidental intervention of destructive elemental forces.
"This outlook is common to all those who see in the Revolution no
deep meaning, but view its outcome with the same sense of bewilder-
ment and helpless outrage one feels at the introjection of a senseless
natural calamity into human affairs." [3]

The American Communist William Z. Foster derided such views as
long ago as 1921. "The Russian revolution," he wrote, "is a standing
miracle to the bourgeois world. . . . [By] all the rules of 'legitimate'
economics it should not have occurred at all." [4]

These arguments are often countered by the diametrically opposed
view that the initiation and triumph of the October revolution were inevitable and inescapable. The former Comintern staff worker Joseph
Berger writes:

> Even if Lenin and the men around him can be said to have "made the
> October Revolution," it is still more true to say that they were made by it.
> I honestly believe that there was a movement which nothing could have
> broken or stopped . . . and it was this movement which brought Lenin
> and his disciples to the fore. I do not wish to minimize the work of prepa-
> ration carried out for decades by the Russian revolutionary movement,
> but the reason why, at a given moment, the Bolsheviks came to power is,
> I believe, because at that moment they had the people behind them. . . .
> Peace, the distribution of the land, government by workers' and peasants'
> soviets—all this, I think, was in accordance with the people's will, and in
> fact the Bolshevik slogans were formulated in response to it. . . . This was
> why the Bolsheviks were able to seize the leadership of the country. [5]

Nor do we find agreement on how to evaluate these problems
among Russian authors of various trends. "What happened?" we hear
so outspoken an opponent of the Russian revolution as Ivan Bunin
exclaim. "The great downfall of Russia happened, and with it the
downfall of humanity in general. This downfall of Russia was not justified in any way. Was the Russian revolution inevitable or not? There
was no inevitability, of course, because in spite of all its shortcomings
Russia was blooming and growing—developing and changing with
fantastic speed in every respect. The revolution, they say, was inevitable because the people longed for land and had hatred in their hearts

for landlords and for all lords and masters in general. But why didn't this supposedly inevitable revolution affect Poland, for example, or Lithuania? Didn't they have landlords, and wasn't there a shortage of land and great inequality in general in those countries? And why didn't Siberia, replete with its antediluvian bonds of serfdom, participate in the revolution? No, there was no inevitability. But the deed was done all the same. And under what banner? It was done in a frightful way, and their banner was and is international, that is, it pretends to be the banner of all nations and to offer to the world, in place of the stone tablets of Moses from Mount Sinai and in place of the Sermon on the Mount, in place of the ancient word of God, something new and diabolic." [6]

An entirely different view was held by the writer and philosopher N. Berdyaev, and he frequently expressed it in his distinctive manner. "It is very important to remember," wrote this prominent Russian writer in his book *The Origin of Russian Communism,*

> that the Russian Communist revolution came to birth in misery, the misery of a destructive war, it was not born out of a creative abundance of strength. Revolution, as a matter of fact, always presupposes misery, always presupposes an intensifying of the darkness of the past. This is the reason for its fateful quality. The new liberal democratic government, which came on the scene after the February revolution, proclaimed abstract humane principles and abstract principles of law in which there was no organizing force, no energy with which to inspire the masses. . . . The position of the Provisional Government was so difficult and hopeless that it is hardly possible to judge it severely and condemn it. Kerensky was a man of revolution, but of its first stage. Moderate people of liberal and humanist principles can never flourish in the elemental sweep of revolution and especially of a revolution brought about by war. The principles of democracy are suitable to times of peace, and not always then, but never to a revolutionary epoch. In the time of revolution people of extreme principles, people who are disposed to dictatorship and capable of it, are those who will triumph. Only dictatorship could put an end to the process of final dissolution and the triumph of chaos and anarchy. . . .
>
> Only Bolshevism could control the situation. It corresponded to the instincts of the masses and their real attitude to things. Russia was threatened by complete anarchy and this was checked by the Communist dictatorship, which found the slogans to which the people agreed to submit. This is the undisputable service of Communism to the Russian state. [7]

The thesis that the October revolution was inevitable was frequently stated by Leon Trotsky as well.

Having themselves arrived in a blind alley, the highly civilized nations block the road to those in the process of civilization. Russia took the road of proletarian revolution, not because her economy was the first to become ripe for a socialist change, but because she could not develop further on a capitalist basis. Socialization of the means of production had become a necessary condition for bringing the country out of barbarism. That is the law of combined development for backward countries.[8]

Of course many present-day Soviet authors also uphold the thesis that the October revolution was unavoidable, although in different terms. For example, V. S. Vasiukov and V. I. Salov contend in their article that because of the disposition of class forces in the country in 1917 "the proletarian revolution was inevitable and foreordained."[9]

What can we say about the arguments we have quoted? We do not think it possible to agree completely with any of them, although each of these authors can cite quite a few striking facts and convincing arguments in defense of his position.

★　★　★

Before considering the question of the inevitability or accidental nature of one revolution or another it is necessary to agree on a definition of the terms *revolution* and *social revolution* themselves. In the social sciences there are virtually no concepts with only one meaning, and most concepts have different meanings in different contexts. This fact results, on occasion, in some highly scholastic arguments. As I see it, the concept "social revolution" is usually used in two senses.

First, social revolution is understood as a fundamental change in the social and economic structure of society, a transition from one socioeconomic formation to another, regardless of the specific political form of this transition. It was this *general* meaning that Marx employed when he wrote in his *Critique of Political Economy:*

At a certain stage of their development, the material productive forces of society came into conflict with the existing relations of production, or— what is but a legal expression for the same thing—with the property relations within which they have been at work hitherto. From forms of development of the productive forces these relations turn into their fetters. Then begins an epoch of *social revolution*. With the change of the economic foundation the entire immense superstructure is more or less rapidly transformed.[10]

In this broad sense, social revolutions are indeed inevitable and inescapable. Direct political action in Germany and Austria-Hungary in

1848–49 was defeated. Nevertheless during the second half of the nineteenth century a fundamental shift from feudalism to capitalism occurred in Central Europe, i.e., a social revolution, which was brought to completion by a series of political actions only after World War I. Likewise, the complex of reforms "from above" carried out in Japan in the last third of the nineteenth century was essentially a social revolution, although it was not accompanied by the collapse of the traditional structural forms of the state or by radical changes in the composition of the ruling classes. And is there any shortage of European examples of former feudal lords being transformed into model capitalists?

From the Marxist point of view, capitalism [the product of those nineteenth-century social revolutions] is not itself the universal and best form of socioeconomic organization. Therefore, the transition from capitalism to a new, more just form of society—which will open up broader opportunities for the development of the productive forces, for science and culture—is both necessary and inevitable. We are of course talking about socialism, various forms of which have appeared on almost every continent, though none of them can be called perfect.

If the question we have posed is viewed from this standpoint, we may regard the October revolution as merely the external form of realization of this profound inner historical necessity, with quite different forms appearing in other countries and at other times.

The concept "social revolution" can also be used in the narrow sense, to mean an abrupt and rapid shift in political power from one class to another as the result of a mass movement of the people or an insurrection.

For example, the Soviet historian Ya. S. Drabkin writes,

> A social revolution is a fundamental upheaval in social life which changes its structure and represents a qualitative leap in its progressive development. . . . [Social] revolution is always marked by the active political intervention of the masses, in which a spontaneous upsurge is combined with a conscious and purposeful effort to achieve, first of all, a transfer of social leadership, i.e., of state power, to a new class or class grouping. . . . It should also be noted that because it is multidimensional and encompasses all basic aspects of the vital activity of society, social revolution differs from narrower, partial upheavals which touch only one or another sphere—for example, political revolutions (coups d'état), which only change the faces in power while preserving the former structure of society and the main lines of policy. It also differs from such phenomena as the

industrial revolution and the scientific-and-technical revolution. At the same time social revolution differs from the gradual changes in society which take place relatively slowly, without direct participation by the masses; social revolution is highly concentrated in time and is characterized by the direct intervention of the "lower classes." In this sense a distinction is commonly made between revolutionary and evolutionary processes, between reform and revolution.[11]

In this narrower sense, a social revolution is determined not only by the inner action of social laws and the relations among social factors which arise inevitably but also by the activity of individual political groups and particular leaders, whose behavior and decisions are not and cannot be totally predetermined. The behavior of entire political parties may sometimes depend on a multitude of subjective and accidental factors, and this inevitably gives an indeterminate or chance coloration to the entire course of specific historical events.

The primitive concepts of "absolute determinism," according to which all events in history were predetermined and could not have happened in any other way, are by no means part of Marxism. Any *specific* historical event, even one having the most significant consequences, is invariably the product of a complex interweaving of necessary and accidental processes. One is therefore obliged to speak, in dealing with a particular event, of the greater or lesser degree of probability of its occurrence, not of its absolute inevitability. In historical and social reality every situation necessarily contains several feasible alternatives, whose realization depends on a multiplicity of circumstances and actions, far from all of which can be foreseen. The facts of history attest that the most likely historical alternative is not always the one that is realized. On the contrary, what would seem to be the most unlikely events often do happen in history. "We do not believe that nations have special callings or that they are predestined," Aleksandr Herzen wrote. "We think that the fates of nations and governments can change in transit, as can the fate of an individual, but we have the right to draw conclusions about the future, basing ourselves on actually existing elements and following the theory of probability."[12] In history there is no "libretto" and the road is not marked out in advance, Herzen observed, adding that if anything in the life of nations and of humanity as a whole was predestined, "history would lose all of its interest and would become boring, unnecessary, and absurd."[13] Any real Marxist could easily agree with Herzen's words.

In studying the events of the years and centuries gone by we see clearly that the specific course of even the most colossal historical events depends not only on the social and economic conditions that have developed but also on the activity of certain "historical" personalities. And the actions and decisions of any person, including the very greatest, are even less predetermined or foreordained than one or another specific political event. Historical events in Europe in the early nineteenth century were closely linked with the deeds and personality of Napoleon. But if we recall the extremely risky undertakings and numerous battles that preceded his being proclaimed Emperor of France, we can say that Napoleon's dictatorship was certainly one of the least probable alternatives; nevertheless, it was the one that came about.[14]

G. V. Plekhanov, in his brilliant article "On the Role of the Individual in History," analyzes the unique case of Napoleon. "Having taken the role of the 'good sword,' needed to maintain public order, Napoleon thereby pre-empted all other generals who might have done the same, or almost the same, as he. Once the social demand for an energetic military ruler had been met, the social organism barred all other military talents from access to the position of military dictator."[15]

The notion that Napoleon played a distinctive role is based, in Plekhanov's opinion, on nothing but a kind of *optical illusion*, which is especially well illustrated by the history of human progress in intellectual matters.

> When particular social conditions confront a society's intellectual representatives with certain tasks, these problems attract the attention of the most outstanding minds until they succeed in solving them. Once they have done so, they turn their attention to other matters. Having solved problem X, talent A thereby directs the attention of talent B away from the solved problem to a new one, problem Y. But if we wonder what might have happened if A had died without solving problem X, we might suppose that the thread of society's intellectual development would have been broken. We forget that in the event of A's death, B, C, or D could undertake the task of solving problem X and in this way the thread of society's intellectual progress would remain unbroken, despite the premature death of A.[16]

There is only an element of truth in Plekhanov's arguments. If Einstein had not discovered relativity theory, some other great physicist would have after a number of years, and the thread of human intellectual development would indeed not have been broken. The basic laws of heredity would have been discovered without Mendel. If Columbus had not discovered America, some other navigator would have after a few years. But human history is not determined solely by such events. If a child is drowning, and the first passerby who sees this happening does not reach out to save it, the next passerby may see the child disappearing beneath the waves. If a wrong order is given, even the greatest military commander may prove unable to rectify the situation, with the result that his army is defeated or an entire campaign lost. Likewise an astronomer who does not notice a comet shooting by on the night sky will never be able to see it again, despite the most careful observation.

It is true that when Napoleon assumed the role of "the good sword," he precluded all other French generals from that role. But even Plekhanov admits that if another, more peaceable general had ended up as military dictator, he might not have roused all of monarchist Europe against himself. And all the ensuing events of the first half of the nineteenth century might have been of a different kind.

Of course there are quite a few thinkers who hold that all actions are predetermined, both major and minor, including those of the greatest historical figures. For example, I. M. Sechenov, the great Russian physiologist, maintained that the actions of all human beings depend on the external and internal conditions of their life and activity, on the effects of the environment and the human biological condition, and that therefore "the apparent possibility" of free will "is merely a delusion of self-consciousness." [17]

"Man is 'free,'" a contemporary American philosopher similarly argues, "in so far as he is able to do what he wants to do, and is 'bound' in so far as he has to do what he does not want to do. But all his actions, whether performed from free choice or under compulsion, have their causes and their effects." [18]

This point of view is not new. The eminent French thinker Charles Montesquieu wrote in 1734 in his book *Considerations of the Causes of the Greatness of the Romans and of Their Decadence:* "It is not chance that rules the world. . . . There are general causes at work. . . . All accidents are subject to these causes. And if *the accident of a battle,* which is to say, a particular cause, has ruined a state, a general cause must have been at work that *made it inevitable* that the state perish in a single battle. In a word, *the dominant trend carries with it all the particular accidents."* [19]

Leo Tolstoy did not concede that accident has any role to play or that strength of will can affect the outcome of great events. The outcome of such events is unforeseeable only because no one knows Destiny or Divine Providence.

The Italian publicist and critic Nicola Chiaromonte analyzed Tolstoy's views as follows:

> [The] nearer [military] leaders are to the top of the hierarchy, the less free they are. At the very top the "man of destiny" is a mere instrument of fate, "a puppet of the gods." . . . The reason for this is simple: the higher place a man is, the stronger his authority and the greater the number of individuals subject to his will, the greater becomes the number of hazards on which the carrying out of his orders depends. The fulfillment of the will of such powerful men as Napoleon or Tsar Alexander requires the coming together of an incalculable number of circumstances. Hence, what is finally accomplished is not their will, but something else, unpredictable and fateful. "The heart of kings is in the hands of God," says Tolstoy, quoting the Bible. . . . The great man is indeed the "man of destiny." . . . He who is endowed with [power] is its instrument, not its master.[20]

Quite recently the American psychologist B. F. Skinner has expressed views denying any freedom of the will. He not only rejects "free will" as an illusion but tries to prove that inner causes have no bearing on a person's behavior; only external causes are of any importance. The aim of survival for any culture consists in arranging the external factors (the milieu) in such a way that they ensure desirable behavior by people. Skinner holds not only that a person's behavior can be foreseen but that it can be controlled like a chemical reaction through what he calls behavioral psychology, which shifts the focus of psychology from the inner world of the individual to his or her outer world.[21]

We cannot agree with such views. It was Herzen who observed quite rightly in one of his letters:

> It would be absurd to regard human beings as exceptions to the general laws of nature and to attribute to them a subjective willfulness not subject to law. However, this in no way prevents people from cultivating within themselves a faculty, consisting of reason, passion, and memory, that can "weigh" circumstances and particular choices of action. This happens, not because of an imagined power of self-will and not because of the grace of God, but because of their own organs, their own abilities, both innate and acquired, which are shaped and combined in a thousand ways by social life. Action understood in this way is undoubtedly a func-

tion of the organism and its development, but it is not so obligatory and involuntary as breathing and digestion. . . . Human beings are moral creatures, i.e., social beings who have the freedom to determine their own actions within the limits of their consciousness and reason.[22]

Tolstoy was absolutely wrong to belittle the possibilities open to Napoleon, Alexander I, or Kutuzov as military commanders. Obviously, there are cases when orders from above do not decide the course of military and political events. In the summer of 1941 or the spring of 1942 Stalin issued quite a few orders that could no longer be carried out, and in 1944–45 Hitler often found himself in the same position. But many examples could be cited of battles and engagements in which it was precisely the will and the skilled leadership of the commander that played the decisive role.

We would go even further than Herzen in recognizing human freedom of choice. The mixture in every human being of the material element with an intellectual one that is not reducible to the purely material makes the actions of individuals unpredictable in many cases, although the effect of such actions on the course of external events may not be overly significant. People are not all-powerful, but the behavior and thinking of any person are by no means totally predetermined by either internal or external factors. Nor are human actions predetermined by "Providence." Thus, everyone has freedom of choice, though it may be very limited; one can make independent decisions and be responsible for one's actions.

Human consciousness is not of course impervious to the effects of many factors, both internal and external. Nevertheless it is not simply a reflection of those factors. As a creature with intellect a person has a certain active capacity, which can, within certain limits, change the course of external material events and processes, both in a person's own life and in human history as a whole.

"We do not believe," Roger Garaudy has written, "in the automatic realization of a future whose history is written in advance and not made by men themselves. Several futures are possible and each one of us is responsible for their actualization."[23]

Without getting lost in a discussion of these complex philosophical questions, let us simply note that our view coincides with that of the Soviet historian Leonid Rendel, who wrote the following in one of his interesting but, unfortunately, still unpublished works:

It is expedient to look at the historical process in a dual way. First, as a process in which people's behavior is determined by objective laws, processes, and external conditions independent of them. This makes it possible to present a true picture of the disposition of the dramatis personae upon the stage of history. Second, as a process *freely directed* by its participants. This makes possible a better evaluation of the negative and positive consequences of the willed choices of the participants in the action.[24]

Moving now to our question about the October revolution, we should state clearly that this event was not simply the result of what was apparently an irrepressible and undeterrable mass movement, nor was it solely due to the purposeful activity of the Bolshevik Party. The victory of the October revolution is inseparably connected as well with the activity of many individual party members, for example, Sverdlov, Trotsky, Antonov-Ovseenko, Raskolnikov, Dybenko. But the main role in the 1917 revolution was unquestionably that of Lenin, whose actions left a far greater mark on the twentieth century than Napoleon's did on the nineteenth century.

In an anonymous review of Alexander Solzhenitsyn's book *Lenin in Zurich*—the weakest, most malicious, and most dishonest of that author's books—the émigré magazine *Kontinent* wrote: "In Zurich Lenin was only on the threshold of that 'gift of history' which his majesty Chance was about to bestow upon him. Lenin's role in preparing the way for the Russian revolution was insignificant. But in this insignificance we can already see the kind of role he was to play in exploiting that revolution."[25]

The falseness of such statements is so obvious they do not require refutation.[26] In reality Lenin's role in the first twenty years of our century was far more significant than that of any of his contemporaries, although in its external aspect his rise to power was of course not so striking as Napoleon's. Moreover the tasks he tried to accomplish were incomparably more difficult. In the last analysis Napoleon merely consolidated and codified in his own way the results of the already completed bourgeois-democratic revolution. Lenin faced the task of organizing a new revolution and carrying it through to victory.

From the earliest days of the Bolshevik Party, which was Lenin's creation, he was irreplaceable as that party's leader. Other Bolsheviks understood this perfectly well and, as a result, when very sharp differences arose, Lenin's threat to resign from the leadership was more effective than all other arguments. Virtually all the Bolsheviks' opponents understood Lenin's role in the same way. "To be left without Lenin," wrote N. Sukhanov, "wouldn't that be the same as tearing the heart out of the organism or cutting off the head? . . . In the party, next to Lenin, there was no one. . . . A few big generals, without Lenin, amounted to nothing, as would several huge planets without the sun." [27]

But Lenin was not a prophet, the earthly representative of some higher power. Berdyaev was completely wrong to regard Lenin as a "man of destiny, a man sent by fate." No, Lenin was an ordinary mortal, not guaranteed against mistakes and none too well protected against the numerous dangers lying in wait for him. We will not speak here of the several well-known attempts on his life, but will refer to a less well-known fact. During his illegal crossing of the border on December 15, 1907, Lenin barely escaped drowning when the ice of the Gulf of Bothnia, not yet solid, gave way beneath him and his two guides.

N. V. Valentinov in his book *The Unknown Lenin* asks the rhetorical question:

> What would have happened if Lenin had drowned in the Gulf of Bothnia on December 15, 1907? Would the October revolution of 1917 have happened? And if it had, would it, without Lenin, have taken the special socio-political form that he "imposed on it by force" with his decrees, defying the Marxism of Plekhanov, who argued that "no great man can impose on society relations that do not correspond to it." In the course of the great historical events consequent to the October revolution, didn't a mere trifle like the thicker layer of ice Lenin leaped on to save himself from drowning—didn't that trifle play a role? Petty accident plays a more important role in the greatest historical events than it is customary to suppose. [28]

There is a certain truth to this argument, for if Lenin's personal fate had taken a different turn in 1907, or in 1914–15, or in 1917–18, the fate of the revolution he proclaimed and organized might well have come out differently.

Similarly, the actions of both the opponents and the temporary allies of the Bolshevik Party were not predetermined. From this angle, too, it is evident that the victory of the October revolution was not inevitable, although it was not accidental either. In any of the periods before the revolution the situation allowed for several different alternative lines of development, and the same was true after the October victory in Petrograd. This is understood by the more thoughtful foreign historians of the October revolution. William H. Chamberlin, the author of a two-volume history of the Russian revolution, by no means regards it as a total accident for Russia and the world. But he wrote in 1967, "This is not to say that every step . . . from the traditional rule of Nicholas II to the revolutionary dictatorship of . . . Lenin was preordained and fatalistically inevitable." [29]

What actually happened, of course, cannot be changed. Nevertheless the study of various alternatives and missed opportunities should also serve as subject matter for history and for historians. This knowledge is useful not only for futurologists or scientific workers in other disciplines. It is useful for practical politicians, too, if they wish to learn something from history. Unfortunately one finds this desire only in a minority of politicians. Hegel's celebrated aphorism that "History teaches us only that no one has learned anything from history" is also true of most of those politicians who never cease to proclaim that they are guided by the one true scientific ideology of the modern world.

two

On the February Bourgeois Democratic Revolution

If one were to accept the thesis we have outlined above, one would have to conclude, likewise, that the February democratic revolution was not absolutely inevitable. The inept way the war was conducted, its increasing unpopularity among the masses of workers and peasants, the growing burdens on the soldiers in the trenches, the worsening economic dislocation, the ferment among the intelligentsia and the petty bourgeoisie—all this made the revolutionary overthrow of the autocracy a likely development. And the probability of just such a revolutionary turn of events mounted steadily with every passing month in 1916 and with every week in January and February 1917. Still it remained only one of the alternatives in the existing historical situation.

The fact is that Russia was pregnant with revolution even before its entry into World War I. The persistence of the essential features of the autocracy, which represented above all the power of the large, semi-feudal landowners; the bureaucratism and corruption; the lack of equality for national minorities; the growing dependence of Russia on foreign capital; the steadily increasing impoverishment of a significant section of the urban and rural population and the simultaneous process of relatively rapid capitalist development—all this wore away and undermined the foundations of the *ancien regime* in imperial Russia.

The Orthodox Church was not of course able to halt these processes. Solzhenitsyn has recently written, "Nay, the truth compels me to say that the status of the Russian church at the beginning of the twentieth century, the age-old degradation of its clergy, its malleability in the hands of the state and fusion with the state, its loss of spiritual

independence, and therefore its loss of authority with the bulk of the educated class and the bulk of the city workers, and—most terrible of all—the shakiness of its authority even among the masses of peasants—this situation in which the Russian church found itself *was one of the main reasons for the irrepressible force of the revolutionary events.*
. . . Alas, the situation of the Russian Orthodox Church at the time of the revolution was totally out of keeping with the profundity of the spiritual dangers baring their teeth at our century and at our nation, which was first in line. The vital forces in the church, which had brought about salutory reforms and the convocation of a Synod— oppressed by the arbitrary government apparatus and bogged down by the drowsy placidity of their colleagues—*failed,* and so visibly failed that the Red Guards' cannonfire crashed down on the roofs and cu- polas of the Synod as it was in session.'' [1] (Solzhenitsyn's emphasis— R.M.)

The possibility of revolution was so evident that even the none-too- farsighted monarchists could see it. After the dissolution of the First State Duma, which had seemed to the tsar too radical, Prince Yevgeny Trubetskoi—who openly termed himself "a landowner and a monar- chist"—wrote to Nicholas II as follows:

> Sire, the peasants' desire for land has irresistible force. . . . Anyone who is opposed to compulsory alienation [of the great estates] will be swept from the face of the earth. The impending revolution threatens us with confiscation and puts our lives themselves in danger. Civil war is only a matter of time. . . . Perhaps the government will succeed now in put- ting down the revolutionary movement through repressive measures. . . . All the more terrible will be the consequent and final explosion, which will bring down the existing order and level Russian culture to the ground. And you yourself will be buried in the ruins. [2]

Although the 1905−7 revolution was defeated, the subterranean forces that produced it continued to grow. The reforms undertaken by Premiers Stolypin and Krivoshein from 1906 to 1912 were aimed at preventing a new revolution. But these reforms were not sufficiently thorough and far-reaching to achieve their goals. While they speeded up economic development in both town and country, they failed to remove the main obstacles to capitalist development in Russia. Con- trary to Trotsky's assertion, Russia had not yet "arrived in a blind alley" and could have developed fairly rapidly on a capitalist basis. But Bunin's opinion that Russia was "blooming and growing" and "changing with fantastic speed in every respect" is profoundly wrong.

In the final analysis, the monarchy chose the war precisely as a means of saving itself, expecting it to be brief and victorious. Far from everyone in the tsar's entourage shared these hopes, however. In February 1914 when the possibility of a military confrontation with Germany was already evident, P. N. Durnovo, ex-minister of internal affairs, warned the tsar that war would lead to revolutionary convulsions of a political and social nature in the defeated countries, and that Russia was by no means ensured against this. In the event of military setbacks, wrote Durnovo, social revolution

> in its most extreme manifestations is inevitable in our country. . . . It would begin with all the setbacks being attributed to the government. In the legislative bodies a furious campaign would be started against the government, as a result of which revolutionary demonstrations would begin in this country. The latter would immediately project socialist slogans. . . . The defeated army would prove too demoralized to serve as a bastion of law and order. The legislative bodies and opposition parties of the intelligentsia would not have the strength to hold back the raging waves of popular revolt which they themselves had summoned forth, and Russia would be plunged into unrelieved anarchy whose outcome does not bear thinking on.[3]

Refusing to heed such prophecies, the Russian monarchy entered World War I. But the war began unfavorably for Russia and, more importantly, became a prolonged and wearing conflict, which only aggravated all the basic contradictions of Russian society.

Nevertheless, in 1915 and 1916 the monarchy still had several opportunities for political maneuver, for retreat, or for compromise with the Duma and the liberals (who were, after all, not asking for very great concessions). After harsh antigovernment speeches began in the Duma, the extreme right-wing group headed by Durnovo sent a new note to the tsar:

> The liberals are so weak, so disunited, and—we must speak frankly— so lacking in talent that their triumph would be as brief as it would be unstable. . . . What would the installing of a "responsible ministry" yield in these circumstances? Final and complete destruction of all the parties of the Right, the gradual swallowing-up by the Cadet Party of the intermediate parties—the Center, the Liberal-Conservatives, the Octobrists, and the Progressists—the parties which at the beginning would have decisive importance. But the Cadets would be threatened by the same fate. . . . and then? Then would come the revolutionary mob, the Commune, the downfall of the dynasty, and pogroms against the propertied classes.[4]

A compromise with the monarchy was sought by those cliques and parties in the Duma who now were united in the so-called Progressive Bloc. It would be a mistake to think that only the "bourgeois parties and factions" of the Duma belonged to this bloc, as academician I. Mints asserts in his three-volume work, which is full of inaccuracies and distortions.[5] The large-landowner element clearly predominated in the Octobrist Party, which was part of the Progressive Bloc. As for the Center faction and the nationalists who participated in the Bloc, here too we find many proponents of the reactionary politics of the great landlords. The formation of the Progressive Bloc showed that Nicholas II and his circle were losing support even among their recently loyal adherents. And although the speeches of the members of the Bloc were sometimes quite harsh and evoked a powerful response in the country, the leaders of the opposition parties, in raising their voices against the government, called only for the most modest reforms for the time being—thinking thereby to forestall revolution. They demanded a "government enjoying public confidence," responsible to both the tsar and the Duma. By no means did they want the full power; rather they sought to share it with the monarchy. One of the leaders of the Bloc, V. Shulgin, wrote several years after the revolution,

> We were born and brought up to praise or criticize the government while remaining under its wing. . . . We were capable in the most extreme case of moving from our deputies' seats to the ministerial armchairs without suffering ill effects—but only on the condition that the imperial guard protect us. . . . But when we faced the possible downfall of the state power, confronted by the bottomless abyss of such a fall, our heads swam and our hearts went numb. Impotence stared out at me from behind the white columns of the Tauride Palace. And the look on its face was terrifyingly contemptuous.[6]

V. A. Maklakov, another leader of the Russian liberals, reflecting later, as an émigré, upon the causes of the revolution, concluded that the liberals were "overzealous" in their criticism of the "historical form of power," i.e., tsarism. Maklakov regretted that the liberals refused to join the Witte cabinet during the first Russian revolution. He regretted that the liberals had not supported the Stolypin government as they should have. And this "repentant liberal" especially condemned the policies of his co-thinkers during World War I. It was after the revolution that Maklakov wrote,

> In the last analysis the war pushed Russia into revolution. Without it there would have been no revolution. But if Russia was able to fight for only three years, after eight years of a constitutional regime, would it be too daring to suggest that if those eight years had elapsed differently, Russia might have been able to hold out to the end of the war? Working constitutionally in cooperation with the public, the healthy elements of the historical form of power could have received the kind of support that would have enabled them to overcome the microbes of dissolution and decay which were growing ever stronger. ... In that case the war would have transpired differently and might have ended differently. . . . These consequences are so immeasurably vast that it is frightening to imagine their full dimensions.[7]

These were only illusions, however, because the "healthy elements of the historical form of power" proved to be too insubstantial in the face of the war. Neither Nicholas nor the empress nor anyone in the court camarilla around them was able to evaluate the situation, and none of them wished to make concessions in any area, even to those who had recently been their supporters. In the tsar's entourage there was no longer anyone of the stature of Stolypin. Nicholas II constantly reshuffled the Council of Ministers and appointed to the key posts representatives of the same untalented monarchical bureaucracy which had not been capable of ruling the country in peacetime and was even less so in time of war.

Of course the blindness of the ruling dynasty stemmed from its class prejudices, from the tsar's unwillingness to surrender even a small share of his power, and the reluctance of the great landowners and top bureaucrats to yield the slightest fragment of their privileges. Nevertheless a decisive role in the developing situation went to such completely undetermined factors, from the historical point of view, as the absymal intellectual level and the weak will of the last Russian tsar and the equally apparent mediocrity of his fanatical wife, who was inclined toward a hysterical kind of mysticism. "Be Peter the Great, Ivan the Terrible, Emperor Paul—crush them all," Alexandra Fyodorovna urged her husband in a letter of December 14, 1916 (she was referring above all to the Duma opposition).[8] Accusing the tsar of being too kind and gentle, the tsarina wrote, "I wish that you would keep them all in hand with your intelligence and experience. . . . They should learn to tremble in your presence. . . . Remember you are the Emperor, and that others dare not presume so much."[9]

Of course Nicholas II was neither kind nor gentle. He was lazy, sluggish, unintelligent, distraught, and lacking in character and audacity. He was depressed by events and incapable of understanding them. Trotsky found a great similarity between the personalities of Nicholas II and France's Louis XVI, who was also overthrown ˙and executed by the people. But the similarity is accidental; revolutions by no means occur only during the reign of weak monarchs.

Nevertheless the disintegration among the upper layers of Russian society undoubtedly quickened the pace of revolution and facilitated its victory. The Rasputin phenomenon was only one manifestation of the moral decay, mental degradation, and impotence of those at the top. The only thing the tsarist court could bring itself to do in search of a way out of the impasse was to prepare for secret negotiations with Kaiser Wilhelm for a separate peace with Germany, a move foreshadowed by the appointment of B. V. Stürmer, an open Germanophile, as chairman of the Council of Ministers. Historians still debate how far Nicholas went in his attempts to establish contacts with the enemy. But even the most timid moves in that direction surely intensified the rumors of treason and hastened the assassination of Rasputin, an event which not only caused rejoicing in the Duma but also brought joy to most of those in court circles.

A palace coup was undoubtedly one of the possible alternatives for Russia in 1916. The leaders of the Progressive Bloc and many influential figures in the Entente pressed for one. Not only politicians but a number of prominent military men took part in discussions on this theme. Alexander Kerensky has testified, "We felt that a spontaneous and uncontrolled revolutionary movement was impermissible in time of war. And therefore we set ourselves the task of supporting moderate and even conservative groups, parties, and organizations, which would prevent the catastrophe of an uncontrolled explosion by means of a palace coup." [10]

N. I. Bilibin, a colonel in the tsarist army, reports that Guchkov, while visiting military units for the Red Cross,

> expressed to me, in private conversation his serious apprehensions about the outcome of the war. We were as one in concluding that the inept operational direction of the army, the appointment of undistinguished courtiers to the highest posts, and finally, the ambivalent behavior of Empress Alexandra, having as its aim a separate peace with Germany, could end

in a military catastrophe and a new revolution which, in our opinion, threatened to destroy the very state. We felt that the only way out of this situation would be a palace coup. The abdication of the throne by Nicholas should be extracted from him by force.[11]

According to Professor Iu. V. Lomonosov, the discontent in Duma circles

was directed almost exclusively at the tsar and tsarina. In the field headquarters and at the general headquarters the tsarina was unmercifully abused; there was talk not only of having her arrested but even of having Nicholas removed. This was discussed even at the generals' tables. But always, in all conversations of this kind, the most likely outcome seemed to be a revolution that would be purely a palace revolution, such as the assassination of Emperor Paul.[12]

However all these "preparations" for a palace coup were too sluggish and lacking in vigor; essentially they were never more than talk. No one, either in the court circles or among the members of the Progressive Bloc, would decisively take the leadership of this whole movement. It goes without saying that this situation was not at all predetermined.

The leaders of the Duma did not lose hope of reaching an agreement with the tsar. Thus, on February 10, 1917 (two weeks before the revolution began) M. V. Rodzianko, president of the Duma, in his last "humble" report to the tsar spoke of the proximity of revolution. The tsar rejected the report. The angry and agitated Rodzianko declared:

" 'I have warned you. I'm convinced that three weeks will not pass before a revolution breaks out that will sweep you away and you will no longer be the tsar. . . .

" 'Where do you get that from?' asked the tsar.

" 'From the entire situation, the way it has developed.'

" 'Well, God will provide. . . .'

" 'God will provide nothing; revolution is inevitable.' "[13]

Some generals were opposed to a coup, for example, General Alekseev. But most of the commanders of the fronts supported the idea of a palace coup, which was at last set for March 1917. As General Denikin, one of the participants in the plot, reports:

Members of the right-wing and liberal circles of the Duma, members of the imperial family, and members of the officer corps all belonged to the circles that had formed. Direct action was to be preceded by a last appeal to the sovereign by one of the Grand Dukes. . . . If that did not succeed, it was proposed that in the first half of March the emperor's train would be stopped by armed force on its way from the General Headquarters (Stavka) to Petrograd. What was to follow was a proposal to the sovereign that he abdicate the throne, and in the event that he did not agree, his physical removal would follow. The proposed successor was Alexis, the legal heir to the throne, and the regent was to be the Grand Duke Michael.[14]

However, time was no longer counted in months, but in weeks and days. As early as January 5, 1917, the Okhrana reported to A. D. Protopopov, the minister of internal affairs,

The mood in the capital is extremely agitated. The wildest rumors are circulating in society, both as to the plans of the governing authority, for taking various kinds of reactionary measures, and as to the projected aims of groups and layers of the population hostile to the government, implying the possibility and likelihood of revolutionary initiatives and excesses. Everyone expects some sort of extraordinary actions either from one side or the other.[15]

The Okhrana probably understood the situation better than any other imperial agency, but no one wished to listen to it any more. On January 6 it reported to Protopopov:

The situation we are now in is very similar to the time just before the first revolution of 1905. The liberal parties believe that in view of the imminence of terrible and inevitable events the governing authority ought to move in the direction of concessions and should hand over the totality of power to the Cadets. The left parties, for their part, argue that the government will not make any concessions, that a spontaneous and anarchic revolution will come, and that then the basis will be laid for transforming Russia into a state free from tsarism and constructed upon new social principles.[16]

The likelihood of a revolutionary turn of events in fact was growing with every day. The revolution was becoming the most likely alternative.

At one time Soviet historical literature almost totally ignored the role of the Duma opposition in the *actual* preparation of the masses for the revolution and the overthrow of the autocracy. Today books and articles have begun to appear in which the authors describe in detail the struggle of the Duma opposition against the tsarist regime, conceding that the anti-government actions and statements of the liberal-bourgeois and moderate-monarchist leaders, regardless of their intentions, helped to bring the masses of workers and soldiers to their feet against the tsarist regime. But, strange to say, some of these authors, who call themselves Marxists, in fact condemn the Progressive Bloc, not for its indecisiveness in combating the tsarist regime, but for its lack of patriotism, for its insufficient support to the throne in time of war. The political parties of the Progressive Bloc are accused of trying to crowd the tsarist bureaucracy out of power and thereby hindering the consolidation of Russia's forces in the struggle against the foreign enemy. This is the position taken by N. N. Yakovlev, author of the book *August 1, 1914.*[17] Yakovlev does criticize the tsarist regime and the Rasputin phenomenon. However, the cutting edge of his criticism is directed at the bourgeois circles who, according to him, not only wanted to seize power but intentionally created difficulties on the battlefront and the homefront and exaggerated the shortcomings and failings of the tsarist war machine, which in 1916, he claims, were not all that great or insuperable.

Yakovlev asks:

> But what about the famous slogan of the bourgeoisie "War to a victorious conclusion"? For those who raised the slogan, it only had meaning for a Russia in which undivided power would be held by the bourgeoisie. A victory for imperial Russia, from the point of view of the bourgeoisie and its ideologists, would have put incredible obstacles in the way of its effort to force the tsarist regime out of power. Hence the extremely complicated tactics of the bourgeoisie and its parties, *whose aim was to create difficulties for the tsarist government in waging the war.* The voguish proposition that "the worse things get, the better" became the operating principle of the bourgeoisie.[18]

Yakovlev rearranges the facts when he tries to prove, for example, that at the beginning of 1917 the bourgeoisie and its agents helped to cause a serious food crisis on the homefront and in the army, as well as a shortage of ammunition, etc.[19]

Yakovlev's entire conception cannot withstand criticism. It differs in no essentials from Solzhenitsyn's indictment of the Cadets for their "frenzied and ill-considered assault in 1916 against Goremykin and Stürmer," which he claims was a tremendous political mistake by the Cadets and a great service to the Bolsheviks.[20]

Certainly the bourgeois political parties sought to win a larger share of power and influence during the war. But that is what any *political* party tries to do. Certainly the Russian bourgeoisie sought to make profits from the war and from military contracts. But the bourgeoisie, in every belligerent country, did this kind of thing at the time. There is no serious basis for charging the Russian bourgeoisie with deliberate sabotage of the military effort of the Russian army.

Yakovlev's "revelations" about the decisive role of the Masonic lodges, or of the "Freemasons" in general, in laying the basis for the overthrow of Nicholas II are equally unfounded. Of course any preparation for a palace coup required some organization. And contacts through the Masonic lodges could have served a useful purpose in this respect. But the activity of these lodges, as can be seen from Yakovlev's own book, had an insignificant effect on the political situation in the country and on the activities of the "conspirators," who never went beyond preliminary discussion and "sounding things out." Yakovlev apparently does not notice that he himself shifts from a description of attempts to create a secret organization *modeled on the Masonic lodges* to a discussion of the Masonic organizations in Russia and their allegedly powerful influence. All this is just as unconvincing as the attempts by some writers in our country and elsewhere to explain the foreign and domestic policies of the United States and certain other Western governments in terms of secret Masonic influence.

At any rate, in the first weeks of February 1917 the tsarist court and administration found themselves almost completely isolated. A situation had arisen in the country, the army, and the capital in which any small incident could set off a universal reaction. "The tense mood in the country could be compared with a barrel of gunpowder; one spark was enough to cause an explosion"—such were the later recollections of S. I. Afanasiev, secretary of the Narva district committee of the Bolshevik party in Petrograd in 1917.[21] The Menshevik leader N. Chkheidze said in a statement before the State Duma on February 14, 1917: "The street, gentlemen, is beginning to speak. Whether this is good or bad, it is a fact, gentlemen, and you cannot get away from it. And I suggest that you cannot fail to take the utterances of the street into account."[22]

Only the ruling dynasty was afflicted with blindness. As late as February 24, 1917, Alexandra Fyodorovna wrote to her royal spouse at General Headquarters: "I hope that this Kedrinsky [meaning Kerensky] in the Duma will be hanged for his dreadful speeches—this is necessary under the laws of wartime and will serve as an example. Everyone wishes and begs that you show your firmness."[23] And indeed the tsar tried to show his "firmness." To a request by Rodzianko, the leader of the Octobrists, that the powers of the Duma be extended, Nicholas replied, as we know, with a decree dissolving that body. During those very days, in response to strikes by working men and women caused by food shortages in the capital, 22 business establishments in Petrograd announced a lockout—that is, a mass firing of all their workers. It is not surprising that the demonstrations and strikes in the capital began to develop into an insurrection. The fate of the incipient revolution was decided by the Petrograd garrison—the Pavlovsky, Litovsky, Volynsky, and Preobrazhensky regiments—which took the side of the workers. After wavering for a while the Cossack regiments also joined the uprising. The workers seized the city's arsenal and the Peter and Paul fortress and freed the prisoners in the jails.

On February 27 Rodzianko sent the tsar a telegram: "The situation is becoming worse; measures must be taken immediately, for tomorrow will be too late. The last hour has come; the fate of our country and the dynasty is being decided." In truth it was the final hour. But when the tsar received this telegram, he said to Frederiks: "Once again this Rodzianko has written me a lot of nonsense, which I won't even bother to answer." [24]

On February 28, 1917, the fate of the monarchy was already sealed. Even the Council of Ministers, some of whose members had been arrested, sent the tsar a telegram asking him to form a "responsible ministry" and stating that the ministers could no longer carry out their functions. The tsar forbade any changes in the government; accompanied by several military units, the tsar's train set out for the capital. In a telegram to the tsarina, Nicholas wrote, "We started out this morning at five. In my thoughts I am always with you. Magnificent weather. I hope you are well and feel calm? . . . With tender love, Niki." [25] But the road to the capital was closed, and the tsar's train was rerouted to Pskov. In the Tauride Palace the Soviet of Workers' Deputies was already in session.

Solzhenitsyn suggests that even at this time the monarchy could have been saved. He writes: "It was not Russia that abandoned the Romanovs, but the brothers Nicholas and Michael who forever renounced Russia for all the Romanovs—and they did this in three days after the first street disturbances in a single city, without even trying to fight, thereby betraying all those officers—a million strong!—who had taken the oath of allegiance to them." [26]

But this is not true. It was Russia that turned its back on the Romanovs. And there were hardly any generals or other officers in those days who, feeling bound by their oath, hastened to die for the Romanovs. Even less were there soldiers ready to carry out the orders of such officers. Well before the abdications of Nicholas and Michael on March 3, 1917, the February revolution had won. That the autocracy came to an end was of course not an accident but the result of historical laws. However, the specific form its end took was by no means the only possible outcome of the political, social, and economic processes at work in Russia at the beginning of the twentieth century.

three

On the October Socialist Revolution

If the February revolution cannot be called an absolutely inevitable event, still less can this be said of the October socialist revolution. Certainly the possibility of a new revolution that would give power to the proletariat (that is, the Bolsheviks) had emerged as early as the spring of 1917. This was why Lenin was able not only to proclaim the slogan "All power to the Soviets" but also to conclude his brief speech at the Finland Station with a call for socialist revolution.

At the First All-Russia Congress of Soviets, when the Menshevik I. Tsereteli made the assertion that in Russia at that time (June 1917) there was no political party that would say, "Give us the power; leave, and we will take your place," Lenin interrupted the speaker to call out loudly: "There is such a party!" He meant the Bolshevik Party, which had a total of 105 delegates out of more than a thousand at the Congress of Soviets.[1]

Bolshevik influence, however, grew very rapidly in June 1917, and this was shown in particular by the July demonstrations, which began spontaneously and very nearly developed into an insurrection. In league with the Menshevik and SR leaders of the Soviets, the Provisional Government succeeded in smashing the incipient movement and driving the Bolsheviks underground temporarily; some of the party's leaders were arrested and others were forced to go into hiding. Bolshevik influence was not broken, however; it continued to grow among the workers, and the party functioned almost openly in working-class districts. At the end of July the Bolsheviks held their Sixth Congress, which adopted a policy aimed at organizing an armed insurrection.

In many respects August 1917 was the decisive month. Relying on the army, the counterrevolution feverishly gathered its forces to stop the revolution by taking advantage of the temporary defeat of the Bolsheviks. It seemed as though the cause of socialist revolution had temporarily lost. At the end of July Lenin wrote: "Every class-conscious worker, soldier, and peasant should ponder thoroughly the lessons of the Russian revolution, especially now, . . . when it is clear that the first phase of our revolution has ended in failure." [2]

The main task for the counterrevolution during these weeks was to rally its main forces—the bourgeoisie and its parties, the officer corps, the most backward section of the Cossacks, and the right-wing leaders of the SRs and Mensheviks. This was no easy task, but it was not an impossible one. At any rate an alliance between Kerensky and Kornilov against the Bolsheviks was considerably more likely in the second half of August than Kerensky's sudden turn against Kornilov, which resulted in a temporary compromise, or quasi-alliance, between Kerensky and the Bolsheviks, the rapid legalization of the Bolshevik Party, and rapid improvement in the chances of a Bolshevik victory in a new revolution. At the time Lenin himself was surprised by this "most unexpected (unexpected at such a moment in such a form) and downright unbelievably sharp turn of events." [3] However, Lenin did not lose his bearings; with surprising rapidity, together with other Bolshevik leaders, he managed to readjust all of the party's policies to take advantage of the new opportunities that suddenly opened up and to carry the revolution forward. "It would be wrong to think," Lenin wrote on August 30, 1917, "that we have moved farther away from the task of the conquest of power by the proletariat. No, we have come very close to it, *not directly,* but from the side. *At the moment we must campaign not so much directly against Kerensky as indirectly* against him, namely, by demanding a more and more active, revolutionary war against Kornilov. A development of this war alone can lead *us* to power, but we must *speak* of this as little as possible in our propaganda (remembering very well that even tomorrow events may put power into our hands, and then we shall not relinquish it)." [4]

Lenin's prognosis proved to be absolutely correct. Kerensky's move against Kornilov turned all the right-wing forces and the Cadets against the Provisional Government. A large part of the officer corps now regarded the supreme commander in chief, Kerensky, with undisguised contempt. His authority, after the defeat of the Kornilov revolt, was so illusory and weak that as early as September 1917 Lenin considered a Bolshevik victory guaranteed and therefore continually prodded the vacillating majority of the Central Committee, urging them to make haste.

When Lenin and his closest collaborators, in October 1917, made the final decision to start an armed insurrection they showed that they knew how to take brilliant advantage of a favorable situation, realizing full well that it could change to their disadvantage within a matter of days.

"Under no circumstances," Lenin wrote to the Central Committee members on October 24, 1917, "should power be left in the hands of Kerensky and Co. until the 25th—not under any circumstances; the matter must be decided without fail this very evening, or this very night. History will not forgive revolutionaries for procrastinating when they could be victorious today (and they certainly will be victorious today), while they risk losing much tomorrow, in fact, they risk losing everything." [5]

Lenin's letter once again shows the tremendous role he played in the revolutionary events that transpired in Russia in 1917. It was Lenin who managed to change the minds of, and reorient, the majority of the Bolshevik party leaders, who did not understand the opportunities that had opened up before them and who at first greeted Lenin's April Theses with hostility. Without Lenin the party would scarcely have been able so successfully to turn to its advantage the succession of political crises in 1917. It was Lenin who outlined a specific tactical plan for the insurrection and worked out a series of immediate measures for the future Soviet government to take. Further such examples could be listed. That is why we cannot agree with those historians who now write about the inevitable and inescapable victory in October. Academician A. M. Rumiantsev was closer to the truth in stating, "The road from February to October was not a straight line; the Bolshevik victory was not, so to speak, 'programmed,' i.e., inevitable from the very start. In order to win the majority of the population to their side, the Bolsheviks had to overcome colossal difficulties." [6]

Likewise, the actions of the Bolsheviks' political opponents were not preprogrammed, in particular, the Menshevik and SR parties, which found themselves at the head of the Soviets after February and at the head of the Provisional Government after the July crisis. These parties (which also considered themselves socialist), in spite of their organizational weakness, were swept onto the center stage of political life by the revolutionary floodtide and for several months held the main levers of political power. However hard the SRs and Mensheviks clung to the idea of coalition with the Cadets, after the Kornilov revolt the Cadets were left out of the formal cabinet (though not by their own wish) and were not represented in the Directory (Council of Five) announced by Kerensky. But during that crucial time, neither the SRs nor the Mensheviks took any significant action to implement their own political programs or to win over the majority of the revolutionary people and army.

One might have expected, for example, that the initiative in solving the land question in Russia in 1917 would have come from the SRs. After all, the central demand in their program was for "socialization" of all privately owned land—"removing it from the status of private ownership by groups or individuals and making it the property of all the people." According to the SR program, "All lands should come under the jurisdiction of central and local self-governing bodies. . . . land use should be equal and should be based on a labor standard, i.e., provide for minimum consumption on the basis of one's own labor or labor as part of a cooperative group." [7]

It had been under the leadership of SR organizations that 242 local peasant mandates had been drawn up in the summer of 1917, becoming the basis for the "Model Peasant Mandate on the Land," published in the newspaper of the All-Russian Council of Peasant Deputies on August 19, 1917. [8]

It was not the Bolshevik *Pravda* but the official newspaper of the SR Party that carried an editorial in September 1917 saying,

> Virtually nothing has been done so far to eliminate the relations of bondage which still prevail in the countryside, particularly in central Russia. . . . A bill for the normalization of land relations in the countryside was long ago submitted to the Provisional Government, . . . [but] this law has bogged down hopelessly in some chancery or other. Aren't we right in maintaining, then, that . . . the dead hand of Stolypin still makes itself felt in the methods followed by the revolutionary ministers. [9]

But it was the Bolsheviks who, immediately after the October victory, proclaimed the Peasant Mandate of the Land a provisional law to be put into effect without fail throughout the territory of Russia. Speaking at the Second All-Russia Congress of Soviets, Lenin said: "Voices are being raised here that the decree itself and the Mandate were drawn up by the Socialist-Revolutionaries. What of it? Does it matter who drew them up? As a democratic government, we cannot ignore the decision of the masses of the people, even though we may disagree with it." [10]

In this way the Bolsheviks made a reality of the programmatic demands of the SR Party, while the SRs, for numerous subjective reasons, could not bring themselves to carry out their own program.

It is well known that the delay in solving the land question was caused by the right-wing SR leaders (N. D. Avksentiev, V. M. Chernov, and A. F. Kerensky), who even authorized the dispatch of military units in a number of cases to prevent unauthorized seizure of large estates. Only in October, when the peasant movement in Russia began to develop into an agrarian revolution and the influence of the Left SRs and the Bolsheviks grew rapidly among the peasantry, did the position of the right wing of the SRs begin to change. Thus on October 16 (29), 1917, a joint commission of the Provisional Government and the Council of the Republic hastily passed a bill which *temporarily* gave the land to the peasants. But this measure failed to make the impression on the masses that Kerensky counted on. And in the local areas few even heard about the bill; communications with the villages were still highly imperfect.

The foreign policy of the Provisional Government was not absolutely predetermined either. As we have said, the palace's attempts to conclude a separate peace with Germany hastened its downfall. The Russian bourgeoisie did not want peace; its slogan was to continue the war "to a victorious conclusion." Therefore, the Provisional Government, dominated by the Cadets during the spring of 1917, sought in every way to firm up the situation in the army and prepare it for a new offensive. However, after the failure of the June offensive the mood in the country and in the army changed abruptly, leading to a change in the make-up of the Provisional Government itself. By early autumn the question of peace became the main political question in the country. The Bolsheviks and the left-wing Mensheviks were both advocating peace. For example, Martov, in a speech before the Council of the Republic, demanded that peace be concluded immediately, for otherwise nothing would be left of the Russian army, and Russia itself would become "the subject of bargaining between the different imperialist groups." [11]

A few days before the October revolution (on October 20) General

A. I. Verkhovsky, the minister of war, gave a confidential report to one of the commissions of the Pre-Parliament on the situation in the army. According to M. I. Skobelev, Verkhovsky's most notable statement was that he had "told all the members of the Provisional Government simply and directly that, in view of the way the question of peace is now being handled, disaster is inescapable. . . . In Petrograd itself not one hand will be raised to protect the Provisional Government, and any columns withdrawn from the front will go over to the Bolsheviks. . . . The government's actions are leading to a disaster. . . ."

To judge from Verkhovsky's own rough minutes and notes, which have survived, the essence of his report was as follows:

> The situation at the front is disastrous. . . . There is no way out. There are no palliative measures for restoring the army's fighting power that are capable of overcoming the destructive influence of the peace propaganda. We are at an impasse. The only possible way to combat the pernicious influence of the Bolsheviks is to pull the rug out from under them by immediately proposing to make peace ourselves. News of peace negotiations . . . will lay the basis for restoring the army to health. By relying on the units that remain most intact we would find it possible to forcibly suppress anarchy in the country.[12]

When Kerensky learned of Verkhovsky's report, he was greatly angered and retired the minister from his post.

However, among the leaders of the VTsIK and Council of the Republic there were few who any longer supported Kerensky. Both the Menshevik leader F. I. Dan and the Right SR leader A. R. Gotz condemned Kerensky's stand:

"The policy of the Bolsheviki is demagogic and criminal," declared Gotz to the Council of the Republic,

> in their exploitation of the popular discontent. But there is a whole series of popular demands which have received no satisfaction up to now. . . . The questions of peace, land and the democratization of the army ought to be stated in such a fashion that no soldier, peasant or worker would have the least doubt that our Government is attempting, firmly and infallibly, to solve them. . . . °Neither we nor the Mensheviks' wish to provoke a Cabinet crisis, and we are ready to defend the Provisional Government with all our energy, to the last drop of our blood—if only the Provisional Government, on all these burning questions, will speak the clear and precise words awaited by the people with such impatience.[13]

But the Provisional Government could not find the firmness of will or the political wisdom to pose the question of peace clearly enough or

in time. This does not mean in any way that such a possibility was totally excluded.

After the victory of the October revolution George Buchanan, the
British ambassador to Russia, sent a telegram to the British Foreign Office advising "that the only safe course is to give Russia back her word
and to tell her people that, realizing how worn out they are by the war
and the disorganization inseparable from a great revolution, we leave it
to them to decide whether they will purchase peace on Germany's
terms or fight on with the Allies. . . . For us to hold to our pound of
flesh and insist on Russia fulfilling her obligations under the 1914
Agreement, is to play Germany's game."

The historian Louis Fischer, after giving this quotation, comments
aptly as follows:

"If the ambassador had sent such a dispatch six months earlier and
persuaded his superiors of its wisdom, and if the other Western am-
bassadors in Petrograd had done likewise and met with equal success,
there might have been no Soviet government. There was nothing
preordained by history or heaven in the development that occurred."[14]

It is also known that a congress of the Right SR Party was held in
Petrograd soon after the October revolution. Most of those who spoke
at this congress saw as the main reason for their defeat the incorrect
tactics of the SR Central Committee, which had proved incapable of
decisive action. A resolution of that congress on the existing situation
stated that a stage of coalition with the bourgeoisie was necessary for
socialist democracy and had rendered great service in 1917, but that
for the future it was not justified and should be abandoned. The party,
the resolution went on, "did not show the necessary decisiveness at
the crucial moments and failed to take power into its own hands in
time, leaving it until the end in the hands of a weakened and colorless
government which had lost all popularity and became easy prey to the
first conspiracy to be hatched."[15]

The Russian bourgeoisie wished to continue the war "to a victorious
conclusion." But it did not wish to carry on the war *regardless* of the
cost, certainly not at the cost of losing power. Within a few months
after the October revolution the counterrevolutionary government of
General Krasnov in the Don region made a de facto alliance with the
German high command and allowed several large German units to
enter the Don territory. The Volunteer Army and Denikin oriented

toward the Western Allies. But as early as August 1918, when World War I was still going on, Miliukov argued, in a confidential letter to Denikin, that it was necessary to come to terms with Germany, to agree to the independence of Poland and Finland, even to benevolent neutrality toward Germany, if only the Germans would help establish a central, national government headed by the Grand Duke Michael.[16]

Nor was there any preordination in the policy of the Provisional Government toward the Constituent Assembly. At any rate the Provisional Government could have convened the Assembly as early as the summer of 1917 and thereby have strengthened its position. As one historian has written, "The Provisional Government did not know how to use its time to its own advantage and did not succeed in accomplishing the task for which it was created. Precisely in this lay its historical failure."[17]

From what we have said it is evident that the October revolution was not at all an absolutely inevitable event; to an even greater degree than the February revolution, it represented the realization of one of the possible alternative lines of Russia's historical development. It was neither accidental nor absolutely unavoidable, but like any historical event, was a combination of accident and necessity.

four

Spontaneity and Organization in the Actions of the Masses in 1917

The question of the relation between spontaneity and organization in the revolutionary movement long preoccupied the Russian revolutionary parties. Pointing to the experience of Western Europe, the Mensheviks argued that mass popular revolutions always begin spontaneously. Therefore no party could "set a date" for a revolution in Russia; the revolution would come by itself and could not be "organized." The party should be ready for revolution; its members should engage in agitation and propaganda, helping to clarify the aims of the revolution and to bring forward leaders of the people. But popular movements could not be directed the way a military commander directs troop movements during a battle.

After the huge demonstrations of January 1905 the Mensheviks wrote, in *Iskra* (which they controlled), that this upsurge of spontaneous, mass proletarian struggle definitively refuted both the liberal skeptics, who had no faith that the "people would speak," and the Bolsheviks, "the utopians of conspiratorial organization," who thought it possible, in the name of "formal organizational discipline, to use the mechanical lever of a body of agents to direct the many millions in the army of the working class to suit their own purposes."[1] The task of Social Democracy, Martov wrote at that time, "is not so much to organize the people's revolution as to unleash it, set it loose."[2] Leading Social Democrats in Western Europe held similar views. "Revolutions do not let anyone play the schoolmaster with them," Rosa Luxemburg wrote. "The masses will be the active chorus and the directing bodies will merely take the 'speaking parts,' that is, will only be the interpreters of the mass will." Luxemburg even considered the Bolsheviks' demands for military and technical preparations for insurrection utopian.[3]

The Bolsheviks had a different view. They did not deny the possibility or importance of spontaneous revolutionary actions such as the January 1905 demonstration of the Petrograd proletariat or the mutiny on the battleship *Potemkin*. Much later, in summing up the experience of the February revolution, Lenin wrote: "It is beyond all doubt that the spontaneity of the movement is proof that it is deeply rooted in the masses, that its roots are firm, and that it is inevitable."[4] But spontaneity by itself is not enough. It was precisely the spontaneousness, the lack of organization, and corresponding fragmentation of the revolutionary actions in the 1905−7 revolution that, in the opinion of the Bolsheviks, were the main reasons for the failure of that revolution. "A people's revolution cannot be timed," Lenin wrote. "But if we have really prepared an uprising, and if a popular uprising is realizable by virtue of the revolutions in social relations *that have already taken place,* then it is quite possible to time the uprising."[5] Lenin likewise entitled one of his articles in the newspaper *Vperyod* "Should We Organize the Revolution?" His answer was essentially in the affirmative.

The 1905−7 revolution did not resolve this dispute. The spontaneous mass actions of the workers, peasants, and sailors at that time were defeated, but such preplanned, organized, and carefully timed actions by the Bolsheviks (with SR participation) as the December armed uprising in Moscow did not lead to victory either.

The February revolution of 1917 was largely the result of a spontaneous eruption of the mass unrest among the working men and women of Petrograd and the soldiers of the garrison who supported them. To the surprise of the authorities even the Cossack regiments, which the government had gradually assembled in Petrograd, Moscow, and other strategic centers from the end of 1916 on, joined the revolution. Resistance by isolated police units was put down in a day or two, the gendarmes disappeared from the streets of the cities, and the revolution swept like a great fire through the whole country and was supported on all the battlefronts. Berdyaev was close to the truth when he wrote: "One cannot even say that the February revolution overthrew the monarchy in Russia; the monarchy fell by itself; no one defended it; it had no supporters." [6] In other words the February revolution occurred approximately in the way that the Mensheviks conceived of political revolution; no one timed this revolution in advance, and no one drew up a plan of how it would unfold, either in Petrograd or the country as a whole. No one afterward could find out the name of the soldier who brought out the Volynsky regiment in support of the striking workers—an event which proved the turning point in the February revolution.

Many learned historians and many participants in the February revolution have written about its spontaneous and unexpected nature. "No one organization can assume for itself," wrote V. Bazarov, "the honor of having led in the first days of the revolution." [7] N. Sukhanov, a prominent participant in the February events, has also testified: "No single party was prepared for the great upheaval. They were all dreaming, having presentiments, and 'feeling things out.' " [8] An SR member, V. Zenzinov, wrote soon after the fall of the monarchy: "The revolution struck like a bolt from the blue and caught not only the government, the Duma, and the existing public organizations by surprise; . . . it was also a surprise to us revolutionaries." [9] Ten years after the revolution the Menshevik O. A. Yermansky recalled: "The streets were taken over totally by the masses of workers who poured out in an avalanche. This was a spontaneous movement which had no clearly formed or immediate goal. Whether there were attempts at some sort of leadership I do not know. It would seem not." [10]

The same thesis, that the February revolution was completely spontaneous and surprising, is repeated in many Western historical studies. "The Revolution to which all the revolutionary parties looked forward," wrote Merle Fainsod, in How Russia Is Ruled, "took them all by surprise." [11] The American historian W. B. Walsh has asserted: "The February—March revolution was in no sense either a Bolshevik or Marxist movement in causation, organization or direction. It was a chaotic happening." [12]

Lenin, too, more than once commented on the predominantly spontaneous nature of the February events. "In February the masses created the Soviets even before any party had managed to proclaim this slogan. It was the great creative spirit of the people, which had passed through the bitter experience of 1905 and had been made wise by it, that gave rise to this form of proletarian power." [13]

However, it is also true that the unexpectedness and rapidity of the revolutionary explosion at the beginning of 1917, which in fact no one could have predicted *in this particular form* and for which no one was prepared, was connected with the tremendous preparatory work of all the revolutionary parties over the preceding years. The "dress rehearsal" of the revolutionary events of 1917 was the 1905–7 revolution. By drafting millions of peasants and workers into the army and training them to handle weapons, the tsarist regime, without intending to, provided military and technical training, and laid the material and technical basis for the revolution. Of enormous importance in the ensuing events was the fact that the junior officer corps, which before the war had preserved its aristocratic character, was filled with replacements from the students and the intelligentsia and from soldiers and Cossacks who had distinguished themselves in the war. The likely allies of the working class, the peasants, were armed and organized in military garrisons in every major city, with especially large garrisons in Moscow and Petrograd.

Of course, one cannot fail to observe that not only the extreme left-wing parties but the liberal-monarchist and bourgeois parties, too, helped lay the basis for the revolution by their vocal criticism of the tsarist government. Many speeches by famous Duma orators were circulated in manuscript or through the newspapers not only in bourgeois and liberal circles but also among the students, intelligentsia, and part of the working class. Miliukov felt that, in criticizing the government, the Duma was restraining the mob and thus helping to protect the authority of the state. But this was an illusion. V. Shulgin was closer to the truth when he persistently asked himself: "Isn't the Progressive Bloc criticizing the government too strongly by asserting that the government does everything wrong? Won't this help the revolution? Are we holding back the revolution or fanning the flames?" [14] To be sure, given the blind, unyielding stance of the dynasty, the activity of the Progressive Bloc objectively helped pave the way for the February revolution.

The activity of the Mensheviks, SRs, Narodniks, and other political groups and parties similar to them, including the various nationalist parties, all helped to bring on the February revolution. The position of most of them was defensist; nevertheless they criticized the government and the monarchy more and more sharply. One of the appeals of the Menshevik Defensists in the fall of 1916 spoke plainly of "removing, overthrowing, or abolishing the regime which has brought the

country to the brink of disaster." It also declared that "the democra-
tization of the country cannot be separated from the defense of the
country." [15]

But the Bolsheviks did much more significant spadework for the revolution, though it was not so noticeable as that of the Progressive Bloc.
Only the Bolsheviks were in fact able to maintain a widespread underground organization in the chief proletarian centers, and many of
its sections penetrated the army as well. In the midst of the war Shliapnikov returned to Russia on instructions from the Central Committee
to take charge of the Russian Bureau. On the eve of February he
wrote in a report to the Central Committee: "By comparison with
others our situation is splendid. It can be said that we are the only
ones who have an all-Russia organization at the present time. . . . .
The Mensheviks, Unificationists and others who had split are re-
joining the party. . . . The political struggle is growing sharper every
day. There is seething unrest throughout the country. A revolutionary
hurricane could break out any day. The atmosphere is ·extremely
threatening." [16]

Almost all the strikes and demonstrations in the capital city in
January and February in 1917 had leaders; they were coordinated by
the Bolshevik district committees and the Petrograd committee. As of
February 1917 the Bolshevik organizations throughout the country
had about 24,000 members, with 600 in Moscow and about 2,000 in
Petrograd.[17] "These people," Sukhanov wrote about the Bolsheviks in
those days, "were buried in a completely different kind of work, keeping the equipment of the movement in repair, forcing the pace for a
decisive clash with the tsarist regime, organizing propaganda and the
underground press." [18]

Despite all the facts we have cited we still cannot deny that the revolution in February was primarily spontaneous; we cannot say that the
Bolsheviks were its chief organizers, or that the revolutionary events
developed according to some secret but precise plan worked out by
the Russian Bureau of the Central Committee. Nevertheless, it would
be equally wrong to argue that the revolution had not been prepared
in any real way and that it caught everyone by surprise. The truth lies
somewhere in between these extreme positions. Trotsky came fairly
close to the truth when he wrote at a later time in his book on the February revolution:

The mystic doctrine of spontaneousness explains nothing. In order correctly to appraise the situation and determine the moment for a blow at the enemy, it was necessary that the masses or their guiding layers should make their examination of historical events and have their criteria for estimating them. In other words it was necessary that there should be not masses in the abstract, but masses of Petrograd workers and Russian workers in general, who had passed through the revolution of 1905, through the Moscow insurrection of December 1905, shattered against the Semenovsky Regiment of the Guard. It was necessary that throughout this mass should be scattered workers who had thought over the experience of 1905, criticized the constitutional illusions of the liberals and Mensheviks, assimilated the perspectives of the revolution, meditated hundreds of times about the question of the army, watched attentively what was going on in its midst—workers capable of making revolutionary inferences from what they observed and communicating them to others. And finally, it was necessary that there should be in the troops of the garrison itself progressive soldiers, seized, or at least touched, in the past by revolutionary propaganda.

In every factory, in each guild, in each company, in each tavern, in the military hospital, at the transfer stations, even in the depopulated villages, the molecular work of revolutionary thought was in progress. Everywhere were to be found the interpreters of events, chiefly from among the workers, from whom one inquired, "What's the news?" and from whom one awaited the needed words. These leaders had often been left to themselves, had nourished themselves upon fragments of revolutionary generalizations arriving in their hands by various routes. . . . Elements of experience, criticism, initiative, self-sacrifice, seeped down through the mass and created, invisibly to a superficial glance but no less decisively, an inner mechanics of the revolutionary movement as a conscious process.[19]

The Bolshevik organizations in Petrograd of course prepared the way for the revolution and prepared themselves for it. But not even they supposed that the events would unfold at such breakneck speed. It is indicative that the Bolsheviks did not schedule any strikes or demonstrations for February 23. The Petrograd Committee projected the decisive demonstration for May 1, 1917 (a general strike and street demonstration).[20] But events outran this projection. It was on February 23 that the spontaneous actions of the Petrograd working women began, soon to be joined as we know by the entire working class of the city. Control of the incipient mass movement was not lost, however. All the party committees immediately joined the movement, seeking not only to give it political form but also to bring their own representatives to the fore.

No small role was played in the events of the first days and weeks of the revolution by individual groups of Mensheviks and SRs, who still had great influence in the factories (the Mensheviks) and among the soldiers of the garrison (SRs). Thus, for example, the leadership of the Petrograd Soviet was actually in the hands of three persons in the first few days after the revolution: Yuri Steklov, who did not consider himself either a Bolshevik or a Menshevik at that time; N. Sukhanov, who belonged to the Menshevik Internationalist group; and N. D. Sokolov, who belonged to the left wing of the Menshevik party in February 1917.[21] It was these three who helped draw up the celebrated Order No. 1 of the Petrograd Soviet, which served to rapidly revolutionize the army. With the return of other, more authoritative Social Democratic and SR leaders to Petrograd, these early activists of the Petrograd Soviet retired into the background.

It is very important to trace Lenin's political course in January and February 1917. Separated from Russia and stranded in neutral Switzerland, Lenin closely followed the events in Russia, Europe, and the whole world through the press and through information that reached him by private channels. Of course he was expecting revolution in Russia and the other European countries and doing everything he could to bring the day of the revolutionary explosion closer. Lenin was certain that the world war would end in a revolution in most of the countries of Europe, but he could not of course predict the exact course of events, either political or military. He also saw clearly that Russia was the weakest link among the warring countries and he thought carefully about the possible alternative lines of development. In his article "A Turn in World Politics," published on January 31, 1917, Lenin wrote:

> It is possible that a separate peace between Germany and Russia *has been concluded* after all. . . . The tsar may have told Wilhelm: "If I openly sign a separate peace, then tomorrow, you, my august counterpart, may have to deal with a government of Miliukov and Guchkov, if not of Miliukov and Kerensky. For the revolution is growing, and I cannot answer for the army, whose generals are in correspondence with K. G. Guchkov and whose officers are yesterday's high-school boys. Does it make sense for us to risk my losing my throne and you perhaps losing your worthy counterpart?"[22]

Lenin's lecture to young Swiss workers on the 1905 revolution is often referred to. In this January 1917 lecture Lenin said in part:

> We must not be deceived by the present gravelike stillness in Europe. Europe is pregnant with revolution. The monstrous horrors of the imperialist war, the suffering caused by the high cost of living everywhere engender a revolutionary mood; and the ruling classes . . . are more and more moving into a blind alley from which they can never extricate themselves without horrendous upheavals. . . . The coming years, precisely because of this predatory war, will lead to popular uprisings under the leadership of the proletariat against the power of finance capital, against the big banks, and against the capitalists; and these upheavals cannot end otherwise than with the expropriation of the bourgeoisie, with the victory of socialism. We of the older generation may not live to see the decisive battles of this coming revolution. But I can, I believe, express the confident hope that the youth which is working so splendidly in the socialist movement . . . will be fortunate enough not only to fight but also to win in the coming proletarian revolution.[23]

It is quite evident that the sentence about the "older generation" who might not live to see the revolution (which broke out in Russia within a month and a half) was only a rhetorical device in that particular context. Lenin actually felt a great certainity that the revolution was not far off. Krupskaya in her reminiscences said: "Never before had Vladimir Ilyich been in such an uncompromising mood as he was during the last months of 1916 and the early months of 1917. He was positively certain that the revolution was imminent."[24]

Lenin's letters to Inessa Armand from December 1916 to February 1917 are also frequently cited. There is much in these letters about émigré squabbles of all sorts, about the state of affairs in Switzerland, and so on. Lenin frequently inquires about Inessa's health, advises her to ski more often, writes about Nadezhda Konstantinovna Krupskaya's illnesses, and about his work on the theory of the state. But this is quite natural. Lenin was interested in many questions—theoretical, personal, and political. But in the same letters we find references to reports from friends in Russia that the mood there is "extremely revolutionary." And in his letter of February 19 Lenin informs Armand: "The other day we had a gratifying letter from Moscow. . . . They write that the mood of the masses is a good one, that chauvinism is clearly declining, and that probably our day will come."[25]

According to the recollections of Willi Muenzenberg, during a meeting in Zurich not long before the revolutionary events in Petrograd, Lenin tried to convince him of the inevitability of a revolution in the near future.[26]

But it would be odd to think that Lenin could predict the exact week or month of the outbreak of revolution in Russia and the rapid pace of its development and to conclude from this that the revolution was "fate's gift to Lenin." A year and a half after the February revolution Lenin said, "Two months before January 1905 and before February 1917 not one revolutionary, no matter how experienced and knowledgeable, no one who knew the life of the people, was able to predict that such an event would break Russia apart." This is the special nature of popular uprisings, most of which—like the February revolution—are spontaneous. "Spontaneous outbreaks," Lenin observed subsequently, "become inevitable as the revolution matures. There has never been a revolution in which this was not the case, nor can there be." [27]

★   ★   ★

If, in spite of everything, spontaneity prevailed amid the unfolding events of the February revolution, the October revolution developed and matured in quite a different way. This is understandable. The February revolution took place in a country deprived of basic democratic freedoms, which was one of the main reasons that the revolution emerged from a spontaneous, and therefore poorly directed, explosion of popular unrest. The situation was quite different before October. The mass of the people had enjoyed virtually total political freedom for more than a half a year. All the left political parties had been legalized, and their numbers had grown rapidly. The Bolshevik Party, because of its program, organization, and discipline, had very quickly become the chief party in the industrial centers during this time. Although the bourgeoisie was in power for several months after February, it could not eliminate the situation of dual power (the Provisional Government on the one side and the Soviets on the other), nor was it able to construct an administrative apparatus that could be at all effective in such a short time and in such a fluid situation. With the old apparatus of the tsarist regime falling apart before all eyes (the prisons were destroyed, as were the police stations; the court system was inoperative; and officers were stripped of their former authority and privileges), the feverish attempts of the bourgeoisie and the Compromiser parties to organize a new apparatus of power achieved no noticeable results.

Under these conditions the Bolsheviks were able not only to carry out active propaganda work but also to build a *political army* for a new revolution. They did a great deal of organizational work to establish real *military support* for the new revolution. Armed Red Guard units with a unified command were established in the factories. The Bolsheviks succeeded in becoming the dominant force in the revolutionary organizations of the Baltic fleet. And their influence grew in many units of the garrison in the capital and on the fronts (especially the Northwestern front).

It was especially important when the Petrograd and Moscow Soviets came under Bolshevik control, because until then the Provisional Government had maintained itself not so much on the support of the army or the state apparatus as on the active, or at least passive, support of the Soviets.

It is true that in September and early October 1917 there was an evident decline in the mass movement, while at the same time the pogromist, Black Hundred, and anti-Bolshevik press was increasing its circulation everywhere, a fact that Lenin's opponents frequently pointed to. But he convincingly refuted these arguments. "Absenteeism and indifference on the part of the masses is due to their being tired of words and resolutions," he said at the Central Committee meeting of October 10 (23), 1917.[28] A few days later Lenin further explained his point of view as follows: "Yes, the masses today are in no mood to rush out into the streets. . . . What is needed for an uprising is not this, but, on the one hand a conscious, firm, and unswerving resolve on the part of the class-conscious elements to fight to the end; and on the other, a mood of despair among the broad masses who *feel* that nothing now can be saved by half-measures. . . . The development of the revolution has in practice brought *both* the workers *and* the peasantry to precisely this combination of a tense mood resulting from experience among the class-conscious and a mood of hatred toward those using the lockout weapon and the capitalists that is close to despair among the broadest masses."[29] (Emphasis in the original.)

Subsequent events showed that Lenin was right. Basing itself on his urging that armed insurrection be treated as an art, the Military Revolutionary Committee of the Petrograd Soviet worked out a plan of action that detailed the deployment of forces in the coming battle; this plan was implemented precisely according to schedule and was crowned with complete success. With somewhat greater difficulty and greater losses the armed insurrection was carried out successfully in Moscow, too. In many other cities it proved possible to avoid an armed insurrection, and power passed into the hands of the Soviets peacefully without any shooting or casualties.

The October revolution was in fact the first great popular revolution in which the spontaneous factor was not of decisive importance and which was carried out in an organized and precise way in virtually total conformity with the plan drawn up in advance. Thus Lenin's idea that it was possible and desirable not only to prepare politically but also to "plan" and "organize" the revolution received full confirmation. It turned out that revolutions, notwithstanding Rosa Luxemburg's opinion, will submit to tutelage after all. Jean-François Revel's book *Neither Marx Nor Jesus* has many paradoxical arguments, more often wrong than right, and much of what he predicted five or six years ago has not been borne out. But it must be admitted that many of his ideas are correct. And this applies to the question of the "organization" of revolution.

> Revolutions . . . are not improvised; and they are not accomplished through doctrinal inflexibility. In the first case, a would-be revolutionary imagines that he will "play it by ear" and proceed by means of dialogue with the people. In the second, a dogmatic revolutionary is concerned only with knowing whether his revolution is like earlier revolutions, whether it is proceeding according to the rules. The true revolutionary, however, follows the path of prepared extemporization, as it were; that is, he excludes no possible expedient, but, once a means is adopted, it is applied rigorously and with technical competence and exactitude. In this case, all that is left to collective inspiration are the basic concepts of historic evolution. So far as the means of execution are concerned, they are evaluated realistically, in the cold light of reason. If revolutions fail, it is because their general concepts are too rigid, precise, and cold, and because the application of those concepts, being ill-defined, does not succeed in changing reality. Unsuccessful revolutions, in other words, are intellectually bureaucratic, and practically amateurish.[30]

The October socialist revolution was not intellectually bureaucratic; on the contrary, it was highly professional in its practical work.

★   ★   ★

Since the October revolution was not the result of a spontaneous outbreak, the question naturally arises, To what extent did the actions of the Bolsheviks contain an element of risk and how great was the danger of their being defeated?

It is not hard to see that in October 1917 the victory of the Bolsheviks in Petrograd and Moscow was for all practical purposes assured. After all, the decision of the Sixth Party Congress in favor of an armed insurrection was no secret to the Provisional Government. That government was fairly well informed about the Bolsheviks' preparations for an armed insurrection in October 1917, though not of the exact timing or details of the operation. But by September and October Kerensky could no longer force the Bolsheviks to retreat or drive them underground, as he had partially succeeded in doing in July. The forces of counterrevolution in Russia were still quite powerful, but Kerensky was no longer in a position to unite them. In the wake of the Kornilov movement his government lost the support of the majority of the officers, generals, and of most of the Cadet Party. The contempt these people felt for Kerensky was undisguised, and many of them even wanted the Bolsheviks to overthrow the Provisional Government. They felt sure that the Bolsheviks would not be able to stay in power even for two weeks and that, after them, a strong, "truly Russian" state would have its turn. For example, the monarchist newspaper *Novaya Rus'* demanded the immediate removal of Kerensky and called for an "interim government" of "irreproachable all-national Russian names," such as General Alekseev, G. Plekhanov, Bishop Andrei Ufimsky, N. V. Chaikovsky, Nikolai Morozov, and a number of fighting Cossacks who had served brilliantly. One of the first tasks of such a government would have been "to restore the good name of General Kornilov, to withdraw all charges against him, and to place him in the sacred position of representative of all Russia."[31]

Kerensky of course had no wish to acknowledge his own isolation and weakness at that time. V. D. Nabokov, a prominent member of the Provisional Government, subsequently wrote: "Four or five days before the October Bolshevik insurrection I asked him (Kerensky) directly what his attitude would be toward action by the Bolsheviks, which everyone was talking about. 'I would be willing to pray aloud that such action would take place,' he answered me. 'But are you sure that you could handle them?' 'I have more forces than I need. They will be crushed completely.' "[32]

As we know, the opening of the Second Congress of Soviets was originally set for October 20. The Provisional Government expected the Bolsheviks to move on that day. On October 16, 1917, G. Polkovnikov, commander-in-chief of the Petrograd military district, reported to a closed session of the Provisional Government that the mood of the Petrograd garrison as a whole was on the side of the Provisional Government and there was no need to fear active participation by these troops in any action by the Bolsheviks. At a meeting of one of the commissions of the Pre-Parliament the same Polkovnikov made the even stronger statement that no military actions by the Bolsheviks would be permitted. All the necessary measures had been taken and, if the Bolsheviks made a move, they would be crushed the moment they began.

Nevertheless the VTsIK postponed the opening of the Congress of Soviets until October 25, expecting the arrival of a number of Menshevik and SR delegates in Petrograd. The Bolsheviks made no move on October 20, nor had they planned to. On that day *Izvestia,* the newspaper of the VTsIK, wrote in an article entitled "Ultimatum": "Their adventure with an armed insurrection in Petrograd is over and done with. They proved to be completely isolated in this adventure, surrounded on all sides not by Kornilovites but by the universal indignation of the entire democracy, and they have already surrendered. . . ."[33]

But this was sheer illusion. Not only in Petrograd but in virtually all of the industrial centers of the country the Bolsheviks had become stronger than their opponents since September 1917—both politically and militarily. Kerensky came to understand this too late. The Western Sovietologist Bertram D. Wolfe interviewed the aged ex-premier in the United States and asked him why he had not suppressed the Bolsheviks the minute they openly declared war against his government. Kerensky replied: "What force did I have to suppress them with?"[34]

Colonel Polkovnikov's assumptions proved to be mistaken. Although only part of the garrison supported the Bolsheviks, the other part emphatically refused to support the Provisional Government and announced its neutrality.

Estimates by Soviet historians indicate that on the eve of the October insurrection there were in Petrograd alone no fewer than 300,000 men in armed worker, soldier, and sailor units on the Bolshevik side. On October 24 the Provisional Government had at its disposal little more than 25,000 men. On the evening of October 25, when preparations were underway for the storming of the Winter Palace, the Bolsheviks assembled about 20,000 Red Guards, sailors, and soldiers before that last refuge place of the Provisional Government. But within the palace there were not more than 3,000 defenders, and many of those left their posts during the night. Thanks to the Bolsheviks' overwhelming superiority there were no serious battles in the capital from October 24 to October 26, and the total number of those killed on both sides was no more than 15, with no more than 60 wounded.[35]

During these critical hours, as all the main strategic points in the city passed under Bolshevik control (telephone and telegraph exchanges, bridges, railroad stations, the Winter Palace, etc.), Petrograd continued on the whole to go about its normal business. Most of the soldiers remained in the barracks, the plants and factories continued to operate, and in the schools none of the classes were interrupted. There were no strikes or mass demonstrations, such as had accompanied the February revolution. The movie theaters (called "cinematographias" in those days) were filled, there were regular performances in all the theaters, and people strolled as usual on Nevsky Prospect. The ordinary, nonpolitical person would not even have noticed the historic events taking place; even on the streetcar lines, the main form of public transportation in 1917, service remained normal. It was in one of those streetcars that Lenin, in disguise, and his bodyguard Eino Rahya traveled to Smolny late on the evening of October 24 from the apartment of M. V. Fofanova, where Lenin had been in hiding during the last few days before October. Louis Fischer, one of Lenin's Western biographers, wrote:

> Outwardly everything had happened so calmly, without casualties, without fighting or disorder, that complete enthusiasm reigned in the Smolny when Lenin arrived on the evening of October 24. Lenin spent the first night in the Smolny; it was late at night, almost dawn, when he went to sleep in the same room as Trotsky (see the latter's memoirs). On the next day, at 2 A.M. on October 26 (November 8), the Winter Palace was taken. The Provisional Government was arrested.

On learning this, Lenin removed his wig and makeup. He appeared briefly before the Petrograd Soviet and then went to the home of Bonch-Bruevich to spend the night. There were no sentries outside the apartment and no bodyguards. Bonch-Bruevich recalled later that he had

> fastened the front door with its chain, hook and lock and loaded and cocked his revolvers. "It's our first night," he thought, "anything might happen." Lenin was given a small bedroom; Bonch lay down on a couch

in another room. Lenin extinguished his light; Bonch too. Bonch was falling asleep when he heard Lenin get out of bed, switch on the electricity,
and start writing. . . . Early in the morning [Lenin] tiptoed back to bed.
He awoke several hours later and appeared in the living room fresh and
smiling. "Happy first-day-of-the-revolution," he greeted the family. [As
Bonch related,] "Soon we headed for Smolny on foot, but after a while
we boarded a trolleycar. Seeing the exemplary order in the streets, Vladimir Ilyich beamed." In his pocket was the Decree on Land, which he had
drafted in pencil during the night. That evening (after the Decree on
Peace had been adopted) Lenin read the Decree on Land to the
Congress of Soviets which approved it unanimously.[36]

Writing about the decisive hours and days of the October revolution
15 years later, Leon Trotsky similarly wrote:

The final act of the revolution seems, after all else, too brief, too dry, too
business-like—somehow out of correspondence with the historic scope of
the events. The reader experiences a kind of disappointment. . . . Where
is the insurrection? There is no picture of the insurrection. The events do
not form themselves into a picture. A series of small operations, calculated
and prepared in advance, remain separated one from another both in
space and time. A unity of thought and aim unites them, but they do not
fuse in the struggle itself. There is no action of great masses. There are no
dramatic encounters with the troops. There is nothing of all that which
imaginations brought up upon the facts of history associate with the idea
of insurrection.

The general character of the revolution in the capital subsequently
moved Masaryk, among many others, to write: "The October revolution
. . . was anything but a popular mass movement. That revolution was
the act of leaders working from above and behind the scenes." As a matter of fact it was the most popular mass-insurrection in all history. The
workers had no need to come out into the public square in order to fuse
together: they were already politically and morally one single whole without that. The soldiers were even forbidden to leave their barracks without
permission. . . . But whose invisible masses were marching more than
ever before in step with the events. . . . The bourgeois classes had expected barricades, flaming conflagrations, looting, rivers of blood. In reality a silence reigned more terrible than all the thunders of the world. The
social ground shifted noiselessly like a revolving stage, bringing forward
the popular masses, carrying away to limbo the rulers of yesterday.[37]

Kerensky, who was still formally the supreme commander-in-chief,
managed to flee Petrograd, as we know, not long before the taking of
the Winter Palace. He was certain he would soon return to the capital
at the head of a powerful phalanx of troops loyal to the government.
But no one had any desire to support him seriously. The Cossack

corps of General Krasnov was deployed not far from Petrograd. Kerensky wished to bring this corps against Petrograd first of all. But the meeting between Kerensky and Krasnov was far from friendly. Krasnov writes in his memoirs:

> I walked up to Kerensky. *The* notorious Kerensky. I had never, not for one moment, been one of his admirers. I had never seen him before and had read very few of his speeches, but everything about him was so disgusting and repellent that it made me sick. Even his self-assurance and the fact that he set his hand to everything and was able to do everything repelled me. When he was minister of justice I said nothing. But when Kerensky became minister of the army and navy everything in me rebelled. In the middle of a war, I thought, how could a person take charge of the military when he understood nothing of military matters. The military art is one of the most difficult, and for that reason it requires training of the will and of the mind as well as knowledge. If dilletantism is undesirable in any art, in the art of warfare it is impermissible.
> Kerensky as a military leader! Peter the Great, Rumiantsev, Suvorov, Kutuzov, Yermolov, Skobelev, and—Kerensky!
> He had destroyed the army and insulted military science, and therefore I regarded him with hatred and contempt.
> And here I was approaching him on a magical moonlit night when reality seemed like a dream. I was approaching him in his capacity as supreme commander in chief, to place my life and the lives of people who trusted me at his complete disposal.

Krasnov recalls that when he reported to his own immediate superior—General Cheremisov, commander of the Northern Front—to inform him of Kerensky's wishes Cheremisov was at first reluctant even to come out and speak to Krasnov.

> His eyes were dull and lusterless and he avoided looking at me. He yawned, either from nervousness or as a way of showing me what great nonsense it was I was telling him. "The Provisional Government is in danger," I said, "and we have sworn our loyalty to the Provisional Government; it is our duty. . . ."
> Cheremisov looked at me. "The Provisional Government doesn't exist," he said wearily but stubbornly, as though trying to convince me. . . . "I order you to detrain your columns and remain in Ostrov. Isn't that enough for you? You aren't going to be able to accomplish anything anyhow." [38]

Kerensky managed to persuade some of the Cossack units to march on Petrograd after all. But after the first few skirmishes with the Red Guards and sailors, Krasnov's Cossacks refused to fight any longer; they demanded a truce and the surrender of Kerensky. The former premier and supreme commander-in-chief fled like a coward from his headquarters by a secret route after dressing up as a woman. Meeting scorn and hatred wherever he went, he soon emigrated from Russia. General Krasnov was arrested but shortly thereafter released on his "word of honor."

In the country as a whole, however, the situation was much more complicated and the balance of forces was by no means as clear and well-defined as in Petrograd. Russia was still at war and there were more than 10 million men under arms and in position on all the different fronts. Not only the body of generals and officers but also the majority of the elected army committees were hostile toward the new power in the capital. Taking advantage of this mood, General Dukhonin, the commander of the Russian army in the field, refused to recognize the Council of People's Commissars (Sovnarkom) or to carry out its orders. This placed the new government in an extremely awkward position, and Lenin's consequent decision to remove Dukhonin and appoint the Bolshevik Ensign N. Krylenko in his place was an extremely risky step. Let us quote Stalin's recollections in this particular case.

> I recall that Lenin, Krylenko . . . and I went to General Staff Headquarters in Petrograd to negotiate with Dukhonin over the direct wire. *It was a ghastly moment.* Dukhonin and Field Headquarters (the Stavka) categorically refused to obey the order of the Council of People's Commissars [on the cessation of military operations and the initiation of peace talks with the Germans—R.M.]. The army officers were completely under the sway of Field Headquarters. As for the soldiers, no one could tell what this army of fourteen million would say, subordinated as it was to the so-called army organizations, which were hostile to the Soviet power.[39]

As we know, Dukhonin refused to recognize the order for his removal; not only would he not begin peace talks with the Germans but he also continued to feverishly assemble forces to combat the Bolsheviks and overthrow Soviet power. At that point Lenin appealed directly to the soldiers in the name of the Sovnarkom, proposing that the regiments at the front directly assume the responsibility for peace talks themselves. "This was unquestionably the right thing to do," Krylenko wrote a year later,

> It was aimed not so much at obtaining immediate practical results from such talks as at establishing the total and unquestionable predominance of the new governing authority on the front lines. The minute the regi-

ments and divisions were offered this right and were given the order to take reprisals against anyone who dared to interfere with the peace talks, the cause of the revolution in the army was won and the counterrevolutionary cause hopelessly lost. . . . And there was no reason to fear that chaos would be produced at the front. The war was paralyzed by this measure. There was nothing to fear from the Germans—they could be expected to take a wait-and-see attitude, and they did. At the same time the danger of counterrevolution at the front was done away with.[40]

Paying no attention to the Stavka under Dukhonin, located at Mogilev, the Sovnarkom sent Krylenko to the front, giving him authorization to conclude a truce. The German command, which also wished to have a truce, recognized the authority of the negotiators sent by Krylenko to the headquarters of one of the German divisions. Krylenko immediately issued an order for a cease-fire on the entire front. A temporary truce was soon concluded with the German High Command and remained in effect until February 1918. Thus Dukhonin was isolated, and all hopes for making the Stavka the chief center for the battle against the new government were dashed. A number of generals, headed by the previously arrested Kornilov, fled to the Don region, and General Dukhonin himself was killed by the sailors and insurgent soldiers who occupied his headquarters.

The overall international situation, however, was much more complicated and hard to predict. Facing the tired, weakened, and demoralized Russian army at the front were the still fairly strong and disciplined armies of the German-Austrian coalition, and the truce with them was not a very firm guarantee against intervention. Moreover, there were millions of soldiers under arms in the countries allied with Russia— Great Britain, France, the United States, and Japan—and the Entente could use some of them to suppress the Russian revolution and reestablish the Eastern front.

When Lenin urged that the socialist revolution be started in wartime Russia, he calculated that the Russian proletariat would very soon have the support of the proletariat in the main European countries. In 1917 neither Lenin nor the other Bolshevik leaders hoped or supposed that a revolutionary Russia would be able to hold out for very long encircled by hostile capitalist powers. The problem was not so much to make the Russian revolution as to *begin* the world revolution, to establish a beachhead for it and to hold out as long as possible— until the revolutions in the other countries "matured." That was

Lenin's chief strategic calculation and that was his main risk, for the countless number of different factors shaping the international situation and determining the course of the war could not be foretold. And Lenin did not delude himself; he knew very well that to raise an armed rebellion in the rear of a fighting army in the midst of a world war was not only to run a risk but to stake everything on one card. The other members of the Soviet government understood this too.

But it would be unfair to accuse the Bolsheviks of playing an overly risky game. It was none other than Engels who wrote: "In revolution, as in war, it is in the highest degree necessary to stake everything on the decisive moment, whatever the odds may be. . . . It is a matter of course that, in every struggle, one who takes up the gauntlet risks being beaten; but is that any reason to confess oneself bested from the start and to submit to the yoke without ever drawing the sword?" [41]

Every revolution contains an element of risk. That was bound to be especially true of the first socialist revolution in history, which in almost every respect was a leap into the unknown. It is understandable that some people take a position of principle against all revolutions and all forms of revolutionary violence, although history has never so far been able to do without this "midwife." Whether some people like it or not, revolutions are not going to stop happening, at least for the time being, in our less than perfect world. Marx expressed the same sentiment as Engels when he wrote in one of his letters: "World history would indeed be very easy to make, if the struggle were taken up only on condition of infallibly favorable chances." [42]

Citing these words of Marx's, Lenin likewise wrote: "To attempt in advance to calculate the chances *with complete accuracy* would be quackery or hopeless pedantry." [43] The Bolsheviks were guided by these postulates in December 1905 and were defeated. But guided by the same concepts in October 1917, they were victorious.

PART TWO

Was the October Revolution Premature?

five

Is a "Premature" Revolution Possible?

Before considering the question of the "timeliness" or "prematureness" of the October socialist revolution it makes sense first to ask a different question: "Is it possible in general to have a premature revolution?" Didn't Marx say in one of his basic works that "no social order ever disappears before all the productive forces, for which there is room in it, have been developed; and new, higher relations of production never appear before the material conditions for their existence have matured in the womb of the old society"?[1] Wasn't it Marx also who said, "Humanity always takes up only such problems as it can solve; since, looking at the matter more closely, we will always find that the problem itself arises only when the material conditions necessary for its solution already exist or are at least in the process of formation"?[2]

It is not hard to see, however, that in this case Marx was talking about social revolution in the broadest sense of the term. In regard to specific revolutionary actions or political movements in particular countries, Marx and Engels always allowed for the possibility of actions that are obviously belated and of actions that are obviously premature. More than once they commented on mistaken attempts by revolutionaries in one or another country to "leap over" as yet uncompleted stages in the historical movement.

The question of how "ripe" a country might be for revolutionary transformation has often been the subject of bitter debate, both in scholarly writing and in politics. The Russian Narodniks of the 1860s seriously believed that Russia was already ripe for socialism and saw in

the village commune the ready-made beginnings of a socialist system.
On the other hand, from 1920 to 1929 all Marxists were certain that
capitalism had already outlived itself, that it would not be able to develop the productive forces any further, and that both Europe and the
United States were on the threshold of socialist revolution. The economic crisis of 1929–33 and World War II seemed to confirm this
interpretation. Who would have thought that forty years later, after
the war and even after the collapse of the colonial empires, capitalism
in Western Europe and the United States would get a "second wind"
and that a new scientific and technical revolution would arise and develop precisely "in the womb" of the capitalist system?

In general, in the history of revolutionary movements in any particular country it has been rare for revolution to come exactly "on time."
Virtually every victorious revolution was preceded by several *premature* and therefore unsuccessful attempts. And only a few of these
premature attempts deserve condemnation because they were marked
by thoughtless and irresponsible adventurism. Many premature actions
were organized by sincere revolutionaries who deeply believed in the
success of their undertakings, but who were incapable of correctly
judging their own strength and the strength of the enemy or, even
worse, were deceived or betrayed. More often premature actions have
occurred spontaneously, the product of the desperation of the oppressed who prefer death in the struggle to the unbearable existence
imposed upon them. The Spartacus rebellion and many less famous
slave revolts were of this kind, as were the peasant revolts of Stenka
Razin and Pugachev, and a multitude of other peasant revolts. The
weavers of Lyons in 1831 and the Communards of Paris in 1871 had
virtually no chance of success, nor did the proletarians of Moscow in
December 1905. But such actions have often enriched revolutionary
thought, given rise to important traditions, produced revolutionary
leaders, and ultimately contributed to the victory of the later revolution.

"Premature" revolutionary actions, or those which have not been
prepared carefully enough, almost always end in defeat. This was true
of the Decembrist revolt in 1825, Babeuf's Conspiracy of Equals in
1796, the Paris Commune in 1871, the December armed insurrection
in Moscow in 1905, and the Canton commune in 1927. But Marx and
Engels gave serious thought to the possibility of the victory of "premature" revolutions, in particular the possibility that the proletariat and its

party might come to power in a situation in which neither the objective nor the subjective conditions were ripe for the implementation of their radical socialist program.

In the event of such a premature political upheaval Engels predicted two possible lines of development.

In the first case the extremist party, having come to power, would carry out, not those reforms which it *wanted* and which constituted the essence of its political program, but only those which it *was able* to under the given social and economic conditions. Engels' predictions in regard to this situation were quite pessimistic.

"The worst thing that can befall a leader of an extreme party," wrote Engels back in 1850,

> is to be compelled to take over a government in an epoch when the movement is not yet ripe for the domination of the class which he represents, and for the realization of the measures which that domination implies. What he *can* do depends not on his will but upon the degree of contradiction between the various classes, and upon the level of development of the material means of existence, of the conditions of production and commerce upon which class contradictions always repose. What he *ought* to do, what his party demands of him, again depends not upon him or the stage of development of the class struggle. He is bound to the doctrines and demands hitherto propounded. . . . Thus he necessarily finds himself in an unsolvable dilemma. What he *can* do contradicts all his previous actions, and the principles and immediate interests of his party, and what he *ought* to do cannot be done. In a word, he is compelled to represent not his party or his class, but the class for whose domination the movement is then ripe. In the interests of the movement he is compelled to advance the interests of an alien class, and to feed his own class with phrases and promises, and with the asseveration that the interests of that alien class are their own interests. Whoever is put into this awkward position is irrevocably lost.[3]

In the second case, Engels conjectured, the extreme party, after coming to power, may try to carry out some of its own political demands, regardless of the objective material conditions. Engels' predictions in this case were even more pessimistic. He wrote in a letter to Weydemeyer in 1853,

> I have a presentiment that, thanks to the perplexity and flabbiness of all the others, our party will one fine morning be forced to assume power and finally to carry out the measures that are of no direct interest to us, but are in the general interests of the revolution and the specific interests of the petty bourgeoisie; on which occasion, driven by the proletarian

populace, bound by our own printed declarations and plans—more or less falsely interpreted, more or less passionately thrust to the fore in the party struggle—we shall be constrained to undertake communist experiments and perform leaps the untimeliness of which we know better than anyone else. In so doing we would lose our heads—only physically speaking, let us hope—a reaction sets in, and until the world is able to pass *historical* judgment on such events, we are considered not only beasts, which wouldn't matter, but also *bêtes* [fools], which is much worse. I do not quite see how it can turn out otherwise. In a backward country like Germany, which possesses an advanced party and is involved in an advanced revolution with an advanced country like France, the advanced party must get into power at the first serious conflict and as soon as *actual danger* is present, and that is, in any event, ahead of its normal time. All that does not matter, however, and the best thing we can do is for our party to have established its historical rehabilitation in its literature ahead of time, should events take such a turn.[4]

Similarly, the outstanding Russian socialist thinker Aleksandr Herzen was not very optimistic in his comments on premature action by the proletariat. He wrote:

After the old bourgeois world has been blown sky high, after the smoke has settled and the ruins have been cleared, there will begin anew, with various changes, some kind of bourgeois world. Because internally it will not have been eliminated and also because neither the world-builder nor the new organization will be so well-prepared that they can replenish themselves as they fulfill their functions.[5]

Almost forty years later, in 1891, Engels returned to the question of the possibility of a *premature* socialist revolution. However, the situation in Germany and throughout Europe was fundamentally different by then. In Germany there existed the strongest mass Social Democratic party in the world, and Engels placed great hopes in it and gave it the support of his tremendous moral authority. Influential socialist parties of considerable size existed in other European countries as well. It is clear from Engels' letters of 1890–91 that he thought Germany stood closest of all to a socialist revolution, owing to the rapid growth of industry there, the expansion of the working class numerically, and the spread of the Social Democratic movement. In estimating how much time might remain before such a revolution, Engels spoke of only some ten years, and he was confident that a victorious socialist revolution in Germany would set off similar revolutions in the other advanced Western European countries. Engels was apprehensive, however, that Russia and France might, in the interim, begin a war against Germany and that Germany would be defeated when faced by such powerful opponents on two fronts. Then the socialist movement would be defeated not only in Germany but in the other countries as well, and as a result, nationalism and the spirit of revenge would reign in Europe for a long time. That was why Engels did not raise the slogan "For the defeat of our own government" in that situation. On October 13, 1891, he wrote to Bebel:

> If the danger of war increases, we can tell the government that we should be ready, provided it makes this possible through proper treat-ment of us, to support it against the external enemy, on condition that it wages the war unwaveringly and making use of all means, including revo-lutionary ones. If Germany is attacked from both East and West, then any and every means of defense is justified. National existence is at stake, and for us also the maintenance of the position and the prospects for the fu-ture which we have won. The more revolutionary the way that the war is waged, the more will it be waged in our spirit. And it may happen that, owing to the cowardice of the bourgeois and Junkers, seeking to safe-guard their property, we shall prove to be the only energetic war party. Naturally, it may also happen that we shall be obliged to take the helm ourselves and act as in 1793, in order to throw out the Russians and their allies.[6]

Ten days later he expressed the same thought in a letter to Friedrich Sorge:

> If the Russians start war against us, German Socialists must go for the Russians and their allies, whoever they may be, à l'outrance. If Germany is crushed, then we shall be too, while in the most favorable case the struggle will be such a violent one that Germany will only be able to maintain herself by revolutionary means, so that very possibly we shall be forced to come into power and play the part of 1793.[7]

Although Engels thought that the rise of the Social Democrats to power in the early 1890s would still have been premature, he did not repeat his earlier gloomy prophecies in this regard. He thought that the German Social Democratic Party was already strong enough to hold power and begin construction of the new socialist society. In view of the fact, however, that subjectively the country was not ready for revo-lution, Engels thought it likely that a new Social Democratic govern-ment would have to use force and even terror to a greater extent than if it came to power under "riper" conditions. At the end of October 1891 Engels wrote again to Bebel:

In order to take possession of and set in motion the means of production, we need people with technical training, and masses of them. These
we have not got, and up till now we have even been rather glad that we
have been largely spared the "educated" people. Now things are different. Now we are strong enough to put up with any quantity of educated rubbish and to digest it, and I foresee that in the next eight or ten
years we shall recruit enough young technicians, doctors, lawyers, and
schoolmasters to enable us to have factories and big estates administered
on behalf of the nation by party comrades. Then, therefore, our entry into
power will be quite natural and will be settled relatively quickly. If, on the
other hand, a war brings us to power prematurely, the technicians will be
our chief enemies; they will deceive and betray us whenever they can and
we shall have to use terror against them, but shall get cheated all the
same. It is what always happened, on a small scale, to the French revolutionaries; even in the ordinary administration they had to leave the subordinate posts, where the real work is done, in the possession of old reac-
tionaries who obstructed and paralyzed everything. Therefore I hope and
desire that our splendid and secure development, which is advancing with
the calm and inevitability of a process of nature, may remain on its natural lines.[8]

Engels' gloomy predictions of 1850−53 in regard to socialists coming to power prematurely were well known to the Russian Marxists.
Engels' letters of the 1890−91 period were much less well known,
and they were only published in full after October. (Not very accurate
translations can be found in various anthologies of the 1920s, and it
was only in 1940, in the first edition of the collected works of Marx
and Engels, that more accurate and complete translations were published.) Regardless of all that, however, the question of whether Russia
was ripe for a socialist transformation, a question that had been discussed in Russian revolutionary and Narodnik circles ever since the
mid-nineteenth century, was also the subject of lively discussion within
the Russian Social Democratic Labor Party, founded at the turn of the
century. Without going through an entire history of this discussion, we
shall merely note that in 1917 the views of the Bolsheviks and Mensheviks on this question differed fundamentally.

six

Socialist Revolution in Russia and the Position of the Mensheviks and SRs

The Social Democrats (Mensheviks) and the Socialist Revolutionaries (SRs) thought of themselves not only as revolutionaries but also as socialists—i.e., advocates of a socialist revolution and the building of socialism in Russia. The Mensheviks also thought of themselves as Marxists, although their approach to the writings of Marx and Engels was pathetically dogmatic; on the other hand, they distorted many of Marx and Engels' statements in an opportunist way. As for the SRs, they did not even formally consider themselves Marxists. Their party arose out of the remnants of the Narodnik groups that had been active in Russia in the 1880s and 1890s.

In February 1917 both these parties actively supported the bourgeois democratic revolution in Russia. However, they continued to hold defensist views as before. In addition, in their effort to strengthen their alliance with the bourgeois parties, the SRs and Mensheviks did anything but force the implementation of such long overdue measures, normally expected of a bourgeois democratic revolution, as agrarian reform, a Constituent Assembly, the proclamation of a republic, etc. As for socialist reforms, the SRs and Mensheviks considered any such thing manifestly premature for Russia.

All the Menshevik factions emphatically took their distance from Lenin's April Theses, regarding that document as mistaken and adventuristic, "written in total disregard of the conditions of time and place." [1]

As far back as 1905–7 G. V. Plekhanov was arguing that the democratic and socialist revolutions in Russia would necessarily be separated by a considerable interval of time. In 1917, when he stood in the extreme right wing of the Menshevik Party, he wrote:

> Since capitalism, in the country in question, has not reached the high stage at which it becomes an obstacle to the development of the productive forces, it is absurd to call on the workers, urban and rural, and the poorest part of the peasantry to overthrow it. . . . The dictatorship of the proletariat will become possible and desirable only when the wage workers constitute a majority of the population. . . . It is obvious that no one among us who has the slightest grasp of the teachings of Marx could speak of a socialist revolution.[2]

Martov, who in 1917 headed the left-wing faction of Menshevik Internationalists, defended a similar point of view.[3] The Mensheviks held that Russia, after February, had a long road of bourgeois development before it. Therefore the Soviets should only act as the "tribune" and "supervisor" of the revolution. This decision was confirmed by the May conference of the Mensheviks, where it was said that since a bourgeois-democratic revolution was under way in Russia, "the working class cannot now pose as its immediate task the socialist transformation of society."[4] Similar arguments were heard in the speeches at the Menshevik unification congress in August 1917.[5]

The SRs held analogous views in 1917, although the programmatic documents of this party were not at all based on Marxism and did not make a sharp distinction between a "bourgeois-democratic" revolution and a "socialist" revolution. For example, the SRs considered it possible to have socialist enterprises under capitalism in the form of cooperative societies. They viewed socialization of the land as a socialist measure and as virtually the main undertaking of a socialist revolution. But such a step, which essentially meant the distribution of all the land to the working peasants on the basis of the number of mouths to be fed or of the "labor standard," remained entirely within the bounds of the bourgeois-democratic revolution, in the view of Marxists.

One could find passages in the program of the SR Party dealing with the socialization of labor and abolition of private property and of the class division of society. And there was the statement that the realization of the party's full program and the expropriation of all capitalist property presupposed the full victory of the working class, the reorganization of society along socialist lines, and if necessary the establishment of the revolutionary dictatorship of the working class. However, the concept "working class" meant something quite different to the SRs than to Marxists. The SR program said, "It must be our aim that all layers of the exploited people, from the industrial proletariat to the working peasantry, *be conscious of themselves as part of a single working class*, see in their class unity the sure means of their own emancipation, and subordinate their partial and temporary interests to the great task of a social-revolutionary transformation." (Emphasis added.—R.M.)[6]

On the basis of this view of socialism, the SRs held that victory over tsarism and the abolition of the large landed estates would immediately open the way to socialist reforms. However, in 1917 a great gap arose between the program and the practical policies of the SRs. In the decisive months after the February revolution the SR Party, which was considerably larger and more influential politically than the Menshevik Party, was in fact under the sway of the Mensheviks on many theoretical questions. Thus the majority of SR leaders after the February victory not only did not push the demand in their program for "socialization" of the land but themselves delayed implementation of agrarian reform in all sorts of ways. Echoing the Mensheviks, the SR paper *Delo naroda* (the People's Cause), for example, carried a lead article saying: "Until socialist revolution has ripened in Western Europe there can be no question of overthrowing the capitalist system in Russia."[7]

"The Social Revolutionaries [SRs] made a feeble and flabby impression even in comparison with the Mensheviks," wrote Trotsky.

> To the Bolsheviks at all important moments they seemed merely third-rate Cadets. To the Cadets they seemed third-rate Bolsheviks. (The second-rate position was occupied, in both cases, by the Mensheviks.) Their unstable support and the formlessness of their ideology were reflected in their personnel: on all the [SR] leaders lay the imprint of unfinishedness, superficiality and sentimental unreliability. We may say without any exaggeration that the rank-and-file Bolshevik revealed more political acumen, more understanding of the relations between classes, than the most celebrated SR leaders. . . .
>
> In the Menshevik-SR bloc the dominant place belonged to the Mensheviks, in spite of the weight of numbers on the side of the SRs. In this distribution of forces was expressed in a way the hegemony of the town over the country, the predominance of the city over the rural petty bourgeoisie, and finally the intellectual superiority of a "Marxist" intelligentsia over an intelligentsia which stood by the simon-pure Russian sociology and prided itself on the meagreness of the old Russian history.[8]

Of course, it would be wrong to say, on the basis of theoretical propositions alone, that all the tendencies and groups in the RSDLP who rejected the April Theses and who felt that their duty was to prepare the proletariat for a prolonged struggle for socialism within the framework of bourgeois democracy—that all such tendencies and groups no longer had the right to call themselves socialists. Among both Mensheviks and SRs there were many sincere socialists who had spent long years in prison and at hard labor for their part in the struggle against the autocracy and who felt they belonged, not without reason, to national contingents of the world socialist movement. In the conditions prevailing in Russia various views on the timing of the socialist revolution and the ways of accomplishing it were justified, and therefore not only the bulk of the rank-and-file Mensheviks and SRs but also a substantial number of their leaders were by no means "agents of the bourgeoisie"—at any rate not in their subjective thinking.

But the Mensheviks and SRs were not only authors of political and theoretical works. In the swiftly changing conditions of 1917 these parties could not evade the most important political actions and decisions. And thus it often happened that the dogmatic desire to act only in accordance with one's earlier doctrines (in the Menshevik case) or, the opposite, the temporary refusal to carry out the promises in one's own program (in the case of the SRs) placed these parties in the position of an objective alliance with the bourgeoisie and the bourgeois parties. And we shall not go into the fact that many Menshevik and SR leaders were also subjectively predisposed toward such an alliance.

Although they were in the leadership of the Soviets after February, the SRs and Mensheviks did not call for "All Power to the Soviets." The dual-power situation also made them uneasy. Recalling Engels' dark prophecies, the Mensheviks were afraid to take power in the country, and on this point the SRs were in full accord with them. According to M. P. Yakubovich, the then-leaders of the Mensheviks— F. I. Dan, I. G. Tsereteli, and A. R. Gotz—and the SR leaders, Viktor M. Chernov and N. D. Avksentiev, were poorly suited in their personal qualities for political activity at a time of rapidly developing revolution, a time of "storm and stress" affecting the mass of the people. These leaders had no understanding of the logic of revolution and feared all "revolutionary excesses."[9] For that reason they eagerly assisted in the formation of the first Provisional Government, which was Cadet and

Octobrist in composition. Invoking the bourgeois nature of the revolution, the Mensheviks and SRs *advocated* that the country be governed by bourgeois parties for the time being and promised their own support and that of the Soviets to the bourgeois parties.

The conduct of the Menshevik and SR leaders did not of course constitute *deliberate* betrayal of the people's interests, as the Bolsheviks then charged and as all Soviet historians still charge. In 1917 the Mensheviks considered themselves a party of the working class; furthermore, they reflected the views of a substantial section of that class, just as the SRs reflected the views of a substantial section of the peasantry and the soldiers. But many of the leaders of those parties were unable to transcend their own doctrinairism; they did not want to take up the tasks of the bourgeois revolution, afraid they would land in the untenable situation which Engels had warned would doom a working-class party.

However, to the Mensheviks and SRs' misfortune, the bourgeois Provisional Government proved completely incapable of carrying out even the most urgent tasks of the bourgeois-democratic revolution. It not only opposed the realization of many long overdue measures normally expected of a bourgeois revolution, but tried at first to restore the Romanov monarchy in some form. The authority of this government in the eyes of the populace and the army declined so rapidly that its downfall became only a matter of time. In the wake of the April crisis, G. E. Lvov, the Premier of the Provisional Government, addressed a letter to N. S. Chkheidze, President of the Petrograd Soviet, requesting discussion of the idea that representatives of the Soviet enter the Provisional Government. This proposal provoked a stormy discussion involving all the factions in the Soviet, and the Menshevik leaders at first rejected Lvov's proposal. However, the Provisional Government kept insisting. The first to speak in favor of entry into the government were the Trudoviks and the People's Socialists (Narodnye Sotsialisty), soon followed by the SR leader Chernov and the Menshevik leader Tsereteli. The first coalition government, formed with their cooperation, was feeble and short-lived, however. And the second coalition government proved equally ineffective. Although representatives of the socialist parties had a numerical majority in the second coalition government, the Cadets continued to decisively influence all government actions. It was this government which tried, under pressure from the Allies, to organize and carry out an offensive in June

1917. According to M. P. Yakubovich, who at that time belonged to the Menshevik left wing and was one of the leaders of the Military Department of the VTsIK,

> The nonsensical decision to start an offensive was taken, though the army was psychologically incapable of an offensive. The soldiers at the front and in the rear were dreaming about the armistice, about the return home, the return to the villages where the landlords' estates were being distributed. . . . How could the soldiers, in such a frame of mind, go to the attack? . . . At best the army was capable of defensive action if the Germans were to attack. But there could be no talk about a Russian attack. . . . [The offensive ended] in a defeat unprecedented in the Russian army, and when the news reached Petrograd it caused a sensation among the workers and even more among the soldiers of the garrison. The result was, of course, quite opposite to that expected by Kerensky and Tereshchenko, by the Provisional Government, which trusted the two Ministers, and by the leaders of the Mensheviks and the Social Revolutionaries.[10]

The outcome of the political crisis and cabinet crisis that broke out in the first days of July is well known. The gigantic demonstration of workers, soldiers, and sailors on July 3 was spontaneous. The Bolsheviks, unable to prevent the demonstration, did everything they could to make it peaceful. Chernov and Tsereteli tried to speak to the demonstrators but, although they were not molested, the crowd would not listen to them. Then the Menshevik and SR leaders, the leaders of the VTsIK and the Provisional Government, out of fear of the demonstrators, committed precisely that sin of sins against which Engels had warned in 1850 and 1853. They called out the Cossacks to disperse the July demonstration, and also called for troops to be sent from the front. Many of the Bolsheviks were arrested. Lenin and Zinoviev went underground, and were forced to find a hiding place in Razliv, a village near Petrograd. The new coalition government, not formed until the end of July, again included seven socialists of various political shadings and an equal number of Cadets and Cadet allies—although by then the SRs and Mensheviks could quite easily have formed a government excluding the bourgeois parties and begun to enact the reforms the people had so long waited for. The political influence of the Cadets (not to mention the Octobrists) had declined precipitously by August 1917, but SR and Menshevik influence continued on the whole to grow. Numerically the SR Party was the largest in Russia in the summer of 1917. The Mensheviks too had grown—to almost 200,000. It was as though the power had fallen into these parties' hands without their wishing it, and their leaders, in confusion and dismay, could not bring themselves to take hold of it and use it. They sought at all costs to maintain their coalition with the bourgeois parties, afraid they would frighten the "propertied elements"—or put more simply, the bourgeoisie—away from the revolution if they put through democratic social reforms which had nothing socialist about them and which were not at all premature, even from the standpoint of these "moderate" socialist parties. This attitude often brought them praise from the leaders of the bourgeoisie. The Cadet leader Miliukov, for example, in one of his speeches declared:

> The socialist parties of the present time have a much more intelligent view of the immediate tasks in the life of Russia; it seems they have absorbed many of the lessons of the past and they accept as an axiom the proposition that the Russian revolution, like all revolutions past and present, cannot end in the victory of socialism and the socialist system, that this revolution is primarily a political revolution and, to use their terminology, a bourgeois revolution . . . , but by no means directed toward the immediate victory of socialism.

Miliukov continued: "The revolution at the present time cannot go farther than the political victory of the bourgeoisie. . . . The socialists have even managed to break with their own traditions and doctrines and have entered the government. This represents a great step forward in their capacity to grasp the principles of statemanship."

At the same time Miliukov had to bitterly admit that the masses "remain receptive to the preaching of an immediate socialist revolution through seizure of the government by the working class," and that a great deal depended on whether the socialist parties could succeed in turning the masses "against the extremist viewpoint of socialist utopianism." [11]

Thus the Mensheviks and SRs—two socialist parties, socialist in their slogans and programs and in the subjective aspirations of most of their members—found themselves in a position even more ambiguous and untenable than the one Engels had predicted and which, in his view, was likely to destroy the reputation of any revolutionary socialist party forever. That is exactly what happened in 1917 to the Mensheviks and SRs. Although they continued to think of themselves as revolutionaries and socialists, the masses began to turn away from them and to give more and more support to the Bolsheviks, whose views on the prospects and possibilities of the revolution were quite different.

To be fair, it must be said that the phrasing of the declarations and resolutions of these two parties became increasingly "revolutionary" as the masses turned away from them. Thus in June 1917, at the "height" of coalitionism, a resolution of the First Congress of Soviets said:

> The transfer of all power to the Soviet . . . at the present stage of the Russian revolution would only weaken its forces by prematurely driving away elements still capable of serving the revolution and would threaten the revolution with disaster. Therefore the All-Russian Congress of Soviets . . . calls on the entire revolutionary democracy of Russia to energetically support the Provisional Government in all its efforts to strengthen and extend the conquests of the revolution.[12]

Many of the Menshevik and SR leaders spoke in quite a different vein in the fall of 1917. "The army is retreating," said Chkheidze, for example, in one of his speeches. "The country's finances have been ruined. The railroads are in a state of total disarray. Industry is falling apart. Famine is stalking the cities. The dissatisfaction of the masses threatens to spill over into forms placing the very existence of the state in danger."[13]

A mid-October appeal of the General Army Committee, in which SR influence predominated, said the following:

> The power should be revolutionary and should resolutely mobilize all the resources needed by the state and all labor power at the disposal of the nation by nationalizing all the most important sources of wealth and means of production and introducing compulsory loans and labor service. . . . Everything has been said and the time for waiting is past. The time has come for the judgment of history. We are on the verge of a new era, the demise of the old and the birth of a new way of life for the peoples of the world.[14]

However neither the SRs nor the Mensheviks were up to the task of beginning this new era or handing down the judgment of history.

The disintegration of the Menshevik Party began well before October, as could be seen from the caucuses of the Menshevik faction at the so-called Democratic Conference. Noah Zhordania, elected president of that faction, later recorded his impressions: "Total confusion.

No one knew what to do or how to proceed. . . . The Mensheviks and Socialist Revolutionaries were equally isolated from the people and from the soldiers." [15] The decomposition and decline of the Menshevik Party was remarked on in the Mensheviks' own press. At the end of September R. Grigoryev wrote in *Novaia zhizn* that the Menshevik wing of Social Democracy "had met its downfall and was on its way to political oblivion." [16] In Plekhanov's *Yedinstvo* Lev Deutsch wrote: "The Menshevik faction is suffering one defeat after another, and one does not have to be a prophet to foretell its rapid demise. Its days are undoubtedly numbered." [17] The Mensheviks' allies, the SRs, also observed this process of disintegration. The SR paper *Delo naroda* commented on the composition of the Moscow regional congress of Soviets as follows: "The congress once again made evident . . . the disappearance from the political arena of the Menshevik Social Democratic Party." [18]

Outwardly it seemed that the SRs were in a better position politically. But for the most part their influence was only significant in the provinces and in those front-line zones farthest removed from the center, i.e., in places where political life flowed at a slower tempo. In the primary and decisive centers of the country the influence of the SR Party, especially of its right wing, by mid-September 1917 had also declined to the minimum. At that point the crisis of the SR Party took the form of a split. The too obvious disparity between the programmatic demands and actual policies of the SR leaders led to the formation at first of a left-wing faction and then of a separate Left SR Party. And whereas the Right SRs were allied with the Mensheviks, the Left SRs were more and more attracted by the idea of supporting and making an alliance with the Bolsheviks.

It must be said that even after October the SRs and Mensheviks repeatedly argued that the already consummated revolution was "premature" and predicted the rapid collapse of Soviet power. When Plekhanov learned of the overthrow of the Provisional Government he addressed an open letter to the Petrograd workers, which said in part: "The events of the past few days distress me not because I do not wish the working class to triumph in Russia but precisely because I favor that with all my heart. . . . We must remember Engels' remarkable words that there could be no greater historical misfortune for the working class than to seize political power when it is not yet ready for it." But Plekhanov's arguments against the policies of the Bolsheviks were too dogmatic and unconvincing:

> In the population of our state the proletariat is not a majority but a minority. . . . It is true that the working class can count on support from the peasants, who to this day constitute the greater part of the population of Russia. But the peasants need land; they have no need for the replacement of the capitalist system by a socialist one. . . . It would seem that the peasants are a highly unreliable ally for the workers in organizing the socialist mode of production. . . . Having seized political power prematurely, the Russian proletariat will not carry out a social revolution but will only provoke a civil war which will ultimately force it to retreat far back from the positions which were won in February and March of this year.[19]

In other words, Plekhanov again tried to convince the Russian workers that "Russian history has not yet ground the grain from which in time the wheaten loaf of socialism will be baked."[20]

Approximately a month after the October insurrection a congress of the Menshevik Party was held. One of its resolutions expressed the firm conviction that the new revolution could not carry out socialist changes, owing to the fact that "such changes have not yet begun in the more advanced European countries and because of the low level of the productive forces in Russia."

★ ★ ★

Separate mention should be made of the position of L. D. Trotsky and his group, who held an intermediate position between the Bolsheviks and Mensheviks during World War I. When the war broke out, Trotsky wrote: "Might not the defeat of tsarism actually serve to benefit the revolution? One cannot dispute such a possibility—and it is not only a possibility. The Russo-Japanese war gave a mighty forward thrust to the events of the [1905] revolution. It may be expected, therefore, that the Russo-German war will produce similar results." But Trotsky was by no means certain at the time that such a turn of events would be desirable. He went on: "Those who think that the Russo-Japanese war caused the revolution neither know nor understand the inner continuity of the events. The war merely speeded up the revolution. But it thereby weakened it internally. If the revolution had developed out of the organic growth of its inner forces, it would have come later, but would have been more powerful and systematic."[21]

Trotsky followed the same logic in his assessment of the possible consequences of World War I:

> In the period 1912–14 Russia was shaken completely out of its state of depression and counterrevolution by a mighty industrial upturn. . . . The movement developed in an incomparably more planned and conscious way and, moreover, on a broader social foundation. . . . On the other hand, the war, in the event of disastrous defeats for Russia, could hasten the onset of revolution, but only at the price of weakening it internally. And if the revolution won out after all in those circumstances, the Hohenzollern army would turn its bayonets against it. . . . It requires no further demonstration that under such circumstances the Russian revolution, even if victorious for a time, would be a historical miscarriage.[22]

Of course Trotsky very soon changed his view. After returning to Russia he endorsed the April Theses and with a group of his supporters joined the Bolshevik Party. He no longer called the revolution in Russia a historical miscarriage. In his *History of the Russian Revolution* Trotsky said of himself (in the third person): "It was only at this July congress that Trotsky formally joined the Bolshevik Party. The balance was here struck to years of disagreement and factional struggle. Trotsky came to Lenin as to a teacher whose power and significance he understood later than many others, but perhaps more fully than they."[23]

Even much later, when he was in exile, Trotsky never wrote that the 1917 revolution in Russia, either February or October, had been premature, although he continued to insist as ever that socialism could not be victorious in one country and that the Russian revolution could only be viewed in the context of the world revolution.

For example, in 1930 Trotsky wrote:

> The crises of Soviet economy are not merely maladies of growth, a sort of infantile sickness, but something far more significant—namely, they are the harsh curbings of the world market, the very one "to which," in Lenin's words, "we are subordinated, with which we are bound up, and from which we cannot escape." (Speech at the Eleventh Party Congress, March 27, 1922.)
>
> From the foregoing, however, there in no ways follows a denial of the historical "legitimacy" of the October Revolution, a conclusion which reeks of shameful philistinism. The seizure of power by the international proletariat cannot be a single, simultaneous act. The political superstructure—and a revolution is part of the "superstructure"—has its own dialectic, which intervenes imperiously in the process of world economy, but

does not abolish its deep-going laws. The October Revolution is "legitimate" as the *first stage of the world revolution* which unavoidably extends over decades. The interval between the first and the second stage has turned out to be considerably longer than we had expected. Nevertheless it remains an interval, and it is by no means converted into a self-sufficient epoch of the building of a national socialist society.[24]

seven

The Position of the Bolsheviks

After the victory of the bourgeois-democratic revolution in Russia the Bolsheviks immediately emerged from underground and began intensive political activity all over the country, but there was no clear and generally accepted opinion among them on the prospects for the further development of the revolution. The bulk of the party leaders who returned to Petrograd and Moscow assumed that the Bolsheviks' main task was to fight to carry the bourgeois-democratic revolution through to completion—above all, to fight for peace, for transfer of the large estates to the peasants, and for the eradication of all vestiges of feudalism and autocracy in Russia. Until all these tasks were accomplished, these Bolsheviks considered it premature to raise the question of the dictatorship of the proletariat and the making of a socialist revolution. In March 1917 there were hardly any leading Bolsheviks who raised the slogan "All Power to the Soviets."

As the basis for their position these Bolsheviks referred primarily to the experience of the 1905—7 revolution, the resolutions of the Third Congress of the RSDLP, and many of Lenin's writings of that period, including such a major work as *Two Tactics of Social Democracy in the Democratic Revolution*. However, the Bolshevik leaders of March 1917 did not realize that after the February revolution a situation had arisen that was completely different from the one in 1905—7.

In 1905—7 a bourgeois-democratic revolution was under way in Russia, but it was only in its beginning stages; it did not win a decisive victory over the autocracy, and the tsarist regime remained master of the situation. Consequently, in Lenin's view, the main aim of the struggle at that time was the overthrow of the autocracy and the establishment of a democratic dictatorship of the proletariat and peasantry, based on a broad alliance of all active revolutionary forces. Only after this dictatorship had achieved all the main tasks of the democratic revolution, and as the consciousness and organization of the proletariat increased, did the Bolshevik Party consider it possible to call for passing on to the socialist revolution.

But in February and March 1917 the autocracy had already been demolished. Along with the bourgeois Provisional Government, Soviets of Workers', Soldiers', and Peasants' Deputies had been formed everywhere in Russia. These in fact constituted the revolutionary-democratic dictatorship of the proletariat and peasantry. There arose the peculiar political phenomenon of *dual power,* with the Provisional Government able to exist only by leave of the Soviets. Thus, the main question of any revolution—the question of power—had already been settled; and the Soviets constituted the real power. However, since the Provisional Government enjoyed the support of the Compromiser parties in the Soviets, it had no desire or ability to solve such extremely important problems of the revolution as peace and agrarian reform. Under these circumstances, the tactics worked out to meet the political conditions of 1905 were no longer applicable. Their effect in 1917 was to put the brakes on the revolutionary struggle.

Only Lenin's arrival in Russia brought the wavering and uncertainty among the Bolsheviks to an end. It was Lenin who raised the slogan of "All Power to the Soviets" and called for a transition from the first phase of the revolution, which had placed power in the hands of the bourgeoisie, to its second phase, which would give the power to the proletariat and poor peasants and make it possible not only to complete all the main tasks of the bourgeois-democratic revolution but also to begin introducing a number of urgently needed measures of a socialist nature. Even for the Bolsheviks this was a new and unexpected approach. In his celebrated April Theses Lenin clearly and precisely stated that, with the transfer of state power to the bourgeoisie the bourgeois-democratic revolution in Russia had been *completed* and that the chief task of that time was to pass "from the first stage of the revolution—which . . . placed power in the hands of the bourgeoisie, to its second stage, which must place power in the hands of the proletariat and the poorest sections of the peasantry." [1] and that it was impossible to break out of "the imperialist war and achieve a democratic . . . peace without overthrowing the power of capital and transferring power to another class, the proletariat." [2] It is not surprising that the

April Theses at first produced consternation and opposition among the Bolsheviks themselves. And it required not only time but great effort on Lenin's part to convince the majority of delegates at the Bolshevik Party's Petrograd city conference and Seventh (April) All-Russia Conference that his position was correct.

As we know, the April Theses were oriented toward the likelihood that the revolution would develop peacefully. Lenin regarded the Soviets as a new form of power, more democratic than any parliamentary republic. He proposed that the Bolsheviks could win a majority in the Soviets through peaceful propaganda work. As for economic questions, Lenin's demands were modest and realistic. The April Theses said in part:

> Nationalization of all lands in the country, the land to be disposed of by the local Soviets of Agricultural Laborers' and Peasants' Deputies. . . . The setting up of a model farm on each of the large estates . . . under the control of the Soviets of Agricultural Laborers' Deputies and for the public account.
>
> 7) The immediate amalgamation of all banks in the country into a single national bank and the institution of control over it by the Soviet of Workers' Deputies.
>
> 8) It is not our immediate task to "introduce" socialism, but only to bring social production and the distribution of products at once under the control of the Soviets of Workers' Deputies.[3]

The April Theses became the basis for the resolutions of the Bolsheviks' April conference. The party's economic program was expanded somewhat at the same time. It was proposed that strict control be established not only over the banks but also over the insurance companies and largest capitalist syndicates, such as Produgol, Prodamet, and the sugar syndicate, and that a fairer system of income and property taxes, along with universal labor service, be instituted. At the same time, a resolution of this conference emphasized:

> In carrying out the above-named measures extreme caution and prudence must be observed, a solid majority of the population must be won over and become consciously convinced that the practical basis has been laid for each such measure, and the attention and effort of the conscious vanguard of the working class, who must help the peasant masses find a way out of the existing economic chaos, should be oriented precisely in this direction.[4]

It was not so much a question of socialist changes as of a series of measures leading up to such changes. It is indicative that resolutions of the Menshevik and SR parties and speeches by their leaders contained similar proposals. Of course in their case the aim was different—to strengthen the home front and forestall a new revolution which might be led by the Bolsheviks. For example *Izvestia,* whose editorial board was totally controlled by the SRs and Mensheviks, wrote in May 1917:

> Many branches of industry are ripe for a state trade monopoly (grain, meat, salt, leather), others are ripe for the organization of state-controlled trusts (coal, oil, metallurgy, sugar, paper); and finally, present conditions demand in the case of nearly all branches of industry state control of the distribution of raw materials and manufactures, as well as price fixing. . . . Simultaneously it is necessary to place all banking institutions under state and public control in order to combat speculation in goods subject to state control. . . . At the same time, the most energetic measures should be taken against the workshy, even if labor conscription has to be introduced for that purpose. . . . The country is already in a state of catastrophe, and the only thing that can save it is the creative effort of the whole nation headed by a government which has consciously shouldered the stupendous task of rescuing a country ruined by war and the tsarist regime.[5]

Lenin commented that this program was excellent but questioned how a coalition of petty-bourgeois and bourgeois parties could carry it out. He understood of course that state control of the banks and monopolies would ultimately lead to their being expropriated. But at the time, he was only referring to the top layer of capitalists and not to total expropriation:

> Socialists are out to make *only* the landowners and capitalists "abdicate" their property rights. To deal a decisive blow at those who are defying the people the way the coal mine operators are doing when they disrupt and ruin production, it is sufficient to make a few hundred, at the most one or two thousand, millionaires, bank, and industrial and commercial bosses "abdicate."
> This would be quite enough to break the resistance of capital. *Even this tiny group of wealthy people need not* have *all* their property rights taken away; they could be allowed to keep many possessions in the way of consumption articles and ownership of a certain modest income.[6]

In April and May Lenin devoted considerable attention to work on a new draft program for the party. In all essentials the economic section of this draft, published in June 1917, followed the same line of thinking as the April Theses.

In comparing the agrarian programs of the SRs and Bolsheviks, Lenin commented that in and of itself the transfer of the large estates to the peasants was a bourgeois-democratic measure, not a socialist one, but that evidently only the proletariat would be able to carry it out. As for the government takeover of highly productive farms, stud farms, etc., that actually was a socialist measure if the big farms were to be used for the benefit of society. He wrote:

> The peasants want to keep their small farms, to set equal standards for all, and to make readjustments on an egalitarian basis from time to time. Fine. No sensible socialist will differ with the peasant poor over this. If the land is confiscated, that means the domination of the banks has been undermined; if the implements are confiscated, that means the domination of capital has been undermined—and in that case, provided the proletariat rules centrally, provided political power is taken over by the proletariat, the rest will come by itself, through "force of example," prompted by experience.
>
> The crux of the matter lies in political power passing into the hands of the proletariat. When this has taken place, everything that is essential, basic, fundamental in the program set out in the 242 mandates will become feasible. . . . This is an issue of secondary importance. We are not doctrinaires. Our theory is a guide to action, not a dogma.
>
> We do not claim that Marx knew or Marxists know the road to socialism down to the last detail. That is nonsense. What we know is the direction of the road, and the class forces that follow it; the specific, practical details will come to light only through the experience of millions when they take things into their own hands.[7]

Lenin was thinking along the same lines in September and the first half of October 1917, when the economic dislocation in Russia had swelled to catastrophic proportions. In those weeks before the revolution he added to his earlier proposals such points as the abolition of business secrets, the nationalization of the syndicates rather than mere control over them, and such a state-capitalist measure as compulsory amalgamation of industrialists and merchants into syndicates, or trade associations.

Of course the implementation of all these measures, Lenin wrote, would be

> a step toward socialism. For socialism is merely the next step forward from state-capitalist monopoly. Or in other words, socialism is merely state-capitalist monopoly *which is made to serve the interests of the whole people* and has to that extent *ceased* to be capitalist monopoly. . . .
>
> Imperialist war is the *eve* of socialist revolution. And this not only because the horrors of the war give rise to proletarian revolt—no revolt can bring about socialism unless the economic conditions for socialism are ripe—but because state-monopoly capitalism is a complete *material*

preparation for socialism, the threshold of socialism, a rung on the ladder of history between which and the rung called socialism *there are no intermediate rungs*[8] (Emphasis in original—R.M.).

Thus the main proposals made by Lenin and the Bolshevik Party in those prerevolutionary months were entirely feasible and quite modest. And Lenin was correct in writing: "We must bear firmly in mind that we have never set ourselves 'insoluble' social tasks, and as for the perfectly soluble task of taking immediate steps toward socialism, which is the only way out of the exceedingly difficult situation, that will be solved only by the dictatorship of the proletariat and poor peasants."[9]

We can see that for Lenin the main thing was the struggle for the political power of the proletariat. He did not give a detailed outline of what the Bolshevik economic program would be after the seizure of power, but only indicated the most important aspects with bold strokes. More than once he told his supporters that the details of the Bolshevik program could be worked out after the seizure of power, because the practical experience and field of vision of party members would then be immeasurably broadened, something a million times more valuable than any program. On all primary and essential questions the Bolsheviks had presented a program of transitional measures pointing toward socialism—an economic program for the next stage of the Russian revolution. When that program had been realized, it would be easier to project the next stage of the journey. This realistic approach to the country's economic problems was an important factor in the Bolsheviks' victory in October.

When Lenin called for moving ahead to the socialist revolution and the dictatorship of the proletariat, he understood very well that the capitalist system in Russia had not exhausted all its possibilities and that Russia was by no means a highly developed capitalist country. He understood perfectly that in Russia there did not exist the *maximum* favorable objective and subjective conditions that would make Russia completely ripe for socialist revolution. He realized that there existed only the *minimum* conditions sufficient for a socialist revolution and the building of socialism. Russia's economic and cultural backwardness was no secret to Lenin.

"But for the war Russia could have gone on living for years and *even decades without a revolution against the capitalists.* The war has made that objectively impossible. The alternatives are either utter ruin or a revolution against the capitalists. That is how the question stands. That is how the very trend of events poses it"[10] (Emphasis added—R.M.).

In this instance Lenin was saying approximately the same thing Engels had said in his 1891 letter to Bebel. It is not hard to detect a difference of tone, however. Unlike Engels, who was distressed at the prospect of socialists having to take power in wartime conditions ten years before the "optimal" moment, Lenin was pleased with the situation and untiringly sought to persuade skeptics in the party that this course of events was the best for the proletariat and the country as a whole.

"Our party will now be threatened with an immeasurably greater danger if we forget [that the question of the Bolsheviks taking power has become very urgent] than if we were to admit that taking power is 'premature.' In this respect there can be nothing 'premature' now: there is every chance in a million, except one or two perhaps, in favor of this."[11]

In reply to opponents who invoked lack of experience and the absence of an apparatus fit to administer the country, Lenin wrote:

"Let those who say, 'We have no apparatus to replace the old one, which inevitably gravitates toward the defense of the bourgeoisie,' be ashamed of themselves. For this apparatus exists. It is the Soviets."[12]

Of course, civilization was still at a low level in Russia. But was it not possible for the proletariat, after taking power, to advance civilization more rapidly than the bourgeoisie? Not long before his death, several years after the October victory, Lenin developed this argument further:

"You say that civilization is necessary for the building of socialism. Very good. But why could we not first create such prerequisites of civilization in our country as the expulsion of the landowners and the Russian capitalists, and then start moving toward socialism? Where, in what books, have you read that such variations of the customary historical sequence of events are impermissible or impossible?"[13]

In general it was Lenin's opinion that many concepts that had been true in the nineteenth century had lost their meaning in the new era that had come—the age of imperialism. Russia indeed remained a backward country, but it had nevertheless entered the stage of monopoly capitalism and imperialism, and therefore the socialist revolution in such a country could not be premature *in general*. And if in 1917 the proletariat was given the chance to take power, it would have been a crime for the proletarian party to pass up the opportunity. For within a few years, the Russian bourgeoisie would have acquired experience in governing, would have built up its own state in place of the shattered tsarist administration, and would have gained economic strength and succeeded in organizing its forces more effectively in every respect. In that case it would have been much harder for the proletariat to defeat the bourgeoisie. Thus, in Lenin's opinion, the country's relative economic backwardness and the weakness of the bourgeoisie offered some extra advantages to the highly mature (in political respects), though not very numerous Russian proletariat.

Lenin calculated that after taking power and putting through not only long overdue bourgeois democratic reforms but some timely socialist changes as well, the Russian proletariat could carry the social and economic development of the country forward much more efficiently and rapidly than could the bourgeoisie. Moreover, Lenin was firmly convinced that Russia would not have to stand alone for long, that the socialist revolution in Russia would hasten the day and smooth the way for the revolution in the other belligerent European countries. Those economically developed countries would in turn help Russia overcome its economic and cultural backwardness more rapidly.

★   ★   ★

To be fair we must note that Lenin voiced some hasty and not quite correct opinions at the same time that he presented his quite moderate, realizable, and very timely program for a new socialist revolution—a program including the energetic implementation of the main tasks of the bourgeois-democratic revolution as well as some initial and urgently needed socialist measures. In a number of statements Lenin made proposals that were not only premature but utopian and unrealizable in general. In the context of the complex and stormy debates of those weeks and months, these proposals went unnoticed for the most part and some of them were published only after the October victory. Moreover, these projects were not reflected in the party's activity during the first few months after the October victory, when the first outbreaks of civil war and the first attempts at imperialist intervention were suppressed. But this part of Lenin's program acquired greater importance within a few months after the October revolution, and we shall discuss this further below.

To understand and evaluate these mistaken proposals and statements of Lenin's in 1917, we must return to some of Marx and Engels' concepts and to certain central problems of socialist theory.

It is well known that Marx and Engels did not discuss at much length or with much willingness their conception of what the future socialist society would be like. Of course the main features were readily apparent from the start. It would be a society in which "the national centralization of the means of production will become the national basis of society, which will consist in the free association of equal producers engaged in social labor according to an overall, rational plan." [14] In a socialist society there would be no anarchy of production, unemployment, exploitation of some by others, or periodic economic crises. Labor productivity and the production of goods needed by society would constantly increase under socialism and the working day would be steadily shortened. Citizens in a socialist society would receive quality education, professional training, and free medical care. They would enjoy all democratic rights, etc., etc.

To be sure, in various works by Marx and Engels many other statements can be found dealing with such questions as the division of labor under socialism and communism and even the nature of family relations. However, the founders of Marxism themselves did not ascribe much importance to these pronouncements. In their view, the people who would live under socialism would solve the problems of their day-to-day lives in their own way. Even after Marx's death Engels was still capable of writing in one of his letters: "The party to which I belong does not put forward any proposals that are fixed for all time. Our views on the features that will distinguish the future communist society from the present society are precise conclusions drawn from historical facts and processes of development, and apart from some connection with these facts and processes, they have no theoretical or practical worth." [15]

Marx and Engels' efforts were primarily aimed at analyzing the contradictions and defects of the capitalist society in which they lived and demonstrating that it was a historically transitory form of society. Their task was to explain the historical mission of the working class as the gravedigger of capitalism, to work out the ways and means of organizing the proletariat as a class, building a revolutionary political party of the proletariat, and laying the basis for its political and economic program. That was precisely the essence of Marxism in the nineteenth century.

Marx and Engels' conception of the specific ways in which the transition from capitalist to socialist society would take place, and of the tasks, special features, and duration of this transitional period were quite undefined. Historical experience had not yet provided sufficient material for recommendations that would be at all scientific, and it was not Marx and Engels' habit to indulge in dreamy speculation. Only after the Paris Commune were Marx and Engels' suggestions on how to proceed with a socialist revolution elaborated more fully. Since, in their view, the Paris Commune was the first historical experience of the dictatorship of the proletariat, they analyzed it in detail, noting both the tremendous achievements and the fundamental errors made by the French workers in their heroic struggle.

It is not hard to see, therefore, that scientific socialism never outlined the prospective form of future society in any truly specific or exact way. In contrast to the analysis of the political economy of capitalism made by the founders of Marxism, or their philosophical conception of history, there remained in their predictions of various kinds more utopian and unscientific elements than in any other part of their creative legacy. Here, along with some truly remarkable prophecies and proposals, one can find quite a bit of what Engels described as of "no theoretical or practical worth."

We must add, however, that as the working-class movement progressed and labor and socialist parties were founded in Europe, the question of how the processes of transition from capitalism to socialism would take place became more and more relevant. Lively discussions on this aspect of Marxist theory developed at the end of the nineteenth century and in the early twentieth during the drafting of socialist party programs. Marx was barely able to participate in this process, but Engels often did. Such issues were also treated in a large number of articles and books by such disciples of Marx and Engels as August Bebel, Karl Kautsky, G. V. Plekhanov, Paul Lafargue, and others.

We will not review in detail what Marx and Engels and their closest disciples thought and said about what the first postrevolutionary measures would be and how socialist and communist society would be organized. Nevertheless, in order to understand a number of major miscalculations made in economic policy after the October revolution, we should comment briefly on what the classical Marxist writers imagined would happen to commodity production and the circulation of money after the victory of the proletarian socialist revolution.

It is well known that Marx and Engels were firmly convinced that under socialism not only the state but the commodity, money, and credit systems also would wither away. The commodity and the commodity system, according to Marx, is a purely capitalist category. "With the seizing of the means of production by society," Engels wrote, "production of commodities is done away with, and simultaneously, the mastery of the product over the producer." [16] Of course Marx and Engels understood that capitalism could not be replaced by socialism in a matter of days and that some sort of transitional period would exist between them, during which capitalist relations, institutions, and customs would be eliminated and new, socialist, relations and institutions created. It is evident from many remarks by Marx and Engels that they were clearly aware that commodity production and credit-and-money relations would persist during the transitional period, although they would be limited in essential ways.

But even this limited use of money and commodity relations would exist only in the transitional period, i.e., "on the road" to socialism. As soon as the socialist epoch had arrived, money would disappear along with all of its functions. In Marx's opinion, accounts would be kept under socialism directly in units of labor time. For this purpose certain "paper certificates" would be needed, but they would not constitute money, since they would not circulate as currency. These certificates, or receipts, would indicate the number of hours put in by a given worker. Of course even under socialism certain material incentives for labor would have to be maintained, since distribution would be according to one's work, not according to need. But material goods would not be obtained through the use of money to "purchase" commodities; a different and more direct system for the distribution of material goods would exist. [17]

It should be said that all these assertions about the "withering away" of money, trade, and commodity production under socialism were not the result of profound scientific probing by Marx and Engels. More emotional factors were at work here, together with the influence of traditional utopian-socialist beliefs and opinions. In such an early work, for example, as Thomas More's Utopia there is neither trade nor money, and consumption is of a primitive communist character. All industrial goods needed by the population are distributed through public stores; vegetables and other agricultural produce are not sold, but given out at "markets," and meat is given out right at the slaughterhouses. There is no private property in Utopia. Thomas More considered money and trade one of the main sources of the prevailing injustice in the society he lived in. Therefore it was a disgrace to wear gold and silver in Utopia; only the shackles of slaves were made of them. Morelly and John Bellers also advocated the total abolition of money and trade in the future society. Robert Owen thought that under socialism the natural measure of value would not be money, but labor itself, measured directly. Therefore special "labor bonds" would be used instead of money.

Only Charles Fourier was more perceptive on this point; he "kept" trade and money in their usual form in his socialist economy. But many "Fourierists" revised these views. Thus Wilhelm Weitling, whom Engels considered the "founder of German communism" and whose views were formed under the influence of Fourier and Blanqui, was especially emphatic in advocating the abolition of money and the entire system of money and commodity relations, making the success of the proletariat's political struggle dependent upon this.

Utopian socialism is one of the sources of Marxism. And although Marx and Engels put considerable effort into transforming socialism from a utopia to a science, they were not able to complete that work in every respect. This is especially evident in Marx and Engels' attitude toward such categories as "money," "trade," and "commodities" in the framework of socialist society. As for Lenin, in the prerevolutionary years he simply and uncritically repeated Marx and Engels' obviously mistaken formulas on this matter.

For example, in 1908 Lenin wrote, "Socialism, as we know, means the abolition of the commodity economy. . . . So long as exchange remains, it is ridiculous to talk of socialism." [18]

As we have said, much of Lenin's attention and effort in April and May 1917 went into the drafting of a new party program, whose economic section was essentially consistent with the propositions in the April Theses. However, in doing this, Lenin could not help but reflect upon the questions of trade and distribution. Unfortunately not all of his thoughts and proposals on such matters pointed in the right direction. For example, a resolution he wrote for a conference of factory committees said:

> In view of the breakdown of the whole financial and monetary system and the impossibility of rehabilitating it while the war is on the aim of the state organization should be to organize on a broad, regional—and subsequently countrywide—scale the exchange of agricultural implements,

clothes, boots, and other goods, for grain and other farm products. The services of the town and rural cooperative societies should be widely enlisted in this effort.[19]

Well before the October revolution bread-rationing cards for the population and the so-called "grain monopoly" were introduced. Such measures of "war socialism" were temporarily instituted in virtually all the belligerent European countries, but in Russia they were not applied as strictly as elsewhere, for there the propertied classes still had many ways of getting around such decrees. Lenin proposed that the grain monopoly and bread cards be utilized, above all, to put into effect the slogan "Those who do not work shall not eat." But he proposed to go farther:

> At a time when the country is suffering untold calamities a revolutionary-democratic policy would not confine itself to bread cards to combat the impending catastrophe but would add, first, the compulsory organization of the whole population into consumers' societies, for otherwise control over consumption cannot be fully exercised; second, labor service for the rich, making them perform without pay secretarial and similar duties for these consumers' societies; third, the equal distribution among the population of absolutely all consumer goods, so as really to distribute the burdens of the war equitably; fourth, the organization of control in such a way as to have the poorer classes of the population exercise control over the consumption of the rich.[20]

There was a certain utopian element in Lenin's persistently repeated proposal for the compulsory organization of the whole population into cooperative societies, because total control over the consumption activities of the population was impossible and unnecessary.

Let us note that among communists and socialists there were quite a few writers who tried in their articles and pamphlets to give a more detailed picture of the future socialist society, hoping thereby to win workers to their cause. Such articles and pamphlets often expressed the view that under socialism there would be neither trade nor money.

Thus, a small pamphlet by S. Grigoryev contains the following passage:

> In a society constructed along socialist lines there would be no buying and selling, there would not be any of what we at the present time call "trade." Trade in the form it has today would disappear completely. Commercial establishments of all sorts would become a thing of the past. Taking their place would be central warehouses and markets, making available everything necessary for a comfortable and free existence for

every human being. And this would not be in exchange for money, because neither money nor commodities nor buyers would exist in socialist society. There would only be producers working for the common good to the extent of their abilities and capacities; they themselves would be the consumers, receiving according to their needs. We should note in passing that with the abolition of the institution of trade a great number of people now employed in commercial occupations (shopkeepers, commercial travelers, salespeople, brokers, etc.) would be set free to participate in socially useful work, and together with these people great energy would be released which is now wasted on the dog-eat-dog struggle for existence based on violence and deception and the chase after profits and pelf.[21]

Such views were quite widespread among the Bolsheviks. That this was no accident or error is confirmed by many of Lenin's pronouncements in *State and Revolution*. (This book was written just before the revolution, although he began work on it during the war, and it was not published in Petrograd until the beginning of 1918.)

Here, for example, is what Lenin wrote while he was in hiding in August or September 1917:

> The selfish defense of capitalism by the bourgeois ideologists (and their hangers-on, like the Tseretelis, Chernovs, and Co.) consists in that they *substitute* arguing and talk about the distant future for the vital and burning question of *present-day* politics, namely, the expropriation of the capitalists, the conversion of *all* citizens into workers and other employees of *one* huge "syndicate"—the whole state—and the complete subordination of the work of this syndicate to a genuinely democratic state, *the state of the Soviets or Workers' and Soldiers' Deputies.*[22] (Emphasis in the original—R.M.)

It is not hard to see how far Lenin had diverged from his own April Theses in this case. In April he had indicated clearly that the "introduction" of socialism was not an immediate task, that in solving economic problems "extreme caution and prudence" were necessary. In April Lenin spoke only of *control* over the banks, insurance companies, and major capitalist syndicates. It is true that after several months he proposed not only that control be intensified but that the largest syndicates and trusts also be nationalized and that there be compulsory syndication of industrialists and merchants. In the circumstances of the war, the time was definitely ripe for all these measures, and they were entirely feasible. But to propose the expropriation of all capitalists and the establishment of a statewide "syndicate," whose workers and other employees would be *all* the citizens of Russia, in the conditions of 1917 was unrealistic and simply an impracticable utopia.

Nor was this a slip of the tongue on Lenin's part. A few pages later in *State and Revolution* we find the following:

> Given these *economic* preconditions, it is quite possible, after the over-throw of the capitalists and the bureaucrats, to proceed immediately, overnight, to replace them in the *control* over production and distribution, in the work of *keeping account* of labor and products, by the armed workers, by the whole of the armed population. . . .
>
> Accounting and control—that is *mainly* what is needed for the "smooth working," for the proper functioning of the *first phase* of communist society. . . . *All* citizens become employees and workers of a *single* country-wide state "syndicate." All that is required is that they should work equally, do their proper share of work, and get equal pay. The accounting and control necessary for this have been *simplified* by capitalism to the ut-most and reduced to the extraordinarily simple operations—which any lit-erate person can perform—of supervising and recording, knowledge of the four rules of arithmetic, and issuing appropriate receipts.
>
> When the *majority* of the people begin independently and everywhere to keep such accounts and exercise such control over the capitalists (now converted into employees) and over the intellectual gentry who preserve their capitalist habits, this control will really become universal, general, and popular; and there will be no getting away from it. . . .
>
> The whole of society will have become a single office and a single fac-tory, with equality of labor and pay.[23] (Emphasis in the original.—R.M.)

These proposals of Lenin's were erroneous and utopian over-simplifications of the traditional aims and program of the communist movement. They were unrealistic and unrealizable not only in 1917 but also in the years that followed. It is no accident that Lenin said nothing about trade. For how could there be any question of trade if all of society constituted a single office and a single factory?

Thus in the prerevolutionary program and proposals of the Bolshe-vik Party there were, along with many quite timely and appropriate proposals, a number that, unfortunately, were premature, unrealistic, utopian, and simply wrong. Marxist economists of the present day can of course see clearly that the views of Marx, Engels, and Lenin on the role of money and trade in socialist society and on the overall organi-zation of socialist production and distribution were mistaken. It was no easy matter, however, to arrive at a more correct view of such issues and categories. And Lenin himself had a decisive part in working out a more correct view. Attendant on the process of reaching such a view, however, were not only theoretical discussions but many rather bloody events, of which we will speak below.

PART THREE

The First Hundred Days
After the
October Revolution

eight

The First Few Weeks
After the Revolution

We have discussed the fact that Lenin convinced the majority in his party of the timeliness and necessity of a "second revolution." Lenin's constant argument was that only the transfer of power to the proletariat would enable Russia to withdraw from the hated war and to offer a just and democratic peace to the peoples and governments of all the belligerent countries. It is not surprising then, that the Decree on Peace was adopted by the Second Congress of Soviets immediately after the resolution placing all power in the hands of the Soviets. Of course the adoption of this decree did not mean an immediate end to the war between Russia and the Triple Alliance. Lengthy and trying negotiations would still be necessary to accomplish that. But the truce that was soon concluded gave the country the breathing spell it needed so badly.

Lenin also argued that only the dictatorship of the proletariat would make it possible to eliminate all the vestiges of feudalism in rural Russia and ensure the rapid and fair resolution of the land question. And as it turned out, the Second Congress of Soviets immediately followed the Decree on Peace with the Decree on Land, under which landed proprietorship was abolished forthwith without any compensation, and all the landed estates and crown, church, and monastery lands were placed under the jurisdiction of rural district (*volost*) land committees and county (*uyezd*) Soviets of Peasants' Deputies to be distributed among the peasants. The peasants were released from all earlier debts and more than 150 million hectares of agriculturally valuable land passed into their hands.

It is hard not to agree that these primary decisions of the Second Congress of Soviets were quite timely. Equally timely were the decrees of the Council of People's Commissars (Sovnarkom) and the All-Russia Central Executive Committee of the Soviets (VTsIK) granting independence to Finland and Poland, and the Declaration of the Rights of the Peoples of Russia, which recognized the right of all the peoples of Russia to self-determination and abolished all forms of national oppression and all unequal treaties between Russia and colonial and dependent countries. Nor can other decisions of the Soviet Government be regarded as inopportune, for example, the decree abolishing social estates, or castes, and ranks, grades, and titles or the decree "on civil marriage, children, and the keeping of records on marital status," which gave women equal rights with men. A long overdue democratic reform was the decree separating church and state, separating church and school, and establishing full freedom of religion. Another very timely resolution of the Soviet government was the annulment of all state loans, which eliminated Russia's colossal foreign debt and freed it from a semi-colonial state of dependence.

This list of long overdue and very timely revolutionary reforms enacted only because of the October revolution could be extended further. Of course there was nothing socialist per se in any of these reforms. They merely constituted an extremely radical way of carrying out the tasks of the bourgeois-democratic revolution, tasks which neither the bourgeois parties nor the Menshevik and SR parties had been able to carry out.

This cannot be said of one measure, which had a plainly socialist tinge—the introduction of workers' control.

Workers' control of production, as one of the most important tasks of the workers' and peasants' government, was announced as early as the celebrated appeal of the Petrograd Military Revolutionary Committee "To the Citizens of Russia!" On November 14, 1917, the VTsIK passed a regulation on workers' control, which had the force of a legislative act of the Soviet government. From then on the factory committees, the shop steward councils, the economic control commissions, and certain other elected workers' organizations in the factories were given the right to intervene in the management of production and to have a say in the orders issued by the administration of any enterprise.

To be sure the work of the Council of People's Commissars, the

VTsIK, the central party institutions, and the Supreme Council of the National Economy (Vesenkha) did not proceed without mistakes and miscalculations during the first few months after October. However, on the whole it moved in the right direction, and for that reason the overwhelming majority of the people supported the Bolsheviks during those months. From November through January Bolshevik influence among the masses grew steadily and universally, while the influence not only of the Mensheviks but of the SRs declined markedly. Specific evidence of this was the "triumphal march" of the Soviets throughout the country, the rapid and almost bloodless victory of Soviet power in all the main parts of Russian territory. This was the best proof of the timeliness of the October revolution, for not only did Soviet territory spread but also—despite the desperate agitation of its opponents, the formation of various underground groups and alliances for "the salvation of the motherland," and attempted uprisings—the social base of Soviet power expanded steadily in the first weeks and months.

The first hundred days of Soviet power were marked not only by the forced destruction but also the automatic collapse of a multitude of state institutions which had persisted in Russia since the time of the tsarist regime, as well as weak and sickly institutions and social formations that had arisen between February and October 1917. At the same time there began the process of creating new, "proletarian" government institutions and adapting some earlier institutions and organizations to the needs and requirements of Soviet power. During these weeks extremely important shifts in the consciousness of the millions of workers, peasants, and soldiers took place. They greeted all of the first Soviet decrees—on peace, land, power, and workers' control— with joy and approval. This mass support for the new organs of Soviet power upset the calculations of all those foreign observers and domestic opponents of Soviet power who were certain that the Bolsheviks would not last for even two or three weeks.

Of course the Bolshevik Party could not fully control the situation throughout the country—the cities, the rural areas, and the front-line zones. For example, a truce was concluded with Germany and Austria-Hungary as early as November 1917 and difficult peace negotiations began. But the soldiers deserted the trenches both individually and in whole units and headed for home, without waiting for the results of the negotiations. Cossack squadrons, regiments, and batteries returned to their *stanitsas* on their own initiative or in response to calls by the local Cossack administrations. The army, until recently so enormous, melted away and disintegrated, stripping the front bare, and there were no forces left with the ability to prevent the rapid destruction of what Lenin called "this sickly organism." It was likewise impossible to control effectively the process under way in the countryside—the distribution of the crown, church, and monastery lands and the large estates. The agrarian revolution had actually begun to unfold in the villages of Russia in the summer of 1917. The October Decree on Land simply gave this revolution a powerful new impetus.

The Decree on Land placed all the large estates and crown, monastery, and church lands under the jurisdiction of district land committees and county Soviets of Peasants' Deputies "until the convocation of the Constituent Assembly." Hardly anyone noticed this qualification in regard to the Constituent Assembly, however, for November and December 1917 were the months in which the agrarian revolution acquired its greatest scope and became an invincible force. Thus, when the VTsIK passed the more elaborate "Law on the Socialization of the Land"[1] later on, it was more of an affirmation and legalization of an already accomplished fact than a starting point for any new agrarian initiative. Moreover, many of the recommendations of this law basically remained only on paper. The first Decree on Land had proposed that the land be distributed on the basis of "a labor standard or a consumption standard." Under the new proposals the amount of land assigned to an individual household for agricultural use was not to "exceed the consumption and labor standard. . . . calculated both by the number of able-bodied persons in the family in question and by the total number of mouths to be fed, including those not able to work." In other words, the new decree did not leave any legal openings for the existence of kulak households, but neither did it provide for the confiscation of kulak land or property.

In reality the kulaks had a great deal of influence in the peasant Soviets, substantial stocks—for those days—of agricultural equipment, considerable livestock, and significant financial resources; they managed to take over a large part of the former estate land, although under the letter and spirit of the law, the land they already possessed was sufficient both in terms of the labor standard and the number of mouths to be fed.

The recommendation that model farms be established on the basis of well-organized farms formerly belonging to large landowners was almost everywhere ignored. A large number of such farms were divided up among the peasants. The peasants' hatred of the landlords, accumulated over the centuries, found release at times in the outright plundering of the landlords' mansions. Often, after the livestock and equipment were divided up, these structures were simply burned, though they could have been used for the needs of the community—e.g., as schools or libraries.

In any event, the peasants obtained their long-awaited land, thanks to Soviet power and the Bolsheviks; at the same time "peace making" began at the front, and peasant youths were able to return home. As a result, the authority of the Bolsheviks and their new allies, the Left SRs, rose substantially in the countryside in November and December 1917. It was at this time that the Left SRs, who completed their organizational development by constituting themselves as an independent party, made the decision not only to support the Bolsheviks in the Soviets but to enter the Council of People's Commissars, the Sovnarkom. The Soviet government became a coalition government, and this significantly strengthened its overall position in the country.

The economic measures of the Sovnarkom and VTsIK during the first hundred days, though they sometimes betrayed signs of improvisation, essentially corresponded to the prerevolutionary Bolshevik program. The State Bank was nationalized along with all privately incorporated commercial banks, the latter becoming branches of the State Bank. Many large businesses and syndicates were also nationalized, and institutions of workers' control were established at most industrial enterprises.

Of course, these revolutionary changes did not immediately bring the desired improvement in the lives of most of the working class. A significant number of office workers in the former ministries and financial establishments, a large percentage of teachers, the upper layers in the railroad union, and many engineers in the businesses nationalized immediately after October went on strike or refused to follow the instructions of the new authorities. A large number of factories had to shut down because of sabotage by their administrations or lack of raw materials and financial resources. Rail transport functioned worse than ever, as did maritime and river transport. In order to crush such sabotage, Soviet government agencies in Petrograd and a number of other cities were forced to arrest some prominent officials. These arrests, however, were of short duration. By order of the VTsIK former ministers of the Provisional Government were released from the Peter and Paul fortress, and General Krasnov was set free on his word of honor. During those first few months Lenin expected to get by without terrorism.

"We are accused," he said, "of making arrests. Indeed we have made arrests; today we arrested the director of the State Bank. We are accused of resorting to terrorism, but we have not resorted, and I hope will not resort, to the terrorism of the French revolutionaries who guillotined unarmed men." [2]

In order to ensure the proper functioning of management in the nationalized businesses and at the same time to lay the basis for further nationalization of large-scale industry, the Supreme Council of the National Economy (Vesenkha) was established under the Sovnarkom in December 1917.[3] In turn the Vesenkha established not only departments for particular sectors of industry but also Councils of the National Economy (sovnarkhozy) for a number of districts and regions (for example, the Moscow Regional Sovnarkhoz, and the Northern Sovnarkhoz which included the provinces of Petrograd, Olonetsk, Novgorod, Pskov, Archangel, Vologda, and Northern Dvina).[4]

Although Soviet power proposed to get by without terrorism, the intensified activities of various underground organizations, organized sabotage, and an increase in speculation required the formation of a special agency to combat counterrevolution. On December 7 (20), a session of the Sovnarkom voted to establish the All-Russia Extraordinary Commission to Combat Counterrevolution and Sabotage (the Cheka). Felix Dzerzhinsky was appointed president. At that time the punitive measures to be employed against enemies of Soviet power included confiscation of property, expulsion, deprivation of ration cards, and publication of lists of counterrevolutionaries. There was no question of having people shot, and capital punishment had formally been abolished.[5]

One of the most important and urgent tasks of the new government was to combat famine in the main industrial centers of the country and to supply food to the armies at the front. The situation in this respect was truly catastrophic. Although the immediate cause of the outbreak of the February revolution had been interruptions in the bread supply to Petrograd and breakdowns in the food supply to the army, the Provisional Government had not been able to improve the situation in any noticeable way in this extremely important sphere. The bread ration in Petrograd before the October revolution was reduced to 200 grams per day, and the food reserves on hand in the city and its environs were virtually exhausted. Alarming telegrams poured in to the capital from all the armies. Food reserves in the front-line depots were sufficient only for several more days. Of the numerous documents on this subject we will cite only one—the reports of Shub and Bukovetsky to the All-Russia Conference of Factory Committees on October 18 (31). Here is what we find in the minutes of this conference:

> In the report on the food situation Shub pointed out that the food shortage made itself felt as far back as the second year of the war. The decline in grain deliveries in 1917 for certain months was 20 to 40 percent of the amount slated for delivery and for the front it was 30 to 73 percent of what was ordered. Grain reserves at the front were good for only three to five days. The 1917 harvest was no lower than average, but the villages categorically refused to give up their grain. It is necessary, through intervention in the regulation of industry, to bring the exchange between town and country back to normal.
>
> Bukovetsky in his report on the financial situation pointed to the consequences of the increase in the government issue of paper money (16,200 million rubles, as opposed to 1,603 million before the war, with the gold reserve shrinking from 1,603 million rubles to 1,298 million). The result was, he said, the devaluation of the ruble to 25, 16, and then 11 kopecks, which falls mainly on the backs of the working class. This financial dislocation should be combated by following a healthy economic policy, regulating production, establishing fixed prices for all manufactured goods, raising direct taxes, and reducing the issue of paper currency. The last measure can be carried out only on the condition that we can borrow successfully within the country, but no one will loan money to the Provisional Government, which has no base of support in even one class of the population.[6]

But the country did have food. Although the grain and potato harvests declined somewhat during the war, total consumption also declined, even in the villages, because of the rise in prices. Especially in the southern and eastern regions and in Siberia the granaries of the large landowners and wealthy peasants held surpluses not only from the harvest of 1917 but from the 1916 harvest as well. But because of the devaluation of paper currency the farmers did not wish to give up this grain at "fixed" prices, and the government did not have a sufficient quantity of the goods needed in the villages; the bulk of Russian industry was producing armaments, and even aside from that was not very highly developed. In order to bring trade and the economy back to normal the war had to be ended. But the peace negotiations might take a long time, and bread was needed right away. The Bolsheviks did not feel bound by any special respect for private property, and having come to power on October 25, they immediately took a series of rapid and effective measures. Groups of Red Guards and units of Baltic sailors were given orders to search all warehouses, stores, and railroad stations. In the first few days, in the capital alone, hundreds of thousands of poods of hidden food stocks were uncovered and confiscated.

An appeal by the Sovnarkom to all army organizations, military revolutionary committees, and soldiers said on this matter:

> There is food in our country. The large landowners, kulaks, and merchants have large hoards of provisions. . . . The counterrevolutionaries are willing to let the soldiers die of hunger rather than submit to the people's power, let the peasants have the land, and let an immediate peace be concluded. The directors of the banks refuse to lend the Soviet government money for the emergency purchase of food. The Council of People's Commissars has taken the most decisive measures. The Commissars of the Council together with sailors, soldiers, and Red Guards are requisitioning food reserves in all parts of the country and sending them to the front. Merciless war is hereby declared upon all speculators, marauders, embezzlers of public funds, and counterrevolutionary officials interfering with the food-supply effort. They will be arrested and imprisoned in Kronstadt. Soldiers at the front! Soviet power will take all necessary steps to provide you with food and expects the necessary supplies to reach you in the next few days.[7]

In November success was also achieved in improving freight deliveries to Petrograd via the rail system and the Mariinskaya river and canal system. Thanks to this, the daily bread ration in the capital increased to 300 grams per capita in November 1917.[8]

The problem of supplying the army with food was eased by its rapidly diminishing numbers, the result, in part, of the demobilization of those in the upper-age brackets and, to a much greater extent, of the spontaneous go-home movement which spread throughout the ranks of the soldiers, numbering in the millions.

To be fair, we should note that a great many of the agencies concerned with food supply under the Provisional Government and various official bodies in charge of supplying the army continued their work after the October revolution and did not join the general strike by civil servants in a number of ministries and offices. For that reason food continued to reach the cities and the front by the same avenues as before, although more obstacles arose than before October. However, the Soviet government could not rely entirely on the loyalty of the civil servants in the former food-supply organizations. With the formation of the Council of People's Commissars, a People's Commissariat for Food Supply (Narkomprod) was established and soon began to function independently, creating its own food-supply agencies in the local areas. I. A. Teodorovich was appointed people's commissar of food supply, with A. G. Shlikhter as his chief assistant. The Council of People's Commissars gave extensive powers to the Food Supply Commissariat, and military revolutionary committees at all levels were urged to provide any and all assistance to the agencies of that commissariat. At this time the first food-requisitioning detachments of workers and sailors were formed in Petrograd and other cities; these units went out into the villages, taking with them goods needed in the villages for exchange purposes and requisitioning booklets for the purpose of confiscating surpluses. According to the memoirs of N. I. Podvoisky, in November 1917 roughly 7,000 people from Petrograd alone went to the villages as members of such detachments.[9]

Another aspect of this problem must be mentioned. Along with the "organized" effort to supply grain to the urban population, "unorganized" trade in surplus food continued almost everywhere. There was a tremendous need for food in the cities, and in the villages there was a tremendous need on the part of all peasants—wealthy, middle-income, and poor—for such products as kerosene, matches, cotton textiles, tools, the simplest kinds of agricultural equipment, as well as nails, sewing needles, kitchenware, and so on and so forth. Food prices had risen during the war, but so had prices on all the manufactured goods needed in the villages. From this reciprocal demand for products a so-called free market (often called a "black market") emerged and began to grow. Despite all obstacles and prohibitions this free market continued to exist. Both the peasants and speculating middlemen found hundreds of ways to bring grain to the cities and exchange it for industrial goods. And although in the very first weeks of their existence Soviet government agencies passed quite a few decrees concerning the struggle against speculation in grain—up to and including "shooting on the spot those exposed as speculators and saboteurs"[10]—such extreme measures were more frequently proclaimed than applied in November and December. The prisons of

Kronstadt were not yet crowded with "bagmen" (*meshochniki*) and speculators, and "shooting on the spot"—if it happened at all—was apparently rare. In general, the existence of the free market was a factor of no small importance in helping the Bolsheviks retain power during their first hundred days.

nine

The Convening and Dispersal
of the Constituent Assembly

Given—among a multitude of pressing tasks—the need to consolidate power, conclude peace with the Germans, and see to the shipment of food supplies to Petrograd, Moscow, and the front, and the question of holding elections for the Constituent Assembly and convening that assembly must not have seemed very vital or urgent to the Bolshevik leaders. Apparently that was the reason the Bolsheviks did not think this problem through completely and, in their handling of it, made a number of serious miscalculations from the standpoint of their own interests. It happens often enough in politics that what seems secondary, and actually is secondary at a particular time, turns out to be extremely important at the next stage of development. Something of that nature happened in the case of the Constituent Assembly.

After the February revolution, and especially after Lenin's return to Russia, the main slogan of the Bolsheviks was "All Power to the Soviets." The call for a Constituent Assembly was actually the main slogan of the SR Party. Boris Sokolov, one of the leaders of that party, subsequently wrote in his memoirs:

> Of all the political parties the Socialist Revolutionary Party was linked with the idea of the Constituent Assembly by extremely close, I might even say organic, ties. The Constituent Assembly embodied the main demands of the revolutionary people and the basic propositions of democratism were focused around it. . . . Those were the considerations that prompted the Socialist Revolutionaries to insist on the idea of an All-Russia Constituent Assembly. It seemed to them, and not only to them, that the crucial thing was to "bring the country to the Constituent Assembly." Theoretically perhaps, and probably in fact, there was a very great truth

in this, but practically this peculiar idealism was fraught with the most exasperating consequences and complications.

This was especially because the people were far from being fully imbued with faith in the saving power of the Constituent Assembly. . . . In the beginning, during the first few months after the revolution, the Constituent Assembly was something absolutely unknown and unclear to the mass of front-line soldiers. . . . Their sympathies leaned completely, openly, and frankly to the Soviets. These were the institutions that were near and dear to them, reminding them of village assemblies. From the very first days, the meetings of the Soviets in the front-line zones attracted a large number of outsiders who often intervened in the business of the Soviets and influenced their decisions. Both the army committee, which the soldiers called "our Soviet," and the Soviets in the capital cities seemed close to them, and their activities comprehensible. During the first few months I more than once had occasion to hear objections to the Constituent Assembly from soldiers, and not from the least intelligent ones at that. To most of them the Assembly was associated with the State Duma, an institution that was remote to them. "What do we need some Constituent Assembly for when we have our Soviets, where our deputies meet and which can decide everything and know how to go about everything?"[1]

Such moods existed not only among the front-line soldiers but among the workers in the cities and the peasants in the villages and hamlets as well. But the Bolsheviks, in their struggle against the Mensheviks and the SRs, did not reject the call for the Constituent Assembly or counter it with the Soviet slogan. The fact was that despite their ostensible support of a Constituent Assembly, for a long time, under pressure from the bourgeois parties, the SRs found all sorts of reasons to oppose the rapid convening of the Assembly, and the Bolsheviks took advantage of this in their propaganda.

In point of fact the social and legal basis for the Provisional Government could only be reinforced in one way—the rapid convening of a Constituent Assembly, which would have raised itself above both the misbegotten remnants of the State Duma and the swiftly radicalizing Soviets. And there were no serious obstacles to the rapid convening of the Constituent Assembly in the spring and summer of 1917. The basic principles for electing delegates to a Constituent Assembly could have been worked out in a few days; the elaborate election-law details of every imaginable kind, which were debated in various commissions, had no essential importance. This work was dragged out unnecessarily and the elections and the convening of the

Constituent Assembly were endlessly postponed as the result of deliberate sabotage on the part of both the bourgeois parties and the Menshevik and SR parties, which had made their coalition with the bourgeois parties. There were several reasons. First, the Provisional Government stated from the outset that it was only a temporary formation and therefore could not assume the responsibility for carrying out social reforms. This government emphatically refused, for example, to carry out the long overdue agrarian reform, arguing that questions of such importance could only be decided by an All-Russia Constituent Assembly. But precisely in order to postpone the implementation of such bourgeois-democratic reforms, the Provisional Government kept putting off the convening of the Assembly. Second, it was not hard to foresee that in the spring and summer of 1917 Constituent Assembly elections would have given a majority, not to the bourgeois parties, which were already losing influence, but to the more leftward-tending parties, especially the SRs and Mensheviks. But at the time those Compromiser parties did not wish to, and were afraid to, take responsibility for the fate of the country. They clung desperately to the bloc with the bourgeois parties (the "propertied" elements), which were supposed to carry out the main tasks of the bourgeois revolution. In those circumstances the convening of a Constituent Assembly would have restricted the SRs and Mensheviks' room for unprincipled political maneuver. Laws would have to be passed and decisions made, but *decisiveness* was what was lacking in the leaders of those two parties, the most popular parties of the revolutionary democracy at that time. Thus, the Kerensky government, which came to power in July 1917 and could have quickly convened the Constituent Assembly, remained under the thumb of the bourgeois parties and continued to put off the elections and the Assembly. It is not surprising that the Bolsheviks added the principle of the rapid convening of the Constituent Assembly to their propaganda arsenal, and this was one of the reasons for their success. As early as April 1917, in reply to the question of whether the Constituent Assembly should be convened, Lenin wrote: "Yes, and as soon as possible." [2]

The Bolsheviks held to this policy through the summer months, contrasting their own readiness to convene the Assembly to the endless procrastination of the Provisional Government.

Not long before the famous June demonstration in Petrograd, the Provisional Government announced a date for the convening of the

Constituent Assembly, September 30, and a date for elections, September 17. However, on August 9, after the new Provisional Government headed by Kerensky had consolidated its power, it postponed the elections to November 12 and the convocation of the Constituent Assembly to November 28. And there was no guarantee that it would abide by those dates either.

The situation changed after the suppression of the Kornilov revolt and after the Bolsheviks, having obtained a majority in the Soviets of the two capital cities, began to win out in the Soviets in other cities and in the army. The slogan "All Power to the Soviets," which had been temporarily withdrawn, was again put forward. In the meantime Lenin had concluded that a peaceful revolution was impossible and he began to urge the Bolsheviks to hasten the preparations for an armed insurrection.

Of course in September the Bolsheviks were not opposed to a rapid convocation of the Constituent Assembly. But the Assembly could only be convened by whoever controlled the administrative institutions; in other words, the initiative could only come from the Provisional Government. For that reason the Bolshevik Party placed its emphasis on the earliest possible convening of the Second Congress of Soviets, expecting to win a majority at that congress and to replace the old VTsIK, dominated by the Compromisers, with a revolutionary leadership.

This new situation forced the leaders of the Provisional Government to change their tactics. They began serious preparations for elections to the Constituent Assembly and tried to establish a certain support for themselves in the form of the Pre-Parliament, which was never anything more than a parody of a representative body. On the other hand, the SR-Menshevik VTsIK began to resist desperately the idea of convening the Second All-Russia Congress of Soviets, arguing that it was no longer necessary since the Constituent Assembly was about to be held. As for the right-wing parties, they feared both the Congress of Soviets and the Constituent Assembly and continued to dream of a military coup and the establishment of a military dictatorship in the country. One of the reactionary dailies, *Novaya Rus'* (New Russia) wrote at this time:

"An increase in the influence of the Bosheviks and the left parties is occurring in the country. Preliminary estimates indicate that in the elections to the Constituent Assembly approximately 30 percent of the

vote will go to the Bolsheviks and no less than 40 percent to the SRs."
Novaya Rus' appealed, "Demand the postponement of the elections;
protest against the new idiocy of the Provisional Government! Make
the government come to its senses! Wake up! Go into action!!! A true
and pure basis for power in Russia can only be provided by our Cossacks." For this reason the newspaper called for the immediate release
of the Cossack leaders and the "purification of the well-springs of
power" by entrusting the formation of a government to the Cossacks.[3]

The struggle around the question of convening the Second All-Russia Congress of Soviets ended as we know with the victory of the
Bolsheviks and the left wing of the SRs, who were in favor of convening the congress. The overwhelming majority of resolutions in local
areas also favored holding the congress, and delegates-to-be began arriving in Petrograd armed with their mandates. Shifting their position
in midstream, the Mensheviks and SRs began to send urgent messages
to Soviets that had voted against holding the congress, advising them
to elect and send their delegates to Petrograd. For this purpose the
opening of the Second Congress was postponed from October 20 to
October 25. The Mensheviks and SRs still hoped to win a majority of
votes at the congress. But when, after long and anxious waiting, the
congress opened in the Smolny Institute on the morning of October
26 it became clear that the Bolsheviks had won a double victory—
power had already passed into the hands of the Military Revolutionary
Committee of the Petrograd Soviet, led by the Bolsheviks, and a majority of delegates at the Second Congress of Soviets were Bolsheviks
or Left SR allies of the Bolsheviks. The subsequent events are well
known: the formation of a Presidium of the VTsIK that was essentially
Bolshevik in composition and the decrees on peace, land, and power.
The First Council of People's Commissars was made up solely of
Bolsheviks: V. I. Lenin, A. I. Rykov, V. P. Miliutin, A. G. Shliapnikov,
V. A. Antonov-Ovseenko, N. V. Krylenko, P. E. Dybenko, V. P.
Nogin, A. V. Lunacharsky, I. I. Skvortsov-Stepanov, L. D. Trotsky,
G. I. Lomov-Oppokov, I. A. Teodorovich, N. P. Glebov-Avilov, and
J. V. Stalin.

A special appeal written by Lenin and adopted by the Second
Congress of Soviets referred to the transfer of all power to the Soviets,
but also included a phrase to the effect that Soviet power would "ensure the convocation of the Constituent Assembly at the appointed
time."[4] As we have already pointed out, the Decree on Land included

a sentence about the transfer of all land in the country to the jurisdiction of district land committees and county Soviets "pending the convocation of the Constituent Assembly." In the same way the second resolution of the Second Congress of Soviets on the formation of a "provisional workers' and peasants' government," stated that the new government would rule "until the Constituent Assembly is convened."[5]

Thus, the new government did not drop the idea of the Constituent Assembly. Was this perhaps only a tactical device? Certainly the overthrow of the Provisional Government and the transfer of all power to the Soviets fundamentally changed the situation in the country. Under these conditions was it necessary or even possible to guarantee the elections and convocation of the Constituent Assembly? Even rank-and-file workers and soldiers had their doubts. Boris Sokolov, the prominent SR functionary whom we quoted above, tells of his participation in a front-line congress on the Southwestern Front held at the very time of the October insurrection in Petrograd. It should be noted that the influence of the Bolsheviks among the soldiers of the Southwestern Front, in contrast to the Northern Front, for example, was very slight. "A majority of the congress," Sokolov acknowledges,

> belonged to the SR Party, which had approximately two-thirds of the delegates. The remaining third adhered to the Bolsheviks or—a small number—to the Ukrainians. However, some of the SRs, primarily those sent by rearguard units in the front-line zone, took an ambiguous position, which could be summed up as follows: Since the Provisional Government no longer exists and since the Constituent Assembly has not yet been convened, all the power in the country ought to go to the Soviets. . . . The disputes that developed on this question showed how contradictory the mood was even among the delegates. . . . They discussed the advantages of the Soviet system over parliamentarism and emphasized the fact, which seemed indisputable to most, that the Soviets were better than the Provisional Government since the "Soviets, you know, are ours." Even the arrival of the former Provisional Government minister Avksentiev at this congress and his many speeches in defense of the slogan "All Power to the Constituent Assembly," did not convince the majority of the congress. . . . The front-line congress, though not by a very large majority, expressed itself in favor of the formation proposed by the Bolsheviks. It spoke out for power to the Soviets—essentially for Bolshevik power.[6]

After the October victory the Bolshevik Party could have taken a number of different positions both theoretically and practically on the question of convening the Constituent Assembly.

The first could have been to abandon the idea of the Constituent Assembly altogether, to declare that the transfer of all power to the Soviets and the formation of the new Soviet government had eliminated the problem of the Constituent Assembly, because Soviet power is a higher form—i.e., workers' power. This of course would have been an incorrect line. Somewhat later Lenin explained why the Bolsheviks could not immediately drop their call for the Constituent Assembly. Although it was clear to the Bolsheviks themselves that the Soviets had taken power "seriously and for a long time to come" the party could not regard as outdated for the masses what was outdated for itself. If among the workers (and, as we have seen from Sokolov's account, among the soldiers as well) the notion of the Constituent Assembly was no longer universally popular, it still enjoyed favor among a substantial segment of the peasantry. Then, a hasty abandonment of the Constituent Assembly could have played into the hands of the counterrevolution, enabling it to take advantage of the illusions about such an assembly which had not yet become outdated.

A second position might have been to postpone the Constituent Assembly elections again, if only for one or two months. As we have said, the Provisional Government had set November 12 as the date for the elections. However, on October 25–26 a new revolution had begun in the country and it spread, not in one day of course, but over a period of several weeks, to all the main areas of Russia. The Second Congress of Soviets had in fact already carried out the principal revolutionary measures which were linked with the idea of the Constituent Assembly in the minds of the people and the army. Even before October, rough estimates had indicated that in the voting for the Assembly the Bolsheviks might receive between 25 and 30 percent of the votes (under the one man–one vote system). But now, when the Bolsheviks had given the land to the peasants and begun peace negotiations, they could expect to significantly increase their representation among the soldiers and peasants. However, given the existing means of communication in 1917, there was not enough time from October 26 to November 12 for the fundamental meaning and content of the first decrees of the Soviet government to reach the remote rural provinces and the outlying sectors of the Russo-German front. In some units on the Southwestern Front the commanders completely hid from the soldiers the fact that the Provisional Government had been overthrown and continued to issue orders and regulations in its name.

But there was not only the problem of a poor system of information.

The October revolution had changed the political face of Russia, and the period up to November 12 was too short for these changes to be reflected in the Constituent Assembly elections. The most important of these changes was the definitive split in the largest party in Russia, the SR Party, and the emergence of the Right SRs and the Left SRs as two separate parties. The split had been in the making for a long time, because the small group at the top of the SR Party, which found itself in the Provisional Government and in the top circles of the Soviets, had not wanted to carry through the policy which the SRs themselves proclaimed in their program and which the majority of peasants expected from them. As early as the summer of 1917 a distinct group of leaders emerged in the SR Party, demanding that their own Central Committee and the Provisional Government carry out fundamental revolutionary changes. By the end of September the Left SRs existed as a separate faction and functioned virtually as an independent party, although formally the split had not yet occurred. But it was at that very time that the lists of candidates for the Constituent Assembly elections were drawn up. The preparation of these lists was under the control of the Right SRs, who predominated in the previously existing leadership of the party. Barefacedly claiming that only a minority of the party and of its active membership favored the left-wing faction, the right-wing leaders drew up lists of candidates for the Constituent Assembly weighted entirely in favor of their own faction. The final split between the Right and Left SRs took place at the time of the October revolution and just after. The Left SRs not only did not walk out of the Second Congress of Soviets, as the Rights did, but supported all of its resolutions and thus helped in the formation of the Bolshevik government. Although at first they did not join the Council of People's Commissars, the Left SRs did join the new VTsIK; they took an active part in the work of all the main local Soviets, and in Petrograd their representatives joined the Military Revolutionary Committee. Immediately after the October revolution the Left SRs selected their own independent party leadership and set the date of their first congress for November 20. Naturally the question arose of having a separate Left SR slate in the Constituent Assembly elections. This question was discussed in particular at the November 6 (19) meeting of the VTsIK— i.e., only one week before the elections themselves. In the days remaining, however, it proved technically possible to distribute the revised slates only to some central regions, not to the country as a whole.

A number of Bolsheviks proposed at that time that the Constituent Assembly elections be postponed, but the VTsIK did not accept that proposal and thereby committed a serious political error. For, as subsequent events showed, the split in the SR Party was not a split into two fairly even factions; the overwhelming majority of that party's supporters favored the program of the Left SRs, while the Right SRs proved to be a group of generals without an army. For example, in Petrograd a total of 16.7 percent of the vote went to the SRs, but of this, 16.2 percent was for the Left SRs and only 0.5 percent for the Right. In Kazan, out of the 21 percent of voters who cast their ballots for the SRs, 18.9 percent were for the Left SRs and 2.1 percent for the Right. The Baltic fleet gave the SRs 38.8 percent of the electorate, the Left SRs receiving 26.9 percent and the Right SRs, 11.9 percent.[7] It is quite obvious that if the new VTsIK or the Sovnarkom had postponed the elections to the Constituent Assembly for a month or two after the October victory, the majority of seats in the Assembly would have gone, not to the Right SRs, as actually occurred, but to the Bolshevik–Left SR bloc. And this would have been especially true because in December 1917 this bloc took distinct organizational forms, with the Left SRs shifting from a policy of support to the actions of the Sovnarkom to direct participation in the Sovnarkom. This governmental bloc became a symbol of the alliance of the working class and peasantry.

The third position open to the Bolshevik Party on the question of the Constituent Assembly, and the one it chose in preference to the other two, was to abide by the date that had already been set by the Provisional Government for the Constituent Assembly elections— November 12 (25), 1917.

As early as October 27 the Sovnarkom which had just been formed passed a special resolution on elections for the Constituent Assembly:

> (1) The elections to the Constituent Assembly should be held at the appointed time, November 12.
> (2) All election commissions, institutions of local goverment, Soviets of Workers', Soldiers', and Peasants' Deputies, and soldiers' organizations at the front, should bend every effort to ensure the free and proper conduct of the elections at the appointed time.[8]

This was a wrong decision, because it was hard to expect that elections could be conducted properly and calmly in a country caught up in a revolution. The Provisional Government had repeatedly postponed the Constituent Assembly elections on grounds much less weighty than a new revolution. The Bolsheviks showed excessive scrupulousness in this case, and subsequently suffered for it in important political respects. It is true that Lenin tried in some measure to correct the mistake after the fact by having the VTsIK pass the "Decree on the Right of Recall" just a few days before the elections. According to this decree voters could, if necessary, recall any deputy from the Constituent Assembly and replace that deputy by a new one. But it was too difficult to put this decree into practice, since the political stance of any particular deputy would only become clear after the Constituent Assembly had begun its work.

The subsequent events are well known. The elections to the Constituent Assembly, which began on November, 12, 1917, lasted for more than three weeks, because of the extremely complicated situation in the country. These elections, in which approximately 50 percent of those qualified participated, gave a majority of seats to the Right SR Party, which had just been removed from power by the October revolution. No sooner had this party's death agony begun than it was granted a new lease on life. It was not until 1918 that a quorum convened in Petrograd, and on January 5, 1918, the first session of the Constituent Assembly was opened. It refused to pass the Declaration of the Rights of the Working and Exploited People submitted to it by the VTsIK and refused to recognize the legality of the Sovnarkom. After a number of ugly scenes and rough altercations the Bolsheviks walked out of the Constituent Assembly and refused to take any further part in its work. In the early morning hours of January 6 the Sovnarkom passed a decree dissolving the Constituent Assembly. Within a day this decree was confirmed and published by the VTsIK. Such a finale could have been foreseen. It is odd that as late as December 1917 both the Bolsheviks and their political opponents still held certain illusions as to the fate of the Constituent Assembly.

For example in mid-December Lenin published his well-known "Theses on the Constituent Assembly." After listing in detail all the reasons why this particular Constituent Assembly could not be considered the legal representative of the peoples of Russia (the results of the elections were already known), Lenin nevertheless wrote:

> The only chance of securing a painless solution to the crisis which has arisen owing to the divergence between the elections to the Constituent Assembly on the one hand and the will of the people . . . , on the other,

is for the people to exercise as broadly and as rapidly as possible the right to elect the members of the Constituent Assembly anew, and for the Constituent Assembly to accept the law of the Central Executive Committee [VTsIK] on these new elections, to proclaim that it unreservedly recognizes Soviet power, the Soviet revolution, and its policy on the questions of peace, the land, and workers' control, and to resolutely join the camp of the enemies of the Cadet-Kaledin counterrevolution.[9]

Of course, all this was quite unacceptable to the Right SRs. Nevertheless many Right SR and Menshevik leaders felt certain for some reason that the Bolsheviks would not dare to touch the Constituent Assembly and would take its prerogatives into account. According to Boris Sokolov, the leaders of the Right SR Party were sure that the Constituent Assembly would be able to defend its rights and that it would need no special protection other than the knowledge that it had been elected by all the people of Russia. This was an especially frequent theme of speeches by the Menshevik leader Tsereteli, who was confident that the Bolsheviks were only trying to frighten their opponents in order to make them more tractable. But it should be remembered that as far back as the Second Congress of the RSDLP in 1903, when the Bolsheviks and Mensheviks still belonged to one party, it was not Lenin but Plekhanov who declared in one of his speeches:

> The success of the revolution is the highest law. And if, for the sake of that success, it would be necessary temporarily to limit the application of one or another democratic principle, it would be a crime to shrink from such a restriction. As my personal opinion I will state that even the principle of universal suffrage must be regarded from the point of view of this highest principle of democracy which I have indicated. Let us hypothetically imagine a case in which we, the Social Democrats, might oppose universal suffrage. . . . The revolutionary proletariat might restrict the political rights of the upper classes, just as the upper classes in their day restricted political rights. As to the suitability of such a measure one may judge only by the rule that "The good of the people is the highest law." And we would have to take the same viewpoint in regard to the question of the life-span of any parliament. If in an outburst of revolutionary enthusiasm the people elected a very good parliament—a kind of "incomparable chamber"—it would be right for us to make of it a Long Parliament; and if elections did not work out well, we would have to try to disperse the parliament not two years later, but if possible, within two weeks.[10]

We repeat: It was not Lenin who said this, but Plekhanov, who after February and after October took a more right-wing stand than Tsereteli. On the other hand, Lenin was not about to wait even two weeks; the decree of the dissolution of the Constituent Assembly was published within two days after the announcement that it had convened.

It is sometimes said that the Bolsheviks' compliance with the previously arranged timing of the Constituent Assembly elections was not a mistake but an expression of political wisdom: The Right SRs, so the argument goes, were sure to expose themselves again in the Assembly. But this is a dubious thesis. In a situation of almost universal peasant illiteracy, extremely poor means of circulating information, and so forth, the Bolsheviks were unable to extract any substantial political capital from their confrontation with the Constituent Assembly. To the contrary, they created a series of political difficulties for themselves. In the summer and fall of 1918 the main slogan used in the struggle against the Bolsheviks, which developed into civil war, was the defense of the Constituent Assembly and the restoration of its authority. Yet the Constituent Assembly could potentially have been used to advantage and made into a central point of support for the gains of the October revolution.

ten

The Economic Situation in the RSFSR in January and February 1918

The Brest-Litovsk Peace Treaty and Its Consequences

A few days after the dispersal of the Constituent Assembly, and in the same Tauride Palace where it had been held, the Third All-Russia Congress of Soviets of Workers' and Soldiers' Deputies opened. Then on January 13, 1918, the Third All-Russia Congress of Peasants' Deputies convened. On the same day both congresses merged under the title Third All-Russia Congress of Soviets. Slightly more than 50 percent of the delegates at the Third Congress were Bolsheviks; the Left SRs had the second largest fraction; together the two parties constituted the overwhelming majority of the congress.

The congress adopted the "Declaration of the Rights of the Working and Exploited People," which the Constituent Assembly had rejected and which was essentially the first variant of the Soviet Constitution. The word "provisional" was dropped from the title of the Soviet government, and it was renamed the "Workers' and Peasants' Government of the Russian Soviet Republic."[1] After passing a number of other important resolutions the Third Congress of Soviets elected a new All-Russia Central Executive Committee (VTsIK) consisting of 306 members; 160 Bolsheviks, 125 Left SRs, 2 Menshevik Internationalists, 3 Anarcho-Communists, 7 SR-Maximalists, 7 Right SRs, and 2 Menshevik Defensists.[2] The Bolsheviks obviously recognized the rights of many political minorities at that time and proceeded on a pluralist basis in the representative Soviet bodies.

Soviet power had been consolidated politically, which Lenin noted with pride in his concluding remarks.

At the same time, however, the economic situation of the young Soviet republic was growing noticeably worse. In the main industrial centers of the country, above all in Moscow and Petrograd, the system of food supply was deteriorating. Narkomprod, the Commissariat of Food Supply, was reinforced; its apparatus gradually replaced all local food-supply agencies. In addition, an all-Russia congress on food supply problems was held. However, grain deliveries did not increase. Available resources—previously purchased grain and the grain privately stored in the port cities and along the railroads—were coming to an end. It was necessary that regular and smooth delivery of grain from the Ukraine, from the Don and Kuban regions, from Siberia, and from the Volga region be organized. However, because of, among other things, the poor condition of the transport system, narrow regionalism, and the shortage of manufactured goods at Narkomprod's disposal, the delivery of grain to the center constantly lagged behind what was planned.

In January and February 1918 Soviet power had already been established in the southern parts of Russia. Narkomprod projected that 1,500 freight cars of provisions would arrive in the central region daily from the south. However, up to March 1, 1918, only about 140 freight cars per day actually arrived from the southern region. Grain shipments from Siberia to the central region in January 1918 were slightly more than half a million poods per month. This was too little. Only 7.1 percent of the projected grain supply reached Petrograd and Moscow in January 1918, and in February, only 16 percent.[3] Discontent grew among the workers, which disturbed Lenin greatly. Nevertheless he placed his main hopes, as before, on requisitioning and confiscation rather than on organizing normal trade. For example, on January 12, 1918, Lenin issued an order to Red Guards headquarters to begin inspection of the railways in Petrograd and vicinity, to discover any freight cars carrying foodstuffs, and to help local authorities apprehend speculators. Two days later, at a meeting of the Presidium of the Petrograd Soviet, Lenin introduced a motion: "All soldiers and workers must be recruited to form several thousand groups (consisting of 10−15 men, and possibly more) who shall be obliged to devote a certain number of hours (say, 3−4) daily to the food supply service."[4]

However, the new government did not yet have the capacity for such all-embracing measures. More important, virtually all "nearby" sources of food had been exhausted, and "3—4 hours daily" was not enough time to find sufficient quantities of grain. Of course the question of forming larger food detachments, to be sent to the grain-producing provinces, had already come up. Several such detachments had been formed and provided by Narkomprod not only with requisitioning books and paper money but with some manufactured goods as well (for example, cloth from army stores). And the formation of several new organizations to assist Narkomprod had begun. For example, on January 30, 1918, the Sovnarkom issued a decree on the formation of an emergency interdepartmental commission for guarding roadways and on the organization of a large number of highway guard units. On Lenin's motion a clause was added to this decree on the need for ruthless struggle against speculation and unauthorized shipment of grain and other freight.[5]

It was easy to pass such decrees of course, but not so easy to carry them out. The peasants in the grain-producing provinces urgently needed a variety of items which only the city could supply. However, they could not obtain these goods through Narkomprod. That was why "bag trading" (meshochnichestvo), far from declining, spread further. As a rule, however, the bag traders did not bring their grain into the city as single individuals. Entire detachments of well-armed men were usually formed for this purpose; often they had recently been soldiers. The Soviet government did not have the forces to stop this flood of speculative trade. The Kuban region, for example, did not deliver a single pood of grain to the center through Narkomprod in January and February 1918, although the bag traders brought millions of poods of grain from the Kuban during those same months. In addition, the workers in various factories in the center did not rely on Narkomprod, but often organized their own food detachments, which were supplied with goods needed in the village. And these goods were exchanged for grain not at the "fixed" price but at free-market prices. For example, such workers' detachments, carrying cotton textiles, went out into the villages from the textile manufacturing city of Ivanovo-Voznesensk. A band of workers numbering 210 persons, carrying not only money but threshing machines and other farm equipment to exchange for grain, traveled to the villages from several factories in Viatka.[6]

Soon Narkomprod began a determined struggle against such local initiatives; in the commissariat's view, such activities undermined the centralized procurement of grain at "fixed" prices. But what could Narkomprod do at the time with its relatively small forces? The villages were all of one mind and the peasants had thousands of ways of hiding grain so that no food detachment could get it by force alone. The peasants demanded goods. Here is what the minutes of a meeting in the Vasily Ostrov district of Petrograd said, for example, about the activities of the workers' detachment from that district in the Don region: "Knowing that Petrograd needs food, we have been trying to persuade the peasants to ship grain. The peasants have promised to support the starving workers, but they ask that cotton textiles and essential farm implements be provided them."[7]

Attempts at outright requisitioning often provoked stubborn peasant resistance; in some cases the peasants not only took the requisitioned grain back home but killed the food detachment members who had seized it. And though the ringleaders of such actions were usually kulaks, many middle peasants supported them. These were the overtures of a veritable war with the peasants over grain, a war which promised nothing good to either side. Even meetings of poor peasants, which passed resolutions against grain speculation and demanded that the rich peasants be relieved of their surpluses, would at times demand, in the same resolutions, that Narkomprod's requisitioning units be withdrawn from their districts, for from the peasants' point of view, these units were engaged in simple plunder. On the whole, the results of grain "procurements" by the food detachments in January and February 1918 were less than modest; the amount of grain obtained was not very great, and most of it went to meet local needs. In the first few months of 1918, neither the food detachments nor Narkomprod was able to break the resistance of the peasants, who did not wish to surrender the grain they had worked hard to grow in exchange for some receipt or for completely worthless paper money.

Although the conflict that arose during these months between the workers on the one hand and the peasants who had just received the land from the working class on the other did not reach the explosion point, it was already providing considerable food for thought.

The new government's success in the area of industrial production was no greater; at any rate industry did not function as well in January and February 1918 as it had in November and December of the previous year. We can see from Lenin's notes that after the October revolution it was not the intention of the Bolsheviks to nationalize a

substantial number of businesses. However, in practice the pace of nationalization went far beyond the original plans. In mid-December
1917, in a draft decree on the nationalization of the banks, Lenin
proposed at the same time the immediate nationalization of all joint-
stock companies, the introduction of universal labor conscription, the
annulment not only of foreign but also domestic loans, and compulsory membership by every citizen in a consumers' society. In addition
the decree proposed that new currency notes be introduced immediately and that all wealthy persons be obliged to keep all their monetary
possessions (over and above 125 rubles per week) in the State Bank
or in the savings banks. The implementation of this decree was en-
trusted to "members of boards and directors of joint-stock companies,
as well as all shareholders belonging to the wealthy classes . . . , who
shall be obliged to continue to conduct the affairs of these enterprises
in good order, observing the law on workers' control . . . and sub-
mitting to the local Soviets of Workers', Soldiers', and Peasants' Deputies weekly reports on their activities." [8]

These proposals of Lenin's were rejected as unfeasible; and they
were not published in full until 1949. They show that Lenin sometimes
tried, in blatant contradiction to his own prerevolutionary statements,
to "implement socialism by decree." Nevertheless, we can see by
other decrees passed in late 1917 and early 1918 that state ownership
was extended not only to such major companies as the Putilov Works,
the Nevsky Drydock, and the Sestroretsk Metals Plant but also to such
minor establishments as a certain Rostokin Paint Factory, a confec-
tionery in one of the county seats of Yekaterinoslavl province, a cardboard factory, and a certain Plo Furriers. And it is a strange thing to
find next to a decree of the Sovnarkom nationalizing the country's entire merchant marine another decree nationalizing the Konovalov factory in Kostroma province. [9]

Altogether from November 1917 to March 1918 about 850 legislative acts nationalizing or "alienating" individual companies, various
monopoly groups, and entire mining districts and sectors of the economy were issued by the central authorities. Lenin himself was subsequently to call this "a Red Guard assault on capitalism." It is true
that a socialist sector was established in Russia's economy during this
period and that the commanding heights of the economy passed into
the hands of the proletarian state. But it is also true that the new state
did not have enough experience or trained personnel to administer all

these establishments, and for that reason the performance of most industrial enterprises failed to improve as a result of their passing into the public sector. This made itself felt quite painfully in the relations between town and country.

In late February the economic difficulties faded into the background against the threat of political and military disaster. The truce with the Germans came to an end, and the Soviet delegation, in spite of Lenin's insistence, simply would not sign the German peace conditions. Trotsky, who headed the Soviet delegation, assumed that the Germans would not begin an offensive. But the German troops on the Eastern front suddenly attacked and began a rapid advance.

It is not our task to describe all the dramatic events involved in the German offensive, the bitter debate over peace, and the peace treaty (which the Soviet government was soon obliged to sign after all—and on more onerous and humiliating terms than before). Lenin desperately defended his point of view both within the Bolshevik Party and against the Bolsheviks' allies in the Soviet government coalition, the Left SRs, and he was unquestionably correct. The temporary retreat and forced compromise represented by the Brest-Litovsk Treaty were essential to Soviet Russia. What interests us in the present context are certain political and economic consequences of the Brest treaty.

Peace was indispensable simply because Soviet Russia could no longer wage war. What had been the Russian army had virtually disintegrated, and time was needed to dispose of this diseased organism and begin to build not only a new social system but a new army as well. However, the signing of the Brest treaty also entailed a serious risk for Soviet Russia. The Entente's position in Europe was quite difficult. By March 1918 only about 20,000 American troops had arrived on the Western front. The aim of the German high command in concluding the Brest treaty was to transfer its troops from the Eastern to the Western front and thus gain a decisive victory over the Allies. But in this case, Soviet Russia, too, would have found itself in a difficult situation in spite of the peace treaty it had signed. On the other hand, the Entente might ignore the express will of Soviet Russia and begin intervention on a large scale in order to open a new anti-German front on Soviet territory. In fact, immediately after the signing of the Brest treaty, the first landings, not yet very large, of British, Japanese, and American troops began in the north of Russia and in Russia's far eastern maritime province.

The Brest treaty had serious consequences inside the country as well. A vigorous faction of "Left Communists" was formed inside the Bolshevik Party, in opposition to the treaty. Although the peasants and soldiers were unconditionally for peace in general, both the Left and Right SR parties emphatically opposed the signing of the treaty with the Germans, and this resulted in the de facto collapse of the short-lived Bolshevik-Left SR coalition.

In any case, the treaty was signed. The remnants of the Russian army were demobilized. Hundreds of thousands of former Russian soldiers began returning from German prison camps, and hundreds of thousands of German soldiers began the trip back to Germany and Austria-Hungary. Starving Russia was freed of the obligation to maintain an army of millions and a large number of prisoner-of-war camps. Millions of peasants and workers, until then dressed in soldiers' greatcoats, were able to join in the constructive labor of restoring the country's war-ravaged economy. Hundreds of thousands of Cossacks also went home with the same passionate desire to get their farms working. These Cossacks, and the bulk of peasant soldiers in general, brought their rifles and grenades home with them. In the spring of 1918 the Russian villages were loaded with every kind of weapon, including machine guns. Millions of peasants had acquired some military science and combat skill and were ready to defend their lands and their recently won rights by force of arms. Industry was able to stop producing weapons and ammunition and begin retooling to produce the goods the country needed. The demands on the transportation system were also eased.

But the Brest treaty not only removed difficulties; it brought new ones with it. The Ukraine was temporarily lost. German troops advanced to the Don region and occupied the Crimea and a large part of Transcaucasia. These were heavy losses for Russia. Looking at World War I as a whole, we may conclude that this greedy advance eastward was one of the German command's biggest miscalculations. As early as March 1918 the German general staff threw its forces into desperate attacks in France, but could not gain a decisive victory. Wasn't this because the German army actually continued the war on two fronts despite Brest-Litovsk?

After the Brest treaty was signed the Soviet government's main concern was to ensure food supplies to the country's industrial regions and to organize the proper functioning of industry to produce the goods the country needed. But the situation in the country in 1918 was quite different from, let us say, the one in 1944. The urban population of the Russian empire in 1913 was 28.5 million, or 18 percent of the total population.[10] If we allow for the fact that in 1918 the territory the Soviet government had to be concerned about was limited to the Russian federation alone, and if we leave aside the relatively small cities in the grain-producing regions, which were able to feed themselves from "local resources," we see that the main problem for the government was the urban population in the non-Black Earth region, that is, at the most 10 million people. Providing these people with at least a minimum supply of food and at the same time rationally organizing their labor in the industrial plants was of course a difficult task, but by no means an insoluble one.

What were the main decisions the Soviet government had to make in order to solve this problem and thereby begin the new, peaceful work of construction in this new and peaceful Russia?

Today after the experience of the terrible civil war, after NEP, and after the tremendous amount of theoretical work done by dozens of scholars (i.e., with the wisdom of hindsight), it is not really very hard to answer this question.

The Soviet government had to establish a system of accounting and control covering everything there was in the country, in particular, everything at the government's disposal—i.e., everything necessary and possible for building the new society.

New nationalizations had to be stopped and order brought into the already nationalized sector.

The war industry had to be switched to peaceful uses, with production of goods essential to agriculture being started first.

The land had gone to the peasants and they were getting ready for the spring planting. The main principles on which relations between town and country would be based in the years to come had to be defined.

The government had goods to exchange for grain but they were in short supply. Money had lost all value and the peasants would not honor it. In this situation it was essential to emphatically abandon the grain monopoly, introduced only as a temporary measure for the duration of the war. Instead a relatively small progressive tax in kind should have been levied on each peasant household; this would have given the state a minimum supply of food for the starving workers.

The peasants should have been allowed to sell or exchange the remaining food surpluses at their own discretion. Every working-class family, indeed every urban family, still had a goodly number of such items as clothing, footwear, dishes, and tools, which they would have been willing to exchange for food. Many city people could have quickly taken up some trade or formed small production cooperatives or businesses. Had they done so, the mounting tensions in the country would have been relaxed; the SRs and Mensheviks would have lost their main slogan of the day (a very popular one not only among the peasants but with many workers as well)—"free trade." The Bolsheviks' popularity, which had begun to decline, would quickly have grown again, and the popularity of their opponents, which was starting to rise, would have shrunk. In other words, the Bolsheviks should have switched in early 1918 to the policy which was later called NEP, a policy they adopted in the much more complicated and difficult situation of early 1921. Unfortunately in 1918 the Bolsheviks were not able to find the optimum solution to the political and economic problems facing them and therefore history took a different and more complicated turn.

PART FOUR

The Difficult Spring of 1918

eleven

The Program of Economic Construction in Soviet Russia After Brest

In early March 1918 there began a period in the history of the young Soviet state which later came to be called "the peaceful breathing spell." It seemed to the Bolsheviks that the most difficult period was behind them. Earlier, in January 1918, at the Third Congress of Soviets Lenin had announced with pride that the Soviet government had held out five days longer than the Paris Commune and that it would not only be able to continue for another several months but would achieve final and lasting victory, realizing the ancient aspirations of socialism.[1]

"We the Bolshevik Party," he wrote in April with unconcealed satisfaction, "have convinced Russia. We have *won* Russia from the rich for the poor, from the exploiters for the working people. Now we must *administer* Russia. And the whole peculiarity of the present situation, the whole difficulty, lies in understanding *the specific features of the transition* from the principal task of convincing the people and of suppressing the exploiters by armed force to the principal task of administration"[2] (Emphasis in the original.—R.M.).

Indeed the chief task of the Soviet government in March 1918 and after was peaceful construction—reviving the dislocated economy, overcoming the universal chaos, organizing accounting and distribution, providing for the proper functioning of production (especially in the nationalized plants), helping the peasants with the spring planting, and establishing an effective and solid basis for the relations between town and country, between the working class and peasantry. It was necessary to bolster the country's transportation system and to organize the regular supply of food to the industrial centers and of manufactured goods to the agricultural areas. It was necessary to take the first steps toward creating a new system of education and culture, and simultaneously to strengthen the various Soviet government agencies and continue building up a strong and politically conscious Red Army.

In what direction and at what pace could and should this work of peaceful construction proceed? To this question the Bolsheviks of course had no ready-made answers. They could not be found in any books, and Marxist theory provided no pat solutions for such specific problems. The Bolsheviks were the first to take the road of socialist construction and had to provide the first answers to many problems of the transition from capitalism to socialism.

The term "the peaceful breathing spell" was introduced in the 1920s, when Soviet historians knew perfectly well how events had turned out in 1918–1921. But in March 1918 none of the Bolsheviks knew that there would only be a respite of three months. Certainly they could assume that there would be more military clashes with one or another group of domestic counterrevolutionaries; and they had to allow for the possibility of foreign intervention: German troops had occupied a considerable part of former Russian territory, and in March and April 1918 came the landings of British, Japanese, and American troops at Archangel and Vladivostok. But on the whole the Bolsheviks expected a period of peaceful development of some length. If from nothing else, this is evident from the fact that in the spring of 1918 the Sovnarkom and VTsIK passed a large number of decrees and resolutions whose implementation would have required many years of peaceful labor—for example, the confirmation of an ambitious plan for soil improvement in Turkmenistan and four regions of European Russia, the establishment of several committees on nationwide electrification, the drafting of a plan for extensive geological surveying, the mechanization of salt production at Lake Baskunchak, and the building of new railroads. In view of all this we shall avoid the term "the peaceful breathing spell" in the present work, referring instead to the peaceful period in the spring of 1918.

One might have assumed that since the Bolshevik Party had coped effectively with the extremely dangerous crises that arose continually from the very first days of the revolution to the beginning of March, the party would be quite able to handle the tasks of administering the country, restoring the economy, and developing it further. One might have supposed that the victory the Bolsheviks had gained would now be consolidated and become irreversible, that the active *revolutionary minority* who had assumed the responsibility of making a new revolution, which had already become a socialist revolution, would be able not only to win the support of the overwhelming majority of the people but also to maintain such support among the soldiers, peasants, intellectuals, and urban petty bourgeoisie as well as among the urban workers.

As in every historical situation, the circumstances that took shape in the spring of 1918 contained various alternatives. By then the Bolsheviks had essentially carried out the main demands of their prerevolutionary program. Power was in the hands of the proletariat, the land had been given to the peasants, and the greater part of large-scale industry and the banks had been nationalized. Russia had signed a peace treaty and was out of the war. The enormous army had been demobilized, which had relieved the government of the most important and burdensome responsibility of the previous several years. In the new situation it was entirely possible for the Bolsheviks to begin introducing the kind of economic policy which was later called NEP— the combination of a socialist sector in large-scale industry, free enterprise in small and medium urban industry, and a certain degree of free trade between town and country. The food requirements of the relatively insubstantial urban population at that time could have been met by a moderate tax in kind, along with relatively free trade for most goods locally and on the province level, and for certain kinds of goods on the national level. This would have brought a rapid revival in industry and agriculture; the majority of peasants and the majority of the working class would have supported such a policy; and the coalition between the Bolsheviks and Left SRs, which was extremely important for the Bolshevik Party, could have been maintained. Some elements of this kind of policy, the most sensible in the given situation, were proposed in March and April 1918 by Lenin (stopping the "Red Guard assault" on capital, bringing order into the nationalized businesses and temporarily calling off any further nationalizations, the employment of bourgeois technical specialists, the admission of foreign concessions under certain circumstances, support for a policy of state capitalism and not only socialism, etc.). Unfortunately, however, Bolshevik policy on the whole followed a different course in the spring of 1918. A certain dizziness from the successes of the first months of the revolution; the absence not only of certain theoretical elaborations but also of practical experience in organizing a socialist economy, especially in a backward country like Russia; and an overestimation of the role of subjective factors—these and a number of other causes led the Bolsheviks to introduce a fundamentally wrong economic policy in the spring of 1918. The machine of revolution, having gained speed, continued to roll along at a rate that was completely unjustified. "Everything was swept along in a turbulent current, flooded with revolutionary enthusiasm," A. V. Lunacharsky was to say in 1921 about those early days. "It was necessary above all to give full voice to our ideals and ruthlessly crush whatever did not accord with them. It was difficult to speak about half measures then, about stages, about approaching our ideal step by step. That was taken to be opportunism, even by the most 'cautious.' "[3]

Also in 1921 Lenin wrote:

> Borne along on the crest of the wave of enthusiasm, rousing first the political enthusiasm and then the military enthusiasm of the people, we expected to accomplish economic tasks just as great as the political and military tasks we had accomplished by relying directly on this enthusiasm. We expected . . . to be able to organize the state production and the state distribution of products on communist lines in a small-peasant country by the direct orders of the proletarian state.[4]

Especially important in this regard was the simple fact that in most cases the Bolsheviks did not know how to go about building socialism, for they were the first to venture on this untrodden path. Quite often they operated by the experimental method, feeling their way forward, using trial and error, and often paying quite dearly for their errors.

We have already discussed the inadequacy of the term "peaceful breathing spell" as applied to the period after the Brest treaty. No one could have known then how long the precarious peace would last and how things would go in Russia and the rest of the world. The most favorable prospect, the one on which the Bolsheviks placed their greatest hopes, was that of socialist revolution in the other European countries, especially in such belligerent countries as Germany and France. And although Lenin proposed some quite extensive plans for peaceful construction in Russia, his main object at the time was for Russia to hold out until the revolution spread to Western Europe and reinforced the victory of the Russian revolution. None of the Russian revolutionaries in the spring of 1918 imagined there could be a rather prolonged period when socialism would be built "in a single country." They viewed the October revolution not as a self-sufficient entity, but as the beginning of the world proletarian revolution.

The generally held view among Russian revolutionaries was that other countries would soon follow Russia, which made them confident of their correctness and strength. But that type of consciousness sometimes prompted the notion that it was necessary to hold out no matter what, by any means necessary, including means that over a longer period of time would weaken the Bolshevik Party's own position and place it in an awkward situation if the European revolution were delayed. And in a number of cases means were employed that were totally undesirable and would be harmful to any socialist revolution.

In any case, the Brest-Litovsk treaty was signed. It was obvious that no matter how long the new peaceful period lasted, it should be utilized to reinforce the dictatorship of the proletariat and consolidate the gains of the October revolution. First and foremost this peaceful phase had to be used to start the war-ruined economy of the country functioning properly, to overcome the chaos and destruction in this sphere, which threatened the country with disaster. The words that Lenin used for the title of a 1917 article, "The Impending Catastrophe and How to Fight It," were particularly apt now, as the symptoms of impending economic and political catastrophe multiplied with every passing day.

In March 1918 Lenin turned his thoughts primarily to the tasks of economic construction. We should note that the "Left Communists" also began to manifest their "leftism" in this sphere. At the Eighth Petrograd Party Conference the "Left Communist" S. Lobov proposed "that private property rights be declared nonexistent in both town and country." The "Left Communist" N. Osinsky (V. V. Obolensky) wrote at the same time, "The civil war is inseparably linked with a decisive liquidation of private property, the introduction of the socialist system, and the direct transition to communism."[5]

Lenin of course took a much more sober view of how to bring the country out of its economic crisis. As early as the Seventh (Extraordinary) Congress of the Bolshevik Party he said: "We have only just taken the first steps towards shaking off capitalism altogether and beginning the transition to socialism. We do not know and we cannot know how many stages of transition to socialism there will be."

Moreover, Lenin added in his polemic against the "Left Communists," "We cannot give a description of socialism; what socialism will be like when its completed forms are reached—this we do not know, we cannot tell. . . . [because] we do not yet have the data for a description of socialism. The bricks of which socialism will be composed have not yet been made." [6]

Although a socialist sector, embodied in the nationalized companies, had already emerged, along with it there existed four other economic structures—state capitalism, private capitalism, petty commodity production, and traditional, patriarchical agriculture (to a large extent, natural farming). Moreover in 1918 petty commodity production and private capitalism remained the dominant economic structures, as before. Plans for the postwar reconstruction and renovation of the country should have been based on this economic reality. Lenin understood this and his plan for "leading up to socialist construction"—a plan most fully spelled out in his pamphlet "The Immediate Tasks of the Soviet Government"—was quite precise and realistic. He spoke of accounting and control as the most important tasks of the day. He proposed that the wave of nationalizations of industrial and other enterprises be stopped and that order be brought into the monetary system. He called for an end to the practice, engaged in by local Soviet government bodies and many other organizations, of exacting contributions from capitalists, merchants, and other wealthy people. Lenin proposed that such contributions be replaced by properly levied taxes. He also discussed the problems of raising the productivity of labor and increasing the material interest of workers and other employees. As for the bourgeois technical intelligentsia and other bourgeois elements who were willing to serve the new government, Lenin proposed that very high pay scales be set for them, to "buy them" until such time as the proletariat could train its own cadres to replace them. (This question soon became the focus of a bitter debate, which we cannot go into.) Lenin proposed that piece rates be treated as the main form of wages for industrial workers. In addition there were many proposals in Lenin's pamphlet on various technical innovations in industry and agriculture. Lenin was quite insistent as well in advocating the encouragement of state capitalism (of course, not to the detriment of socialism). He argued not without reason that in such a petty-bourgeois country as Russia the development of various forms of state capitalism would be a good thing, for state capitalism could easily be subjected to regulation and was only one short step away from socialism.

All of these ideas of Lenin's are justifiably cited even today as examples of his far-sightedness and ability to look reality soberly in the face. Nevertheless, in Lenin's plan for "leading up to socialist construction" there was a fundamental shortcoming, partially connected with the shortcoming in Marxist theory we spoke of previously. In his pamphlet "The Immediate Tasks of the Soviet Government" Lenin did not write anything about *organizing trade,* although with the end of the war, trade was sure to become the most important regulator of economic life. Only trade combined with accounting, control, and a rational system of taxation could have restored Russia's health and provided a stimulus for renewed and rapid economic progress. This purpose could have been served by local trade, by trade on a nationwide level, and by private, cooperative, and state trading. Among the many slogans Lenin raised in the spring of 1918 we find one for socialist competition, another for accuracy and frugality, but the slogan which became the dominant one a few years later, "learn how to trade," is missing. Yet without trade, without conceding a certain freedom for private initiative and trade to the tens of millions of peasants and artisans, Russia could never have raised itself out of the chaos and ruin of those years.

In early January 1918, in his theses on the necessity for signing a separate peace with the Germans—even on very onerous terms—in order to win time for peaceful construction Lenin wrote:

> The reorganization of Russia on the basis of the dictatorship of the proletariat and the nationalization of the banks and large-scale industry, coupled with *exchange of products in kind* between the towns and the small-peasant consumers' societies, is quite feasible economically, provided we are assured a few months in which to work in peace. And such a reorganization will render socialism invincible both in Russia and all over the world, and at the same time will create a solid economic base for a mighty workers' and peasants' Red Army.[7]

Lenin was mistaken of course in his estimate of "a few months" and his concept of "exchange of products in kind." But in March and April 1918, unfortunately, he continued to enlarge upon his mistaken theory of direct product exchange between town and country and his completely unrealistic plan for the universal organization of the population into cooperatives; under this plan all inhabitants of a particular region would belong to a cooperative which would hand over to the state the goods produced by the members of the cooperative and receive from the state a certain quantity of consumers' goods (for distribution among the members of the cooperative).

In this case Lenin's position came close to that of many "Left Communists," who in the spring of 1918 called for the abolition of money and considered the rapidly increasing inflation a good thing, because it would ultimately lead to the exchange of products without money. To be sure the Commissariat of Finance and the State Bank energetically opposed such views. Those organizations were seriously concerned about the disruption of the country's financial system. For example, I. E. Gukovsky, the deputy commissar of finance, in reporting to the VTsIK on the state of finances in the republic, argued that it was necessary to strengthen currency circulation and the Soviet system of banks. And although the VTsIK approved the basic points in Gukovsky's report, the "Left Communists" who took part in the discussion accused him of abandoning socialism and of having a "superstitious regard for money and a superstitious dread of a budget deficit."[8]

Although he refuted the "Left Communists," Lenin did not express himself very clearly in regard to trade and money, and some of his ideas hardly differed from the arguments of the "Lefts." Thus in his "Rough Outline of the Draft Program" of March 1918 Lenin wrote:

"At first state monopoly of 'trade,' subsequently replacement, complete and final, of 'trade' by planned, organized distribution. . . . while not (for the time being) abolishing money and not prohibiting individual purchase and sale transactions by individual families, we must, in the first place, make it obligatory by law to carry out all such transactions through consumer and producer communes."[9]

Lenin himself later acknowledged that this was a mistake—the party's and his own. Thus in a speech in the fall of 1921 he said:

"We assumed that we could proceed straight to socialism without a preliminary period in which the old economy would be adapted to socialist economy. We assumed that by introducing state production and state distribution we had established an economic system of production and distribution that differed from the previous one."

Earlier in the same speech he had said:

"In estimating the prospects of development we in most cases—I can scarcely recall an exception—started out with the assumption—

perhaps not always openly expressed but always tacitly implied—that we would be able to proceed straight away with socialist construction." [10]

Unfortunately most current works dealing with the party's economic policies ignore the complex history of the *formation* of those policies and the fact that they cannot by any means be considered absolutely correct. For example, A. P. Butenko, in an article entitled "Developed Socialist Society," writes:

> V. I. Lenin, following the theory of Marx and Engels, carried their teachings further in application to new conditions. . . . and came to a number of new conclusions constituting an extremely important creative addition to the Marxist theory of socialism.
>
> The most important of these conclusions of Lenin's are the following: (1) socialist production is production in which, on the one hand, there is public ownership "of all the major means of production," and on the other, "cooperative" enterprises (i.e., not publicly owned); (2) the transition to socialism does not eliminate commodity production and in a characterization of this period such categories as commodites, prices, the market, profit, and economic accounting remain in force; (3) distribution should be organized not on the basis of deliveries from public stocks but through direct exchange of products by means of commodity-and-money relations, i.e., trade; (4) the most important incentives for socialist construction should be personal, material interests, a personal, material stake in socialist construction, linked with an accounting of the quantity and quality of the labor of each worker. [11]

Of course Butenko cites quite a few references from Lenin's works in support of his arguments. But he deliberately passes over the fact that all of these works date from 1921 and 1922 and that in the first years of Soviet power Lenin thought and wrote quite differently. Was it not Lenin who argued in 1917, for example, that a system should be introduced in Russia in which "all citizens . . . should work equally, do their proper share of work, and get equal pay. . . . The whole of society will have become a single office and a single factory, with equality of labor and pay." [12]

At the time of NEP Lenin wrote that "the basic elements of our economy have remained the same." [13] From these words the conclusion is often drawn that Lenin's views remained the same from 1918 to 1921. However, Lenin was quite clearly referring to the sameness of the "basic elements of our economy" and not of "economic policy"—especially since economic policy in the spring of 1918 was wrong in many respects.

Only rarely does one find in Soviet economic literature a different point of view on the development of economic policy in the first years of Soviet rule. Thus, Iu. E. Volkov and A. K. Krukhmalev write in their article "The Creative Development of the Marxist-Leninist Doctrine of Socialism:"

> These [economic] tasks were solved, not in a day, but gradually, through constant creative exploration, with accumulated experience being taken into account. At first, in late 1917 and early 1918, the organization of socialist economic life was thought of as the unitary, state-wide planned production and distribution of products to be accomplished by bringing the entire population together in consumer and producer communes and gradually transforming society into a "single cooperative" with direct exchange of products replacing trade (and this concept found its reflection in Lenin's writings, too); it was thought that this would be accompanied by the gradual abolition of money, the naturalization of economic relations, etc. Even in the detailed plan for the peaceful work of laying the economic foundations for socialism, elaborated in the spring of 1918 ("The Immediate Tasks of the Soviet Government" and other works by Lenin), there was no consideration of the question of what correlation there would be between our economy and the market and trade, that is, of their utilization as necessary economic levers for the building of socialism. Still less could this question be considered under the circumstances of foreign intervention and civil war.[14]

Of course this kind of approach to the analysis of our economic history is much more productive, although Volkov and Krukhmalev do not raise the question of whether, given a different economic policy from the one followed in 1918, the civil war might have been quite different in scope and whether there would have been any need to introduce and defend war communism at all.

★   ★   ★

The party's mistaken theoretical orientation very quickly led to mistaken policies. It is true that the time from the end of March to the end of June 1918 was not very long. And many serious economic and political mistakes were made later on, which fall outside the scope of our present essay. But in those spring months quite a lot was done that the Bolsheviks had to pay dearly for afterward.

As we have said, the idea of direct exchange of products between town and country occurred to Lenin even before the revolution. This question was also raised in January 1918, for example, at the First All-Russia Food Supply Congress. In February the Soviet government

Anti-tsarist demonstration by Cossacks. Tsar Nicholas II abdicated in March 1917. The placard reads "Down with the monarchy! Long live the republic!" (Popperphoto)

Behind one of the barricades in Liteiny Prospekt, Petrograd, February 1917.

The head of a demolished statue of Tsar Nicholas II lies on the ground.

Kerensky (below "X") visiting the Russian Front in June 1917. (photo: E. P. Stebbing)

The demoralized army in retreat from the Front, 1917. (photo: Florence Farmborough)

Firing from the rooftops, Kerensky's troops mow down a demonstration by Petrograd workers, July 1917.

A Bolshevik military patrol car operating in the Nevsky Prospekt, Petrograd, during the battle between the Bolsheviks of Lenin and Kerensky's followers (July 1917?). (Popperphoto)

Lenin in disguise.

On the night of October 24, the Winter Palace, headquarters of the Provisional Government, was stormed by Red Guards, shown here massed before the base of the Alexander column.

Photograph made in 1917 by Florence Farmborough, a nurse of the Imperial Army, who described the photo as depicting a former Russian soldier attacking the furnishings in a prosperous home.

Trotsky, Lenin, and Kamenev.

The Petrograd Soviet (photographed during the early 1920s), one of 10,000 city and village soviets set up in 1917.

Peasants forming a line for food rations, 1917. (photo: Florence Farmborough)

ВСѢМЪ ЧЕСТНЫМЪ ГРАЖДАНАМЪ!

ВОЕННО-РЕВОЛЮЦІОННЫЙ КОМИТЕТЪ ПОСТАНОВЛЯЕТЪ:

Хищники, мародеры, спекулянты объявляются врагами народа.

Лица, виновныя въ этихъ тягчайшихъ преступленіяхъ, будутъ немедленно арестовываться по спеціальнымъ ордерамъ Военно-Революц. Комитета и отправляться въ Кронштадтскія тюрьмы впредь до преданія ихъ Военно-Революціонному суду.

Всѣмъ общественнымъ организаціямъ, всѣмъ честнымъ гражданамъ Военно-Революц. Комитетъ предлагаетъ: обо всѣхъ извѣстныхъ случаяхъ хищенія, мародерства, спекуляціи немедленно доводить до свѣдѣнія Военно-Революц. Комитета.

Борьба съ этимъ зломъ—общее дѣло всѣхъ честныхъ людей. Военно-Революц. Комитетъ ждетъ поддержки отъ тѣхъ, кому дороги интересы народа.

Въ преслѣдованіи спекулянтовъ и мародеровъ Военно-Революціонный Комитетъ будетъ безпощаденъ.

Военно-Революціонный Комитетъ.

Петроградъ.
10 ноября 1917 г.

Poster issued by the Revolutionary Military Committee on November 10, 1917, declaring hooligans, profiteers and speculators to be enemies of the state, and asking for all cases of theft, robbery, and speculation to be reported.

turned all of its attention to the situation on the battlefront. But as early as March the Commissariat of Food Supply reported to the Sovnarkom that only by supplying the villages with what they needed, i.e., essential goods, could the hidden grain be "brought to light." The report therefore proposed that product exchange be organized on a state-wide level, with grain being paid for partly with goods and partly with money.[15]

On March 26, 1918, the Sovnarkom issued a decree "on the exchange of products for the strengthening of grain deliveries."[16] The second clause of this decree stated: "A certain proportion, specified in article 3, of the following products are to be used in the exchange of products to obtain food: fabrics, thread, dress goods, leather, woolen goods, footwear, galoshes, matches, soap, candles, kerosene, high-quality ironware, glassware, etc." (The list of products needed in the villages was quite long.)

Farther on, the same decree stated that all businesses, producers, cooperatives, and craft workshops engaged in the manufacture of these products should deliver them according to a definite plan and at fixed prices to the Commissariat of Food Supply, and that the commissariat should issue instructions on the procedure and standards for the exchange of these products for the grain and other foodstuffs that were to be procured under the state plan.

The aim was to organize a system of exchange of products in such a way that every village cooperative or association (but not individual peasants) would receive from the Commissariat of Food Supply the manufactured goods they needed in proportion to the quantity of grain and other agricultural products they delivered. Only part of the grain was to be "traded for goods," however; a considerable amount of grain and other agricultural products was to be surrendered for money or special receipts, for which the commissariat promised to deliver a certain quantity of goods and money at a later time.

At first the leaders of the Supply Commissariat had the rosiest expectations. The most varied estimates indicated that the deficit in the grain-consuming regions was on the order of 150—180 million poods, while in the grain-producing provinces, according to the same estimates, surpluses of 600—700 million poods had accumulated.

However, the attempt at direct exchange of products worked out very poorly from the start. First of all, the country had a shortage of the manufactured goods needed in the villages. By April the Supply

Commissariat had established an "exchange fund," in which there were about 400 million meters of cotton textiles, 2 million pairs of galoshes, 200,000 pairs of shoes, and 17 million poods of sugar, as well as kerosene, matches, ironware, and agricultural tools. But all these products, gathered from all over, met only 10 to 15 percent of the most urgent village needs. And it was impossible to organize the production of more such goods very quickly. The big plants which had been working on defense contracts had to be retooled. There were of course quite a few small businesses, workshops, and rural and urban handicraft establishments. The bulk of this layer of the "petty bourgeoisie" supported the October revolution and constituted an important potential reserve for expanding the social base of the proletarian dictatorship. According to the estimates of economists, in 1918 there were in Russia 350,000 rural establishments of the cottage-industry type, in which more than 1.2 million persons worked.[17]

However, these artisans and craftsmen did not respond enthusiastically to the decree of March 26. Because of the depreciation of the currency all the so-called "fixed prices" were a fiction. No one wanted to surrender their products for next to nothing. Therefore most craftsmen and artisans evaded the decree and found opportunities not only to sell their products at "free" market prices but also to organize their own means of exchange with the villages, which was much more advantageous to them.

In any case, the Supply Commissariat decided to begin its direct product exchange with the villages. The agencies of the commissariat began to ship the "exchange fund" to the villages primarily by rail. At 1918 prices this fund was valued at approximately one billion rubles. Altogether, going by not very precise figures, about 40,000 freight cars of various types of goods were sent into the villages. At first it was assumed that no less than 120 million poods of grain would be obtained in return for these products. But things went badly from the start. First, the local agencies of the Supply Commissariat were functioning quite poorly. There were cases in which freight cars full of manufactured goods would stand unloaded for a month at some remote junction. But the main reason for the failure was the negative attitude of the peasants themselves toward this type of exchange. Because of the famine, market prices for food had risen much faster than prices for manufactured goods. The Supply Commissariat failed to take this trend into account; on the contrary, it set rather high "fixed" prices for manufactured goods and rather low "fixed" prices for grain and other foodstuffs. A pood of grain was equal in "fixed" prices to one horseshoe, or half an arshin of inferior calico, or 200 grams of nails. Apparently the people in charge of the commissariat had a very unclear concept of how prices are determined. Consequently their "fixed" prices were often not only dozens of times lower than the market value, but two or three times lower than the prime cost of the products themselves. Probably no one in the commissariat had any idea of these production costs. As a result, the "fixed" price for potatoes was four times greater than that for rye.[18]

According to Supply Commissariat reports, 30 to 35 million poods of grain were procured through direct exchange of products (instead of the planned 120 million). But even the figure of 30 to 35 million is probably inflated. For according to the March 26 decree, direct exchange of products with the village was still a voluntary matter. In view of that, the peasants more often than not refused to engage in such exchange. They preferred, even at a risk, to use the "free" market to dispose of their surpluses, and that market continued to exist in spite of all prohibitions. This way the peasants could obtain a much larger quantity of manufactured goods for their grain than through the Supply Commissariat. Second, despite all of Moscow's appeals it did not win compliance with the provisions of the Sovnarkom decree requiring centralization of product exchange. Many factories continued to send "their own" carloads of manufactured goods into the provinces, exchanging these goods for grain not at the "fixed" prices but at the prices on the local markets. Both county and provincial authorities would try to obtain a little more grain for their own starving workers and would arbitrarily increase the prices Narkomprod had set for foodstuffs. In a number of provinces freedom to trade was even announced "temporarily," with various highway and checkpoint detachments being withdrawn or suspended.

In those early months of 1918 the press invariably referred to violators of the monopoly of the grain trade as "bag traders, speculators, swindlers, kulaks, and bloodsuckers." Many of the apprehended bag traders were severely punished and all their grain taken away, often after they had transported it hundreds of miles. However, the situation could not be changed; the trains were overflowing with bag traders, many of them dressed in soldiers' uniforms, well armed, and inclined to defend one another and their grain. For it was not a question of individual evil intentions in this case but of the majority of the population of the country.

In 1922 an excellent book was published in Moscow, by the economist N. D. Kondratiev. This book, *The Grain Market,* can still be obtained without any difficulty at the Lenin Library or the Historical Library in Moscow. Kondratiev analyzes the situation on the grain market from the beginning of the war to the end of 1918 and cites a great many reliable and precise figures indicating, in particular, that many of the expectations, decrees, and orders of the Sovnarkom and the Commissariat of Supply were based on unfounded projections and were highly impractical.

First of all, who were the so-called bag traders? In the case of peasants, they were not kulaks, of course, but ordinary peasants—middle peasants and poor peasants (although they also sold the grain of their kulak neighbors for a price). According to Kondratiev, a poll was taken as early as 1917 in 627 settlements of Kaluga province, which was counted as one of the grain-consuming provinces at that time. In the villages and hamlets where the poll was taken (from August 1, 1917, to January 1, 1918), there were found to be bag traders in 94 percent of the peasant families and only 6 percent of the families got by without grain brought in from outside. In these 627 settlements (accounting for 30 percent of all the villages and hamlets in the region) 187,500 persons were found to be engaged in bag trading—approximately 500,000 for the province as a whole. Although only 50 percent of the bag traders returned home with grain, those who returned to their native villages brought, on the average, as much as 10 poods of grain each. The figures indicate that without the bag traders as much as 40 percent of the population in the province might have died of hunger. Kondratiev also reports that from January to May 1918, according to a questionnaire of the All-Russia Union of Office Workers, some 85 percent of industrial workers and 77 percent of office workers, students, and individuals of other categories resorted to the purchase of grain on the free market in Moscow.[19] Of course it was not only peasants who functioned as bag traders in those years. Quite often members of working-class or office-worker families would take their personal possessions or articles they had made themselves and head for the countryside, singly or in groups, in search of grain. Workers themselves would go, hoping to earn some bread by helping the peasants in their work; or they would go to stay with relatives who still lived in the countryside. Are we then supposed to call all of these people "speculators" or "freebooters"?

In a later work, in which Lenin continued to justify the monopoly of the grain trade, he cited statistics for 26 provinces indicating that in 1918 urban workers, both white-collar and blue-collar, obtained *half* of the grain they consumed from bag traders and the other half in the form of rations from the government. Of course the "bread ration" was ten times cheaper than bread on the free market. However a family simply could not survive on the bread ration alone.

The main point Lenin makes is that without the ration the workers could not have survived and suggests that therefore the grain monopoly was absolutely necessary. However this is not a very convincing argument. The same ration could have been provided through a simple tax in kind, as occurred later in 1921–22. But in that case there would have been no need to form roadblock detachments, or highway detachments, or food detachments, or a multitude of other outfits and organizations! Moreover, half of the food needed by industrial and office workers could have been obtained, not at ten times the cost, but perhaps at five times—and without the risk of ending up in one of the concentration camps, which were already jammed full of bag traders and speculators.

It is a fact that in 1918 the free market provided more than half of the grain consumed by the population, and without this market the urban population would not have been able to hold out under the burdens of the postwar economic dislocation. That is why, throughout the years of the civil war, the Soviet government did not close down the celebrated Sukharevka market, which became a synonym for the free market in general. In this gigantic country of petty-bourgeois peasants, neither "surplus" grain nor "surplus" manufactured goods would have been forthcoming if in every large city there had not existed a half-forbidden free market; therefore each city had its own Sukharevka. But after all, the risk and the limited scale of this trade had to be paid for. As early as the beginning of 1918 the grain monopoly had forced out and destroyed the previously established forms and systems of private trade in food; with the entire previous apparatus of the grain trade destroyed, its place was taken by the bag traders. But as Kondratiev rightly observed, if three or four bag traders traveled some 200 or 300 versts to obtain—with considerable difficulty—two or three or even ten poods of grain, the tremendous overhead expenses incurred

were necessarily reflected in the price of the grain, regardless of
whether the grain went directly to the consumers in the bag traders'
families or was put up for sale. In addition the trips taken by millions of
bag traders dislocated the transport system, which was already dislocated enough, and diverted thousands of people into unproductive
work in the roadblock detachments, for example. A small book by a
certain N. A. Orlov, who was active in the Commissariat of Food
Supply, was published in 1919. Its purpose was to justify the commissariat's policies in the grain monopoly. In this book the author refers to
bag traders, swindlers, and speculators as "human dust." But not sur-
prisingly, even this author admits at one point that it would have been
much better "if a hundred big grain sharks had been engaged in this
forbidden private trade, had worked in the open and been guided to
some degree by commercial ethics and, above all, by real economic
considerations." [20]

Actually in 1917 and 1918, when all the previous forms of food
supply for the urban population had been virtually destroyed and new
forms were being born amid great travail, the entire population of the
grain-consuming provinces was in effect thrown onto the road in a pil-
grimage for grain. Under these conditions the policy of so-called fixed
prices, the monopoly over the grain trade, and the formal prohibition
against free trading, which destroyed or, more precisely, pushed back
the free market, served not so much to ease the situation for the population as to produce a rise in the illegal free price of grain, so that in
three years, from 1915 to 1918, there was more than a hundredfold
price increase!

Of course certain objective factors were also involved. There was a
10 to 20 percent decline in total grain production, and the production
of agricultural implements, fertilizer, sugar, textiles for public consumption, etc., also declined. It is obvious that the world war did not improve the supply of industrial and agricultural goods to the population.
Nevertheless the overall food-supply situation in 1918 deteriorated to
a greater extent than did the production of grain and many other
products. There were stocks of grain in the country; the grain-producing provinces had quite a lot. But the shipment of grain to Moscow
kept declining; from July to October 1917 it averaged 21 pounds per
person monthly; from May to June 1918 it was only 7.6 pounds per
person monthly. There were a number of days every month when
bread was not issued to the population at all.

At the end of the book from which we have quoted the above figures, N. D. Kondratiev writes:

> One thing can be said with certainty. The task of regulating and rationalizing the national economic processes and in particular the processes on the grain market and in the supply of bread were extremely complex. The concept of replacing the spontaneous factors in economic life by rational planning was immeasurably more difficult to put into practice than to work out theoretically and ideologically. We have seen that the regulatory measures sometimes did not bring the positive results that were expected, and the unexpected results can by no means be regarded as indications of success in regulation. Direct indications of positive effects from regulation were very few. That is why we can state that we do not know what would have happened to the country if the system for regulating the market had been different or if the system had not been developed so extensively. At any rate the existing system of regulation was not bringing and did not bring the country out of the intensifying food crisis. It cannot be excluded that, in general, the country could not have escaped this situation. It is possible that it would have ended up in this crisis even without the introduction of the regulatory system. But that does not prevent us from evaluating the then-existing system of regulation in a way that is fairly cautious and, we feel, fairly solidly grounded in an analysis of the facts.[21]

Another serious mistake of the Soviet government agencies was to continue and intensify measures to nationalize industry, extending them essentially to medium-sized and small industry (in spite of Lenin's call for the "Red Guard assault on capital" to be stopped). Although the central authorities actually reduced the scale of nationalization (according to the estimates of the historian V. Z. Drobizhev, only 20 percent of businesses changed their status as a result of actions by the central government in 1917 and 1918), local authorities from April to June 1918 in effect undertook the total nationalization of all medium-sized and small industry. The overwhelming majority of such businesses were nationalized, confiscated, or "sequestered" by local Soviets, trade unions, and local Sovnarkhozy. To a large extent industry was "seized by the local revolutionary organs of the proletariat on the spot."[22]

The decree abolishing the right of inheritance passed in April 1918 was an obviously hasty and unjustified measure which roused the discontent of the petty bourgeoisie in both town and country. This decree stated in part:

Inheritance by law and by religious testament is hereby abolished. After the death of the owner, the property belonging to that person (both movable and immovable) becomes the state property of the RSFSR. . . . Until the decree on universal social security is changed, any needy relatives in the direct line of descent who are incapable of working ("needy" meaning not having a minimum living income), as well as full brothers and sisters and half brothers and sisters and wives and husbands of the deceased, will receive their livelihood from the property left behind.[23]

Vacillations in Bolshevik policy and a number of unquestionably mistaken trends were reflected in such a document as Lenin's rough draft, "Basic Propositions on Economic and Especially on Banking Policy," which was written in April 1918 but not published until 1933:

1. Completion of nationalization of industry and exchange.
2. Nationalization of banks and gradual transition to socialism.
3. Compulsory organization of population in consumer cooperative societies (plus commodity exchange).
4. Accounting and control of production and distribution of goods.
5. Labor discipline (plus tax policy).

This document also included reference to "the most vigorous and severe measures for raising the discipline and self-discipline of the workers and peasants" and a reference to "unqualified and immediate centralization."[24]

Such a program was unrealistic and mistaken in its very essentials.

In 1918 the conditions did not exist for "completing the nationalization of industry and exchange," nor was it necessary. It was a mistake to call for "compulsory organization of the entire population in consumer cooperative societies." The organization of any cooperatives, whether production cooperatives or consumer cooperatives, could only be voluntary. The references to "vigorous and severe measures for raising discpline and self-discipline" were at variance with the programmatic demands of the Bolsheviks for class-conscious discipline. It must be said that this kind of extremist note in Lenin's writings was exceptional and evidently was prompted in this case by the exceptionally difficult situation in April and May 1918. But although the document in question was not published, such thinking was reflected in a number of actual measures which had serious consequences and brought Soviet power to the brink of disaster.

twelve

The Masses Turn Away
from the Bolsheviks

The political force on which the October revolution based itself was by no means the majority of the population. The Bolsheviks never concealed this fact; on the contrary they made it clear and justified it. Lenin frequently said that for the victory of the socialist revolution the Bolsheviks did not have to wait for an "arithmetical" majority. Victory was possible with the existing forces, and it would be criminal to let the opportunity slip by when a reliable and energetic minority (the working class of Petrograd, Moscow, and the other major industrial centers; the soldiers of the garrisons in the two main cities and in the less remote front-line zones; the Baltic sailors) were willing to follow the Bolsheviks.

Nevertheless the Bolshevik Party did not fail to seek support from the majority of the population. The Bolsheviks were confident that after they had taken power and put into effect their program of revolutionary reforms, bringing peace and giving the land to the peasants and the factories to the workers, those measures would bring them the support of the overwhelming majority of the workers and the peasants as well; in that way the dictatorship of the proletariat would be consolidated.

Although events by no means developed "according to plan," they did follow this general pattern until the spring of 1918. The entire country was still turbulent and in flux; the political moods of the masses, the ebb and flow of confidence and distrust, were subject to change rather quickly. The days of mass rallies and demonstrations were not over. Moreover, even after several Cadet and monarchist papers were suppressed, the papers of other parties (various SR and Menshevik factions, Anarchists, and "Left Communists") continued to appear without much interference, informing the news-hungry population of events in Russia and the rest of the world. All this provided a fairly sensitive barometer of political moods, and this barometer showed both a rise in sympathy for the Bolsheviks in the first few months after October and a decline in their popularity in the spring of 1918.

Lenin, too, acknowledged this fact later on. He admitted that the entire fate of the revolution depended on the petty-bourgeoisie, who constituted a huge majority of the country's population. Lenin said that this element "was at first in favor of the Bolsheviks when they granted land and when the demobilized soldiers brought the news about peace." However, it turned against them when,

> to promote the international development of the revolution and to protect its center in Russia, they agreed to the treaty of Brest and thereby "offended" patriotic sentiments, the deepest of petty-bourgeois sentiments. The dictatorship of the proletariat was particularly displeasing to the peasants in those places where there were the largest stocks of surplus grain, when the Bolsheviks showed that they would strictly and firmly secure the transfer of these surplus stocks to the state at fixed prices.[1]

It must be said of course that although the Bolsheviks made many mistakes, the principal bourgeois parties were unable to derive any perceptible advantage from them; even less so were the monarchists. Those parties increased their strength in the spring of 1918 mainly in the Cossack regions, where in general no party to the left of the Cadets had any influence before 1917. Thus, it was the Cadets and the more right-wing constitutional-monarchist parties and groups that took advantage of the errors of the first local agencies of the Soviet government in the Don, Kuban, and Urals region. By May of 1918 virtually all of the Don region was under the rule of General Krasnov— not without assistance from the German troops—and in the Kuban region the Volunteer Army, the core of which was made up of the officer caste, expanded its forces. These armies and lesser formations revealed their full strength at the end of 1918, after the military coup in Omsk and Admiral Kolchak's advent to power in Siberia. But in the meantime, in May and June 1918, the errors and miscalculations of the Bolsheviks created some favorable political odds for the Mensheviks and both SR parties.

One could no longer of course refer to the SRs as one party. By the spring of 1918 the Right SRs had hardly any rank-and-file members remaining in their local organizations in many provinces. In counties where in 1917 the Right SRs had had organizations that were large for those times—between five hundred and several thousand members—after the dispersal of the Constituent Assembly only minuscule groups, with from ten to twenty members, remained. They had to suspend publication of their papers and discontinue organizational activity altogether.

Disarray increased noticeably among the Mensheviks as well. After October the small right wing of this party, headed by A. Potresov, persistently favored armed struggle against the Bolsheviks. Fyodor Dan and his supporters called for continued negotiations with the Bolsheviks, hoping for a split in their ranks. An emergency congress of the Menshevik Party was called to discuss these questions; it was held in Petrograd from November 30 to December 7, 1917. The right wing at this congress, headed by Lieber and Potresov, condemned the October revolution as "not conforming to historical law" and "not proletarian" and called for a new coalition with the Cadets to overthrow the Bolsheviks. Their own forces were melting away, and they were ready for anything. "To hope that Bolshevism can be 'given a haircut' and made presentable is unfounded," Potresov declared. "It is part of the nature of Bolshevism not to let its hair be cut. It is intransigent. It can be broken but there is no bending it. And the idea that we could bend it is laughable." [2] Potresov was not far off the mark when he said at the same congress: "Our party is in a disastrous situation. It has been swept almost entirely from the political arena." [3] That was the case. The basic results of the Constituent Assembly elections were known at the time and the Mensheviks had received less than three percent of the vote. However, a more cautious line, to which Martov also lent his support, won out at that congress. These Mensheviks hoped that negotiations could be conducted with the Bolsheviks and that a homogeneous socialist government could be formed, at least after the Constituent Assembly.

However, in the spring of 1918 the Mensheviks' situation began to change somewhat. With the famine worsening and the overall economic situation deteriorating some workers, including those in Petrograd, began to listen again to the Mensheviks. The Mensheviks and both SR parties raised the idea of an All-Russia Workers' Congress, which could be counterposed to the Soviets.

The Right SRs became more active, both in the center and in local areas. The Eighth Council of the Right SR Party was held from May 7 to May 14. After bitter disputes, it proclaimed that the main goal of the party was to prepare for an armed uprising against the Bolsheviks and the Bolshevik-dominated Sovnarkom and for the formation of a democratic government elected by the Constituent Assembly. The SR Council favored continuation of the war with Germany and reestablishment of the coalition with the Entente.

Most important for the fate of the country in those months, however, was the position of the Left SR Party, since most of the peasants and petty bourgeois still followed it. The Left SRs had left the Sovnarkom in the spring of 1918, but their representatives continued to work in a number of agencies of the Sovnarkom and VTsIK, particularly the Cheka and the command staff of the fledgling Red Army.

The Anarchists also made their presence felt by stepping up their agitation in the spring of 1918. Their main demand at the time was that all governmental power in the country be transferred to the trade unions and that the All-Russia Council of Trade Unions be regarded as the highest body of state power in the RSFSR.

The turn of the masses away from the Bolsheviks was reflected also in the statistics on party membership at the Fifth All-Russia Congress of Soviets, where the number of Bolsheviks declined by 40 and the number of Left SRs increased by 115. But the elections to county Soviets were even more indicative. Table 1 gives the statistics on party representation in 100 county Soviets elected from April to August 1918, in comparison to the party representation in these same Soviets on March 14, 1918.[4]

Table 1. Party Representation in 100 County Soviets Compared

Party	On March 14, 1918 (percentage)	From April to August 1918 (percentage)
Bolsheviks	66.0	44.8
Left SRs	18.9	23.1
Right SRs	1.2	2.7
Mensheviks	3.3	1.3
Maximalists and Anarchists	1.2	0.5
Non-Party	9.3	27.1

We can assume that in other counties, especially in the border regions of the former Russian empire, the elections to county and region (okrug) Soviets must have shown an even greater decline in the

Bolsheviks' authority and influence. It must be kept in mind that elections to the Soviets were not based on equal representation, and the fact that the Bolsheviks were still the ruling party likewise affected the outcome. But the political trend was obvious.

Bolshevik influence fell off especially sharply in the grain-producing provinces, where there were surplus stocks of grain and where most of the trains of the Supply Commissariat were sent. These were the Black Earth regions of southern Russia, a considerable part of the Volga region, and Siberia. These areas covered a large part of Russian territory and in them the counterrevolution found fairly solid support. Lenin later realized and admitted this. "We could not," he wrote, "give the peasants in Siberia what the revolution gave them in the rest of Russia. In Siberia the peasants did not get the landed estates, because there were none there, and that was why it was easier for them to put faith in the White Guards."[5] Elsewhere Lenin referred to Siberia as a land of "well-fed peasants, solid and successful farmers not at all inclined toward socialism."[6]

Nevertheless, through January and February 1918, the "triumphal march" of Soviet power did continue through southern Russia and Siberia despite the feverish efforts of local anti-Bolshevik groups to establish their own Dumas, Cossack Army governments, ersatz Constituent Assemblies, and so forth. For example, in February 1918 the Provisional Government of Autonomous Siberia headed by P. Ya. Derber, an SR, was established in Tomsk. But the fate of this "government" hardly differed from that of the Kaledin government in the Don region. Before February was over the Tomsk Soviet had arrested a large number of the officials of this government, had the arrested men driven to the nearby Taiga Junction, and let them go, although it forbade them to return to Tomsk. But by April and May the various "experiments" of the Commissariat of Food Supply and of the local food organizations had undermined the Bolsheviks' influence in Siberia and made the position of the young Soviet government in that extremely important region highly precarious.

As we have said, the first stumbling block encountered by the Bolsheviks in their relations with a party as close to them then as the Left SRs was the Brest-Litovsk treaty, which did not even have full support among the Bolsheviks themselves. But the signing of that treaty was absolutely necessary in the spring of 1918 and the risk Lenin took in that case was justified. Lenin knew very well that the signing of the

treaty would not be popular among the petty-bourgeois masses, but
he was sure this treaty would not stay in effect very long and he
therefore undertook this risk with full and conscious deliberation.

Louis Fischer, a Western biographer of Lenin who is far from sym-
pathetic to his subject, has written:

> As a statesman, Lenin observed, weighed, and reasoned, and arrived
> at decisions on the basis of reality. Power did not go to his head. It
> cleared it. . . . [For] Lenin, power was too precious to be squandered on
> consistency. His responsibilities compelled a cold, objective assessment of
> circumstances, compelled a sober, practical unsentimentality stripped of
> illusions, slogans, cant, pride, attachment to theory, and attachment to
> past stands and statements. He paid lip service to what Stalin called "the
> potentiality" of European revolution but excluded it from his calculations.
> He judged the concrete situation. The situation in 1918 demanded peace
> at a high price. He saw this from the beginning and was ready to pay. He
> thereby saved the state he had created.[7]

Unfortunately, in regard to economic organization and food supply
Lenin did not make such a cold, objective assessment of circumstances
or display such sober practicality stripped of illusions and attachment
to past views and statements. And this cost the Bolsheviks dearly.

Another non-Bolshevik author, known to Lenin and praised by him
as a fairly objective observer, N. V. Ustrialov, wrote in *Under the Sign
of Revolution:*

> The policy of requisitioning and confiscation aroused organic protest on
> all sides, and the ban on trade was universally violated. If any had chosen
> to abide by the Communist decrees, they would have starved to death in
> a couple of weeks, for you could get nothing "legally" except the cele-
> brated *vosmushka* [eighth of a pound] of bread of dubious quality and a
> ladleful of slops made from rotten potatoes. The entire country, including
> the Communists themselves, lived in violation of the Communist decrees;
> all of Russia "engaged in speculation," and it naturally followed that any
> number of official grounds could be found for "punishing each and every
> citizen."[8]

In general one could say without great exaggeration that by the
early summer of 1918 the Bolsheviks had lost much of the confidence
they earlier won among the peasants, especially middle peasants, as
well as among artisans and even a section of the industrial workers. Of
course the other parties rushed to take advantage of this.

Unrest over Bolshevik economic policy was so great in the grain-
producing provinces that local Soviet agencies were forced to suspend

the grain monopoly and the policy of fixed prices. Stalin, who was sent to Tsaritsyn in June 1918, telegraphed Lenin.

> Arrived in Tsaritsyn on the sixth. Despite the muddle in all spheres of economic life, order can be established. In Tsaritsyn, Astrakhan, and Saratov the grain monopoly and fixed prices had been suspended by the local Soviets; there is a bacchanalia of profiteering. I have managed to introduce rationing and fixed prices in Tsaritsyn. The same must be done in Astrakhan and Saratov, or else all the grain will leak out through these profiteering channels.[9]

This telegram was sent on June 7. It is obvious that Stalin could not have accomplished the introduction of rationing and fixed prices within a day of his arrival in Tsaritsyn; he only succeeded in having a resolution to that effect passed by the local Soviet. Nevertheless by employing the most savage measures Stalin was able to procure several million poods of grain and a large number of cattle. However only a small quantity of this food was successfully sent to Moscow. Stalin did not follow through on his assurances that eight or more freight trains could be sent daily by the route of Tsaritsyn—Povorino—Kozlov—Ryazan—Moscow. Krasnov's victory on the Don, the temporary successes of the counterrevolution in the Northern Caucasus, and the actions of the Czech Legion soon obliged Stalin to shift his attention from food to military problems. Going into the reasons for the unfavorable situation and the failure of his mission in the south, Stalin observed in a letter to Lenin: "The unfavorable situation described above is to be explained by (1) the fact that the former front-line soldier, the 'competent muzhik,' who in October fought for Soviet power, has now turned against it (he heartily detests the grain monopoly, the fixed prices, the requisitions, and the measures against bag trading)."[10]

It was not only the "competent muzhik," however, who was affected by the mood of unrest, but a considerable section of the working class, especially in the provinces. For example, as early as May 25, 1918, I. D. Pastukov, president of the Izhevsk committee of the Bolshevik Party in Viatka province, and F. Fokin, secretary of the Izhevsk party committee, reported to the Central Committee that the SRs and Anarchists had intensified their activities in the factories and that Bolshevik influence among the workers had declined as SR and Anarchist influence rose. The party committee asked that experienced party workers be sent from Moscow to Izhevsk to help salvage the situation.[11] The Central Committee was unable to send anyone; dozens of telegrams with similar requests were arriving in Moscow daily from all parts of the country. On June 1 the Izhevsk committee repeated its request, reporting that a new city Soviet had been elected with the Bolsheviks in the minority.[12]

To conclude this part of our discussion, let us ask the question: Wasn't it possible to form a socialist coalition government instead of a one-party government in 1918 or late 1917? Certainly it was possible, as was shown by the experience of the brief coalition with the Left SRs. Some sort of bloc with the Left Mensheviks was also possible. Such proposals had come from the Bolsheviks themselves but were rejected by the Mensheviks, although according to Ivan Maisky, these proposals had been discussed by the previous Central Committee of the Menshevik Party and some members of the party were willing to accept the proposals.[13] The Brest treaty was a very serious obstacle to the formation of such a coalition, but it was a passing thing. A more serious impediment to restoring the coalition, at least with the Left SRs (and possibly with the Left Mensheviks later on), was the Bolsheviks' mistaken economic policy in 1918. In principle Lenin was by no means opposed to a coalition between Communists and Socialists; everything turned on certain practical disagreements over questions which neither the Bolsheviks nor the other socialist parties could resolve at that time. Thus, Lenin never regarded the experience of the Russian revolution on this question as either binding on all other countries or exclusive to Russia alone. In his "Greetings to Hungarian Workers" in 1919 (on the occasion of the socialist revolution in Hungary) Lenin wrote the following:

"Hungarian workers! Comrades! You have set the world an even better example than Soviet Russia by your ability to unite all socialists at one stroke on the platform of genuine proletarian dictatorship."[14]

All these historical circumstances are very important today, when there are so many disputes over the issues of one-party rule and pluralism.

★ ★ ★

As was to be expected, the various measures aimed at organizing the direct exchange of products, as with the attempts to buy grain from the peasants with devalued currency notes, ended in failure. Although the purchasing price for grain was raised threefold, the devaluation of the currency proceeded at a still faster pace.

Meanwhile the food situation in the cities and main industrial provinces grew worse and worse, particularly in early May 1918. The delivery and distribution of bread fell to nearly half of what it had been in April. People were beginning to starve in many areas.

There were two main ways in which the Soviet government could have solved this problem at that time. First was the road of compromise. Concessions should have been made to the bulk of the peasantry and at least a relative freedom to trade permitted. This would have immediately eased the growing tension, calmed the peasants and workers, and moderated the conflicts between the political parties in the Soviets. The old rule of the Russian village, "One spring day feeds the whole year," should not have been forgotten. The main effort in the villages should not have been to whip up class warfare and internecine strife but to get the spring planting done as well as possible, not excepting the great estates which were now in the hands of the peasants.

Second was the road of violence. The Bolsheviks knew there was grain in the villages. They knew the peasants were hiding it because they did not wish to surrender it for receipts, paper money, or an insignificant amount of manufactured goods. This was a powerful economic pressure on the young Soviet government, and those who were leading the peasantry at the time (the Left and Right SR parties) were sure that in view of the threat of starvation the Bolsheviks would be forced to yield.

Which road to choose? In 1921, in a much more difficult and complex situation, when there was total economic chaos, when the peasants were more embittered than ever, and there was obviously less room for maneuver, the Bolsheviks chose the road of retreat and compromise, the road of NEP. They permitted relative freedom to trade and replaced "surplus-grain appropriation" with the tax in kind. Thus they saved the Soviet state from destruction.

But in the spring of 1918 the Bolsheviks chose the road to violence. They chose to take grain from the peasants by force in order to feed the starving industrial and office workers in Russia's urban regions.

On May 13, 1918, the VTsIK and Sovnarkom published a decree "On Granting the Commissariat of Food Supply Extraordinary Powers." What was in fact a food dictatorship was introduced in the country. The published decree stated:

> The peasant bourgeoisie, having accumulated in their cash boxes enormous sums of money, which they extorted from the state during the war, remain stubbornly indifferent to the groans of the starving workers

and poor peasants; they will not bring their grain to the collection points, thinking to force the government to raise prices again, so that then they can sell their grain at fabulous prices to grain speculators and "bag traders." The greedy stubbornness of the village kulaks and rich peasants must be brought to an end. . . . Only one way out remains—to answer the violence of the grain owners against the starving poor with violence against the grain hoarders. Not one pood of grain should remain in the hands of the peasants beyond the amount required for the sowing of their fields and the feeding of their families until the next harvest.[15]

It is not hard to detect the inconsistency in this decree. After talking at first about kulaks and speculators, the authors of the decree go on to refer simply to the peasants, in whose hands not one pood of "surplus" grain is to remain. And how was the amount of grain needed for sowing to be determined? If all of a peasant's surplus stocks were taken away, he would sow a smaller area the following year. Why labor for nothing? And if the new harvest was small, what then?

Another question immediately arose: Who would extract the surplus grain from all the villages in the vast expanse of Russia? The apparatus of the Commissariat of Food Supply was not very big, and only about five percent of its staff were Communists. With what forces and by what means would the food dictatorship be implemented? A natural reply was to centralize and expand the food detachments made up of industrial workers. The loosely organized formation of such detachments had been going on since the winter of 1917–1918. The decree on the food dictatorship stated that the People's Commissariat of Labor should carry out an emergency mobilization of workers throughout the country for this special purpose. Lenin took a personal interest in the formation of such units. On May 10, 1918, he sent a worker named Ivanov to the Commissariat of Food Supply with the following note:

> The bearer—Andrei Vasilievich Ivanov—is a Putilov factory worker. . . . I told him about yesterday's decree and the decision that the Commissariat of Labor was to urgently mobilize workers. I gave him my opinion as follows:
> Unless the *best* workers of Petrograd build *by selection* a reliable workers' army of 20,000 people for a disciplined and ruthless *military* crusade against the rural bourgeoisie and against bribetakers, famine and the ruin of the revolution are inevitable. Please confirm this to the bearer and give him a brief statement that you will grant such detachments the fullest plenary powers on precisely such conditions. Please give him such a statement to be *read in Petrograd* and return this letter to the bearer.[16]

For nearly all of May 1918 Lenin's main work was the organization of the "crusade" for grain. He wrote a long letter, "On the Famine," to the workers of Petrograd, urging them to take the initiative in this matter of the highest importance for the fate of the revolution. Prominent members of the Central Committee, armed with special powers, were sent to the grain-producing provinces, their chief assignment being to collect grain and ship it to the center. The Central Committee sent A. G. Shliapnikov, the commissar of labor, to the Kuban region and Stalin to Tsaritsyn.

The results of this campaign, which Lenin led, were not very impressive, however, and many party leaders were less than enthusiastic in their responses to Lenin's appeals. We know, for example, that A. I. Rykov, president of the VTsIK from 1918 to 1921, spoke against the dictatorship of the Supply Commissariat at the Sovnarkom meeting of May 9, proposing that, instead of the introduction of the grain monopoly, food and grain policy be changed. The leaders of the party's Petrograd organization, then headed by Grigory Zinoviev, likewise did not favor sending tens of thousands of the city's best workers to remote provinces for grain. In their opinion it would hurt the revolutionary cause in the long run to disperse the Petrograd proletariat and in effect stop the work of many of the city's factories. Present-day Soviet historical literature, in discussing the events of 1918, as a matter of course condemns the views of Rykov and Zinoviev as anti-Leninist. We cannot agree with that judgment, however. The working class itself, including the Petrograd workers, did not respond with any particular enthusiasm to Lenin's appeals. By the end of May 1918 there were not even 2,000 or 3,000 workers in all the food detachments under the Supply Commissariat; and although they were given the impressive-sounding title of "Food Army" they were unable to fulfill their assignment of requisitioning surplus grain. Beside this Food Army, additional food detachments were set up under the Military Food Bureau of the All-Russia Central Council of Trade Unions, but by the end of May 1918 there were only several thousand persons in these units too.

Lenin then proposed that the entire country be placed under martial law and nine-tenths of the work of the Commissariat of War be centered on assisting in the grain-collection effort. Lenin's proposals for using the Red Army to collect grain were quickly discussed and approved by the Bolshevik Party Central Committee and the Sovnarkom. But the Red Army was then just being formed and its capacities were not very great. Moreover, it was soon required for direct combat purposes.

On June 1, 1918, a proclamation of the Sovnarkom entitled "All Out for the Struggle Against Famine" was published in the central newspapers. It said in part:

> The food situation in the republic grows worse every day. Less and less grain is reaching the grain-consuming areas. Famine has already arrived: its fearful breath can be felt in the cities, in the factory centers, and in the grain-consuming provinces.
>
> The hungry and tormented workers and poor peasants who have bravely endured all the burdensome consequences of the criminal imperialist war, are asking the government agonizing questions:
>
> Why is there no bread? . . .
>
> What should the workers and poor peasants do to get out of this situation and to keep famine from destroying the gains of the revolution? . . .
>
> Weeks and months will go by before the rigorous enforcement of the law on the grain monopoly and all the new attendant measures bring the desired results. . . .
>
> Meanwhile bread is needed today and tomorrow. Famine has already arrived, and will not allow for any more delays.
>
> How and where are we to get bread in the next few days?
>
> Workers and starving peasants, comrades, you know where the grain is. Almost all the surplus grain is in the hands of the village kulaks. Having grown rich during the war and accumulated huge sums of money, they don't have to sell their grain and they are hoarding it, waiting for the prices to rise, or selling it at speculative prices. . . . Having profited from the war, they now want to profit from the famine. Together with the big bourgeoisie, which finds the grain monopoly not to its taste, the village kulaks demand the abolition of the grain monopoly and a change in the fixed prices. . . .
>
> The kulaks do not want to give their grain to the hungry and will not give it, no matter what concessions the state makes to them. The grain must be taken from the kulaks by force. A crusade must be launched against the village bourgeoisie. . . . As fast as you can, form armed detachments of firm and steadfast workers and peasants who will not give in to any enticements and place them at the disposal of the central authorities. . . . The detachments you form, together with the disciplined units of the Red Army, led by experienced and tested revolutionaries and specialists in food procurement, will march out to win the grain from the village bourgeoisie.
>
> Merciless war against the kulaks!
>
> Thus and only thus, comrades, workers and starving peasants, will you conquer famine and march on to further victories on the road to socialism.

This proclamation was signed by the chairman of the Council of People's Commissars Vl. Ulyanov (Lenin), and the people's commissars Trotsky, Tsiurupa, Lunacharsky, Chicherin, Shliapnikov, Petrovsky, Lander, Vinokurov, and Gukovsky.[17]

It is quite significant that in all of these thunderous proclamations one finds threats against the kulaks, peasants, bagmen, and speculators but that nowhere is there a word about helping the peasants in the spring planting or in working the land, nor was any concern shown for the future harvest, as though the republic needed grain only in the spring and summer. But how were the industrial and office workers, and the peasants themselves, to eat the following autumn and winter?

As was to be expected, all the other parties opposed this "crusade" into the countryside. The Right SRs who protested energetically; so did the Left SRs, until recently the Bolsheviks' allies and the most influential party in the villages in that period. The Left SRs' newspaper *Znamya truda* (Banner of Labor) was filled with protests against the Bolshevik policy.

As for the Mensheviks, they opposed the organization of food detachments, citing the interests of the working class.

The writer Konstantin Paustovsky, who was a young reporter in 1918, has left us a description of one of the sessions of the VTsIK at which the question of the food detachments was discussed.

The speakers' list was coming to an end. Then Martov stood up and asked for the floor in a sluggish voice. The room started to sit up. A premonitory rumbling ran along the rows. Bent and swaying, Martov slowly climbed up to the speaker's stand, surveyed the room with unexpressive eyes, and began to speak, slowly, quietly, reluctantly. He said the decree seemed to need more exact juridical and stylistic editing. . . .

Martov fumbled for a long time in his notes, failed to find what he was looking for, and shrugged his shoulders irritatedly. The room was now convinced there would be no explosion. Newspapers started to rustle again. . . .

Suddenly a shudder ran through the room. I did not realize right away what has happened. Martov's voice was thundering from the tribune, shaking the very walls. It poured out in a fury. He had torn up the dry and boring notes from which he had been reading and tossed them in the air; they sailed and circled like snow and settled on the front rows of chairs. Martov was shaking his two fists in front of him and shouting breathlessly: "It's treachery! You've dreamed up this decree just to clean all the discontented workers, the finest flower of the proletariat, out of

Moscow and Petrograd. And to stifle the healthy protest of the working class!"

After a moment's silence the whole audience jumped to their feet. A storm of shouts echoed through the room. Separate cries cut through. "Get down!" "Traitor!" "Bravo, Martov!" "How dares he!" "The truth hurts!"

Sverdlov rang his bell furiously, calling Martov to order. But Martov went right on shouting, more frenzied than ever. He had put the room to sleep with his pretended indifference and now was getting it all back.

Finally Sverdlov denied Martov the floor, but the latter went right on speaking. Sverdlov then formally expelled him for three sessions, but Martov just waved his arms and went on making accusations, one more sinister than the other. Sverdlov summoned the guard. Then, finally Martov left the speaker's stand and for deliberate effect walked out of the room to a storm of whistling, foot stamping, and applause.[18]

It was clear that the peasants would not give up their grain voluntarily. Hence the reference, in all proclamations addressed to the workers, to the need for ruthless suppression of resistance by kulaks and speculators. In practice this meant terror.

And in fact severe measures were provided for in the decree on the food dictatorship for those who hid grain or speculated in it. Lenin wrote in his amendments to this decree:

> Emphasize more strongly the basic idea of the necessity, for salvation from famine, of conducting and carrying through a ruthless and terrorist struggle and war against peasant or other bourgeois elements who retain surplus grain for themselves; . . .
> Lay it down more precisely that owners of grain who possess surplus grain and do not *send it* to the depots and places of grain collection will be declared *enemies of the people* and will be subject to imprisonment for a term of not less than ten years, confiscation of their property, and expulsion forever from the community.[19]

However, these measures also proved insufficient, and soon the Cheka and the food detachments were given the right to shoot saboteurs and speculators (although, to judge by materials published in the USSR, this right was not very often exercised by the food detachments before the late summer of 1918).

In justifying reinstitution of the death penalty, which the Bolsheviks a year before had opposed more emphatically perhaps than any other party, Lenin declared:

> A revolutionary who does not want to be a hypocrite cannot renounce capital punishment. There has never been a revolution or a period of civil

war without shootings. Our food supply has been reduced to an almost catastrophic state. We have reached the direst period in our revolution. We are facing the most distressful period of all—there never has been a more difficult period in workers' and peasants' Russia—the period that remains until the harvest. . . . [They talk] of the decrees abolishing capital punishment. But he is a poor revolutionary who at a time of acute struggle is halted by the immutability of a law. In a period of transition laws have only a temporary validity; and when a law hinders the development of the revolution it must be abolished or amended.[20]

In mid-June the terror intensified. On June 16, 1918, P. I. Stuchka, the people's commissar of justice, signed an order saying: "Revolutionary tribunals are not bound by any restriction in choosing the means to combat counterrevolution, sabotage, and the like."[21]

This terror, begun in order to overcome the difficulties in connection with grain, was soon extended to the cities as well. After the assassination of V. Volodarsky, a member of the Presidium of the Petrograd Soviet, by Right SRs, Lenin sent the following letter to Zinoviev, then head of the Petrograd Soviet:

> Comrade Zinoviev, Only today we have heard at the [Central Committee] that in Petrograd the *workers* wanted to reply to the murder of Volodarsky by mass terror and that you (not you personally, but the Petrograd Central Committee members, or Petrograd Committee members) restrained them.
> I protest most emphatically! . . .
> The terrorists will consider us old women. This is wartime above all. We must encourage the energy and mass character of the terror against the counter-revolutionaries, and particularly in Petrograd, the example of which is *decisive.*[22]

Of course the intensification of mass terror, especially in the countryside, provoked a storm of protest from the Mensheviks and Right SRs. In this situation the VTsIK passed a resolution to exclude totally from its membership all members of the Menshevik and Right SR parties and "to propose that the Soviets of Workers', Peasants', Soldiers', and Cossacks' Deputies also remove representatives of these factions from their midst."[23] As we know, expulsion of the Left SRs from the Soviets took place within a month, in July 1918 [after the Left SR uprising against the Soviet government].

The actions of the food detachments in the countryside and all the "exceptional measures" that were decreed did not go unanswered by the peasants. As Kondratiev reports, "The village, flooded with sol-

diers after the spontaneous demobilization of the army, replied to
armed violence with armed resistance and a whole series of revolts.
That is why the period . . . up to the late autumn of 1918 was a time
of nightmarish and bloody conflict in the grain-growing areas of rural
Russia." [24]

thirteen

The Poor Peasants' Committees
and
the Beginning of the Civil War

Despite the Sovnarkom's appeal the formation of food detachments in the cities progressed very slowly during the first ten days of June. In mid-June units having a total strength of 3,000 workers were placed under the Chief Administration of the "Food Army" (the Supply Commissariat actually established such an administration). By the end of June the Food Army numbered 4,167 persons.[1]

In spite of everything Petrograd provided most of the Food Army personnel. All of Moscow and its neighboring industrial centers provided less than a thousand persons. From other cities even fewer people were placed at the Supply Commissariat's disposal for service in the Food Army.

But what could these few thousand people do in the limitless expanses of Russia's provinces, when the rural population was inclined to be hostile to the Bolsheviks? The small and poorly armed units of workers could not break the resistance of the villages and often were wiped out to the last "food soldier."

It should be borne in mind that the Bolsheviks always considered themselves the party of the working class and had virtually no party branches in the countryside.

In the multivolume *History of the CPSU* we find that at the end of 1917 in the entire country there were only 203 rural party cells on record, with a total of 4,122 members. Citing these figures, the historian M. A. Kitaev further informs us as follows:

The network of rural party organizations grew slowly in the first half of 1918. According to statistics from the county party organizations in 48 provinces and from rural district organizations in 155 counties in 33 provinces, as of February 1918 there were only 52 county committees and 16 rural district committees in operation. As a rule the size of these party organizations was small. The Taldom district organization in Tver province, founded on February 28, 1918, had 12 members. By April 1918 there were only 590 Communists on record in the counties of Yaroslavl province.[2]

In many of the grain-producing provinces, in Siberia, and in the Cossack villages of the Don region, people had heard of the Bolsheviks but had no first-hand knowledge of them. In these areas nothing was known of the Mensheviks either; the leading position on the left was held by the SR groups of various hues, the People's Socialists, and sometimes the Anarchists. Of course in most villages and hamlets there were no party organizations whatsoever. It is not surprising that in the hostile environment of such rural areas, far from Bolshevik influence, the small food detachments were not able to accomplish much.

When this became apparent, the concept arose among the Bolshevik leaders that it was necessary to *split the village* and thus create some sort of rural social base for themselves. This was essentially the aim of the new decree by the VTsIK of June 11, 1918, having the modest title "On the Organization and Supply of the Rural Poor."

According to this decree, among the principal activities of the poor peasants' committees (established by the decree) would be the distribution of grain, vital necessities, and farm implements, and the rendering of assistance to the food detachments.

The decree also stated that part of the confiscated grain should be given to the poor peasants themselves, with "a reduction from the fixed price"—in fact this meant for free. Although a poor peasants' committee was formally an organization of the rural poor, it very quickly became the real power, a kind of village revolutionary committee, which pushed the local Soviet into the background. Until then the middle peasants and kulaks had played the main role in the Soviets, especially since they constituted the majority of the rural population. In fact it was soon proposed that the poor peasants' committees take over all formal authority from the "contaminated" local Soviets.

There can be no question that the formation of the poor peasants' committees greatly facilitated the work of the food detachments. By uniting the poorest layers of the peasantry, these committees created a social base in the countryside for the Bolsheviks and gave real meaning to the idea of the *dictatorship of the proletariat and poor peasantry.* In this respect the poor peasants' committees not only strengthened the dictatorship of the proletariat but probably saved it from immediate destruction. Lenin was therefore correct when he said, at a later time, that the formation of the poor peasants' committees had been the "turning point; it showed that the urban working class, which in October had united with all the peasants to crush the landowners, the principal enemy of the free, socialist Russia of the working people, had progressed from this to an alliance with the poorest section of the peasantry in order to bring 'socialist consciousness' to the village."[3]

One can find a great deal of literature of various sorts in the USSR about the poor peasants' committees. However, such works usually purvey the idea that, with the formation of these committees, "the socialist revolution was brought from the city to the countryside," that "the socialist revolution began in the countryside in the summer of 1918," and so on. This is a highly debatable thesis. It is true that the poor peasants' committess at that time lent support to Soviet power in the cities and introduced the "spirit of intense class struggle" to the villages. But it is also true that the poorest peasants, unlike the proletariat, were not at all the vehicle of socialist ideas, nor could they be. The main aim of the very poor peasants was not to organize socialist, collective, or state farms of some kind, but to divide up village land and property anew; and with the formation of the poor peasants' committees such a redivision actually began.

If the October revolution was accompanied by the elimination of the large estates, the formation of the poor peasants' committees was followed by the abolition of kulak property, i.e., large peasant farms. However, this first "de-kulakization" in Soviet history led, not to the formation of large collective farms, but to the appearance of a great many new small and medium-sized farms. This new reapportionment of the land was on a vast scale—approximately 50 million hectares were taken from the wealthy peasants, out of a total of 80 million in their possession.[4] Some of the draft animals, farm implements, mills, and household goods of these wealthy peasants were also taken—as a rule, without compensation. Actually the property of the wealthy peasants had been acquired only partly from their exploitation of the propertyless; part of it was the fruit of many years of hard labor by the enterprising peasant families themselves. In the Soviet literature on this subject one finds the argument that part of the equipment taken from the kulaks was transferred to centers from which it was available for rent by the peasants in general or was turned over to communes. But few such cases can actually be cited. In the general confusion of the new redivision of property such cases were an insignificant minority. Most of the land, equipment, and other possessions simply fell into the hands of very poor peasants and former agricultural laborers.

There was also a reaffirmation of the official ban on the renting of land and the hiring of labor—a ban which in fact was not respected before the summer of 1918. Nevertheless the "de-kulakization" of 1918 differed from that of 1929–1932 in an important way: The families of the former kulaks were allowed to keep part of their land, their homes and household plots, and some of their possessions, equipment, and draft animals. Thus they were converted into middle peasants, but were not forcibly deported from their native villages or regions.

As we have noted, the formation of the poor peasants' committees and their activities in 1918 helped in supplying food to the cities and assisted the work of the food detachments. These committees strengthened the Bolsheviks' social base in the villages, although their formation and activities could by no means be called a "socialist revolution." Nevertheless, the fact should not be suppressed that this "final and decisive battle against the kulaks"—to use Lenin's phrase—was also an extremely risky venture. Certainly the formation of these committees and their energetic work against the kulaks (more than 100,000 such committess were formed in the 33 provinces of the RSFSR alone) struck a very powerful blow against capitalism in the countryside. But not only would it be very risky to call this first "de-kulakization" a rural socialist revolution. There is also the problem that the dividing up of the kulaks' land and the increase in the number of middle peasants had nothing in common with the Bolsheviks' own prerevolutionary program on the agarian question. There was danger in the fact that a very painful blow had been delivered to the productive capacities of the Russian village, for in place of the more productive and commercially more successful farms of the wealthy peasants, new poor peasant farms and middle-peasant farms were established, which produced little or no grain for the market. Thus in solving the urgent problem of the moment—supplying bread to the cities and to the needy layers of the village population—the Commissariat of Food

Supply greatly complicated the solution to that problem not only for the distant future but for the near future as well. The harvest of 1918, in spite of the demobilization of millions of working farmers and their return to the villages, was smaller than the 1917 harvest, a fact obviously connected with the "agrarian revolution" that blazed up in the countryside. Moreover, it was far more difficult, later on, to take the "surplus" grain from the middle peasants and poor peasants (to feed the still starving cities) than it had been to take the grain from the large landowners and the rural bourgeoisie.

But the main danger was not even that. The formation of the food detachments and poor peasants' committees aggravated the political situation to an extreme degree. In reaction to the Bolsheviks' policies an especially powerful wave of unrest arose in the grain-producing agricultural regions, in Siberia, in the Volga region, and in the Northern Caucasus, as well as in a number of regions populated by non-Russian nationalists. The situation was such that the smallest spark could ignite the conflagration of civil war.

And there was no shortage of sparks. The Cossacks and the peasants were both exhausted from four years of imperialist war and, of course, did not wish to take up arms again. They had been given peace and land thanks to the Bolsheviks, and therefore supported the October revolution and Soviet power. But they did not wish to give away, free of charge, the grain they had labored to grow, and many of them were ready to take up arms over this question. The absence of masses discontented with Bolshevik policy had meant that civil war was not possible in late 1917; but now that such masses were on the scene, their presence made civil war virtually unavoidable in 1918.

Cossack revolts had already occurred in the Don and Kuban regions and on the Ural River, and the counterrevolutionary regime of General Krasnov controlled virtually the entire Don region. However, at the time these Cossack revolts were confined to Cossack territory. Having overthrown Soviet power in their own areas, the Cossacks had no desire to go further and conquer all of Russia for the White generals. The Volunteer Army was waging a stubborn fight in the Northern Caucasus. However, it had no hope at that time of breaking through to the central and vital areas of the country. Foreign intervention in and of itself was not a great danger then. The British, American, French, and Japanese troop units which had landed on Soviet terrority, were relatively small. The soldiers of the Entente were also ex-

tremely exhausted from the world war, which was still going on, and
they did not wish to start a new one on Russia's limitless expanse.

In the summer of 1918 quite a few underground "centers" and
"leagues"—made up primarily of Cadets, monarchist officers, Right
SRs, and some other political groups—appeared in Moscow, Petrograd, and other cities. But none of these groups had much discern-
ible political influence; they placed their main hopes on foreign intervention, some looking to the former "Allies" of Russia and some of
the Germans. Agents of the Entente and native Russian counterrevolutionaries were holding secret talks with leaders of the Czechoslovak
Legion, which was on Soviet territory. Typically, many of the Russian
rightists who were negotiating with the French to obtain money for
anti-Soviet activity called the SRs and Mensheviks as "pernicious" as
the Bolsheviks.

However, all this petty intrigue, as well as the isolated revolts in the
border regions, could not have had a major effect on the fate of the
young Soviet republic so long as the majority of peasants supported
Soviet power. The formation of the food detachments and the poor
peasants' committees decisively altered the political situation in the
Russian countryside.

It was true that the Bolsheviks won for themselves a more solid basis
of support in the villages from the poorest layers of the peasantry. But
they temporarily lost the sympathy and support of the overwhelming
majority of the middle peasants, who constituted the bulk of the peasantry. This was the main danger.

The new developments found formal expression in the final break
between the Bolsheviks and the Left SRs. Relations with this party had
worsened since the time of the Brest treaty, when the Left SRs voted
at the Sixth Congress of the Soviets against ratification and withdrew
their representatives from the Sovnarkom. However, on many questions the Left SRs, who were the second largest faction in the VTsIK,
continued to support the Bolsheviks, especially so far as the struggle
against bourgeois counterrevolution and foreign intervention was concerned. There was no unanimity among the Left SR leaders even on
the question of participation in the Soviet government. At the second
congress of this party in April 1918 such leaders as Maria Spiridonova,
Kolegaev, Natanson, and others advocated reentering the Sovnarkom.
But the other group, which was led by Kamkov, Shteinberg, and D. A.
Cherepanov and which favored remaining outside the government,
won the vote.[5]

The Soviet literature on this subject often asserts that after the split with the Bolsheviks the Left SRs began to express the interests, not of the working peasantry, but of the kulaks, and that the working peasants began to move away from the Left SRs. The facts do not support this conclusion, however. We have already stated that the elections to the Soviets held from April to June 1918 showed exactly the opposite—a decline in the number of Bolshevik representatives and an increase in the number of Left SRs in almost all the local Soviets. K. V. Gusev in *The Collapse of the Left SR. Party* analyzes the social base of that party and comes to the fundamentally correct conclusion that it was the party of the working peasantry, that is, peasants who did not exploit the labor of others. L. M. Spirin agrees, but prefers to speak in *Classes and Parties in the Russian Civil War* not of the "working" peasantry, but of the middle peasants—a term more commonly used among Marxists.

Nevertheless, in almost all books and articles where the tragic split between the Bolsheviks and Left SRs is discussed, the entire blame for the split is placed on the Left SRs and their policies. In reality a large share of the blame in this case lies with the Bolsheviks, even though the policies of the Left SRs during those months were also marked by a number of mistakes.

Gusev asserts that "the social base of the Left SRs changed depending on their policies at different stages of the revolution."[6] This mistaken point of view is corrected by Spirin:

> It is not the policy of any party that determines its social base, but the social base that determines the policy. Such was the situation with the Socialist Revolutionary Party. The change in its policies and tactics occurred because tremendous social and economic shifts took place within the very layers of the peasantry whose interests it reflected. And these were very broad layers, going all the way from the poor peasants to the well-to-do middle peasants, and the rich peasants. Hence the great range in the oscillations of the SRs. When the Soviet government began to wage a struggle in the summer of 1918 not only against the kulaks but against the wealthy middle peasants who had grain surpluses and refused to surrender them to the workers' state, the Left SRs gave their full backing to these peasants, and thereby objectively became a party defending the interests of the rural bourgeoisie.[7]

We can agree with a great deal in Spirin's arguments but not with his last sentence. For it was not only the kulaks who had grain surpluses but virtually all of the middle peasants, both the "well-to-do" and the "ordinary" middle peasants. No enterprising peasant farmer regarded his own stocks of grain as "surpluses." First of all, this was his own grain, which he had grown by his own labor on his own land. Second, the peasant did not know what the next year's harvest would be like or what events the next year would bring. Thus he regarded his "surpluses" as necessary insurance, a reserve supply, and as a tradable commodity by which he could obtain, not paper money, but the manufactured goods he needed. Thus the peasants' resistance also had its own justification. For the food detachments took almost all their grain by force and paid almost nothing, and in this way not only frustrated these peasants' economic efforts and their confidence in the future but also deprived them of any incentive to labor in their fields in the subsequent years.

Spirin gives us the "thinking" of the Bolsheviks and of the SRs in defense of their respective policies. The SRs apparently favored fixed prices and the grain monopoly, but only under circumstances in which prices would really be fixed—i.e., based on a stable currency—so that the peasant could use the money he earned to obtain the manufactured goods he needed. The Bolsheviks said in reply, "What can you do if the proletariat does not have that kind of currency or manufactured goods? Are the workers supposed to die of hunger?" In Spirin's opinion the SRs had no rational answer to that question. But that is not quite so. If we look closely at the bitter debates in the spring and summer of 1918, we can easily see that the proposals of the Left SRs were much closer to the intelligent solution that the Bolsheviks found in the spring of the 1921 in a similar situation—a tax in kind combined with permission for free trade, i.e., combined with a capitalism that was not yet outdated either economically or in people's thinking.

But in the spring and summer of 1918 the Bolsheviks did not reach this intelligent solution; they mistakenly resorted to mass violence. For this reason we cannot blame the Left SRs alone for all the dramatic events of summer 1918. At that time their policies reflected not so much the position of the rural bourgeoisie (whose progressive role in rural Russia, incidentally, had not yet been exhausted) as much as the position of the working peasant, the middle peasant, who was also opposed to the food detachments and poor peasants' committees. And although there was nothing specifically *socialist* in the policies of the Left SRs in the spring and summer of 1918, there was also nothing socialist in the policies of the Bolshevik-led poor peasants' committees. Many Bolshevik leaders were guided by the revolutionary demands of the moment, and looked to the world revolution or the European revolution, which they were convinced would arrive at any moment, to solve in passing the more difficult problems of the Russian revolution. But events took a different course. The European revolution did not arrive, and in Russia there were smoldering hotbeds of civil war which could potentially burst into flame at almost any time. All that was needed was a pretext; and it was soon found, in the form of the revolt of the Czech Legion in Russia.

What exactly did the Czech Legion represent? It had been organized during World War I among Czechoslovak prisoners-of-war who no longer wished to fight on the side of Austria-Hungary. It numbered approximately 50,000 soldiers and officers, and in 1916 began to take part in military operations as part of the Russian army on the Southern Front. Overall leadership of the Czech Legion was assumed by the Czechoslovak National Council, headed by Masaryk and Beneš, and its main purpose was to win Czechoslovak independence. We must assume that the Bolsheviks sympathized with this aim and understood the desire of the Czechs and Slovaks to fight against the Hapsburg empire, which continued to oppress their nation even after the Brest treaty was signed. However, the presence on Soviet territory of the well-armed Czech Legion, which considered itself at war with Germany and Austria-Hungary, was obviously an undesirable situation for the Soviet government, as it must have been for the Czechoslovaks themselves. Negotiations were begun, resulting in a decision to allow the Czechoslovaks to leave the territory of the RSFSR. It was decided that the Czech Legion would gradually be transferred through Siberia to Vladivostok and from there through the United States to Western Europe.

Because of the dislocation of the transportation system the evacuation of the Czech Legion proceeded slowly. By mid-May 1918 only 16,000 Czechoslovaks had reached Vladivostok. The remainder were spread out along the Trans-Siberian railway, with major units still located in the Volga region and in the Urals, from Penza to Cheliabinsk. The situation was complicated by the fact that under the terms of the Brest treaty trainloads of former German prisoners-of-war were travelling along that same one-track railway. Germany was in a hurry to get its soldiers back, and the Soviet government, not wishing to provoke a conflict, gave a certain priority to the evacuation of the German prisoners-of-war. In addition, various insurgent bands were active along the Trans-Siberian railway, Japanese troops had landed in Vladivostok, and there had been military clashes in a number of regions in Siberia and the Far East; all of this taken together hampered the evacuation of the Czech Legion. This whole situation gave rise to a great many rumors, which were often deliberately inspired by the enemies of the Soviet government.

The Commissariat of War, headed by Trotsky, began negotiations to evacuate part of the Czech Legion through Archangel. But neither Britain nor France would respond to the Soviet proposals. The troops of the Czech Legion found themselves in a difficult situation, and rumors circulated among them that the Soviets intended to surrender the Czechoslovaks to the Germans. It should be noted that as early as January 1918 the Czech Legion was officially made part of the French Army and was being supported financially by the Entente. Since the Entente had already begun military intervention in northern Russia in the spring of 1918, it did not consider it logical to remove from Russia a well-armed military unit already in position there. Thus secret negotiations began with the Czechoslovak National Council on the use of the Czechoslovak troops as a vanguard for the Entente forces in Russia. But the mood of the soldiers in the Czech Legion was such that the Legion's commanders could not bring themselves to interfere in the internal affairs of the RSFSR. Both the Bolsheviks and their opponents conducted propaganda among the Czechoslovak troops. It is indicative that the founding congress of the Czechoslovak Communist Party took place in Russia during these very weeks. On the other hand, it is important to note that there are quite a few Russian officers of counterrevolutionary inclination in units of the Czech Legion, not to mention the presence of various Entente emissaries. Still, most of the soldiers' committees (which had been formed after the February revolution and which had considerable authority) opposed any interference in Russian affairs and favored the most rapid possible evacuation.

A congress of representatives of the Czech Legion was called for Cheliabinsk in mid-May 1918 to discuss the situation. The decision of the congress was that the Czech troops would not surrender their weapons but would make their way to the Far East by force if necessary. The situation had reached a point of extreme tension. "In this white-hot situation," as the story is recounted by doctor of historical sciences A. Klevansky, there occurred the so-called Cheliabinsk incident. On May 14, an object was thrown out of a westbound train loaded with German prisoners-of-war, and a Czechoslovak soldier was wounded by the flying object. This led to a clash, as a result of which several prisoners-of-war were beaten and one killed. An attempt by the Cheliabinsk Soviet to clarify the circumstances of this incident resulted in action by the Czechoslovak Legionnaires to disarm Red Army soldiers and to seize the center of the town and the railroad station.[8]

We can see that Klevansky presents the heart of the "incident" as being quite cloudy. Be that as it may, the situation grew even more tense along the line of the Legion's evacuation. Clashes with Czechoslovaks began to occur in other places as well. Heavy fighting broke out, for example, in Omsk, where the Czechs smashed a unit of the Soviet of Workers' Deputies, killing and wounding approximately 300 people.

When the Soviet government received the first reports on the incipient revolt it found itself in a difficult situation. Extreme reactionary circles in Germany were campaigning for a new offensive into the heart of Russia. Delay in evacuating the German prisoners-of-war could provoke Germany into renewing the conflict. It is not surprising that the local Soviet authorities tried to curtail the irresponsible actions of the Czechoslovaks. But it was also necessary to do everything to calm them down and evacuate them eastward as quickly as possible. Unfortunately things did not work out that way.

Among the causes of the Czech revolt that Klevansky cites in his article is "Trotsky's irresponsible telegram" demanding that any armed Czechoslovak be shot and all other Czechoslovaks be confined in prisoner-of-war camps. But of course Trotsky at that time was not acting as a private individual. He was people's commissar of the Soviet government for the army and navy. Everyone considered him, not without reason, to be the second most important and influential figure in the Soviet government. We do not know whether Trotsky discussed this telegram with Lenin and the other members of the Sovnarkom. But even if he acted on his own authority, the Czechoslovak legionnaires who found out about this telegram at the end of May could not help but regard it as a decision of the Soviet government as a whole.

The text of the telegram was as follows:

Order of the People's Commissar of War on the disarming of the Czechoslovaks.

From Moscow, May 25, 2300 hours. Samara, railroad, to all Soviets along the railway from Penza to Omsk.

All Soviets are ordered, on pain of criminal charges, to immediately disarm the Czechoslovaks. Every Czechoslovak who is found armed on the railroad is to be shot on the spot. Every troop train in which even one armed Czechoslovak is found is to be entirely emptied of Czechoslovaks, who are to be detained in a prisoner-of-war camp. Local military commissars are under obligation to carry out this order immediately, and any delay is equivalent to base treason and will bring severe punishment down upon the guilty. At the same time reliable forces are to be sent into the rear of the Czechoslovak units with the assignment of teaching a good lesson to those who will not comply. Honest Czechoslovaks who surrender their weapons and submit to Soviet authority are to be treated as brothers and given all possible assistance. . . . The present order is to be read to all troop trains of Czechoslovaks, and all railroad personnel where the Czechoslovaks are located are to be informed of its contents. All military commissars are to report on the implementation of this order.

Number 377. People's Commissar of War, L. Trotsky[9]

Trotsky's order was unquestionably a harsh and irresponsible document. It was absurd to expect that the well-armed and well-organized Czech Legion would voluntarily surrender its weapons to the still quite small and weak military units of the local Soviets, and the Red Army which was still in the process of formation. Stranded in a foreign country with a revolution going on and finding it hard to understand the events swirling about them, the Czechoslovak troops considered their weapons and their organization the only assurances they had for returning to their homeland. And since all sorts of armed bands were operating around and about, it was necessary at least to defend the railroad against them. In this situation it was absurd to suppose that the Czech Legion would submit to Trotsky's threatening order. On the contrary, the mood of many rank-and-file legionnaires changed abruptly after they learned of it. It is not surprising that the revolt of some scattered Czechoslovak units, which began on the night of May 25 and the morning of May 26, spread to the entire legion after Trotsky's order became known. The aim stubbornly pursued by emissaries of the Entente—to transform the Czech Legion into a strike force for foreign intervention—was now easily realized. Moreover, Trotsky misled the local military commissars and the still weak Soviets by composing his order the way he did. For he did not have at his disposal any reliable forces that could be sent into the Czechoslovaks' rear to "teach a good lesson to those who will not comply."

The military units of the local Soviets and of the Red Army, which was only beginning to be organized, along with small workers' detachments, fought bravely against the Czech revolt. But they could not gain the upper hand. Only in a few cities, and then only for a short while, was it possible to disarm small groups of Czechoslovaks. In other cities and at every important juncture along the Trans-Siberian railway the Czechoslovaks came out on top. On May 28, Nizhneudinsk fell, on May 31 Tomsk, on June 7 Omsk, and June 15 Barnaul, and on June 18 Krasnoyarsk. Of course the Soviets' battle against the insurgent Czechoslovaks, Siberian Cossack units, and other counterrevolutionary groups that joined them did not end there. A substantial part of the Siberian Red Army retreated into the more remote regions of the territory or into the taiga and began a guerrilla war to wear down the enemy. Nevertheless the defeat was obvious. The vast expanse of Siberia, with its riches, above all its great grain reserves, had been lost to European Russia.

But matters did not end with defeat in Siberia. Soviet Russia soon lost the Urals altogether to the Czechoslovak troops, followed by a large part of the Volga region.

What was the main reason for these defeats, which coincided with a number of severe defeats in the Don and Kuban regions? After all, the 50,000 soldiers of the Czechoslovak Legion were a drop in the bucket in the immensity of Russia. And if the bulk of the rural and urban population had supported the Bolsheviks, the Czechoslovaks and all the counterrevolutionary groups that joined them would have been rapidly defeated. However, it was mainly the workers in Siberia, the Urals, and the Volga region who supported Soviet power, and there were too few of them. A large part of the peasantry was hostile to the Bolsheviks in these areas, and that was the main reason why the victory of the enemies of Soviet power was assured. Lenin himself later acknowledged that the Siberian peasants in 1918 were "the best human material against the Communists." And that meant not only the kulaks. It was the middle peasants, who gave their support to the SRs and were hostile to the Bolsheviks at the time, who were decisive in those areas where, as Lenin put it, "the counterrevolutionary movements, the revolts, and the organization of counterrevolutionary forces had the greatest success." [10]

The victory of the counterrevolution in Siberia, the Urals, and the Volga region placed Soviet Russia in an extremely difficult situation.

The Czechoslovak Front was quickly formed, and three men were assigned to it—the people's commissar A. Kobozev, M. A. Muraviev as
commander in chief, and G. I. Blagonravov as commissar. Muraviev
was a Left SR, whose party was engaged in a bitter polemic with the
Bolsheviks at that time. But this former tsarist officer had performed
creditably in organizing the defense of Petrograd in October and November 1917. Therefore the Commissariat of War had confidence in
him. However, after the July uprising of the Left SRs, the discussion of
which falls outside the scope of the present work, Muraviev himself
tried to start a revolt in the Red Army. In the course of this attempt he
was killed. (Similar events occurred in Red Army units in the Northern
Caucasus.)

The Left SR revolt, although it was quickly suppressed, was nevertheless a blow to the unity and stability of the Red Army and complicated the situation for the Soviet government. Throughout July and
for the better part of August the incipient civil war and the battles with
the Czechoslovaks went badly for the Red Army. The territory of Soviet Russia was steadily shrinking and famine in the cities was growing
worse. The Soviet republic, which had originated less than a year
before, stood on the brink of disaster.

Meanwhile in the camp of the counterrevolution it was by no means
the Cadets or monarchists who predominated in the summer and early
fall of 1918, but the petty bourgeois parties, primarily the SRs and a
section of the Mensheviks, as well as local separatists of petty-
bourgeois coloration. It was precisely these parties that were dominant
in almost all the puppet governments that arose in Siberia, the Urals,
the Volga region, and in Northern Russia. These were the parties that
were raised up high by the mounting wave of dissatisfaction among
the peasants and a section of the workers and petty bourgeoisie. And
behind the backs of these forces the counterrevolution of the generals,
the monarchists, and the Cadets was organizing and gathering
strength, soon to take center stage as the main anti-Soviet force in the
late autumn of 1918. Then the three big campaigns of the Entente (of
1919 and 1920) would take place, those which Soviet schoolbooks
portray as the main aspect of the civil war in the USSR.

When this counterrevolutionary power of the generals and landlords
came to the fore, clearly intent on destroying all the results not only of
the October revolution but of the February revolution as well, the situation was made easier in some respects for the Soviet government,

because it produced a new turn—in the attitudes of the middle peasants and of peasants in general. However, the course and outcome of the civil war in Russia, and its various stages, require separate investigation. The sole aim of the present book has been to briefly review some of the problems of the October revolution and of the economic policy followed by the Bolsheviks, primarily from March to June 1918.

Some Conclusions

We have examined some of the problems and special aspects of the October revolution. We considered the question whether the October revolution was inevitable and answered in the negative: any historical event represents the realization of one of the possible alternative lines of development.

In part II we tried to show that the October revolution was not premature insofar as its main accomplishments were concerned. It instituted reforms that were long overdue or that, in the context of the world war, could only have been accomplished by a proletarian revolution.

However, with the further course of the revolution the Bolsheviks went too far and tried to solve tasks for which neither the objective nor the subjective conditions existed. The consequences were painful—especially the resumption of civil war and the end of the "peaceful breathing spell."

Not long after the beginning of World War I Lenin put forward a number of central slogans to delineate Bolshevik policy in regard to the war. One was "Turn the imperialist war into a civil war." This was a general appeal for the workers in all the belligerent countries to turn the weapons they were using to slaughter each other against their oppressors—those chiefly to blame for the world war.

However, between this Bolshevik slogan and the savage civil war that raged in Russia from 1918 to 1920, there was neither a logical connection nor a cause-and-effect relation. It would be a great error to suppose that in this case the Bolsheviks put into effect a prearranged program. Of course, the February revolution was accompanied by a brief outbreak of civil war in the capital. The fact that the troops of the

Petrograd garrison turned their guns against the police and took the side of the working class was a crucial reason for the autocracy's being overthrown so quickly. But after the victory of the February revolution the situation was such that the revolution could progress in a relatively peaceful way. And when Lenin advanced the slogans "All power to the Soviets" and "Long live the socialist revolution," he did so from the perspective that the socialist revolution would proceed peacefully. The suppression of the July demonstration and the Kornilov revolt represented, new though brief outbursts of civil war, after which there again arose, only briefly, the possibility that the revolution would develop peacefully—a possibility that was lost entirely by the early autumn of 1917.

Of course, as with virtually all social concepts, the concepts of "civil peace" and "civil war" can be viewed in both a narrow and a broad sense. Broadly, any armed confrontation between classes, any open manifestation of violence, constitutes civil war. From this standpoint, the October revolution itself was an act of civil war. The whole period of the "triumphal march" of Soviet power was also attended by many acts of civil war and violence. Recall, for example, General Kaledin's revolt on the Don, or the fighting outside Petrograd with Kerensky's and Krasnov's units (see Glossary, "Fighting Outside Petrograd").

But in the narrower sense, civil war should obviously be taken to mean a regular war between large armies, one of which is organized by the counterrevolution and the other by a new revolutionary government, or one favoring fundamental changes. Such a war may spread over the entire territory of a country, go on for many years, and be fought with unusual ferocity.

Thus, for example, the seventeenth-century bourgeois-democratic revolution in England was accompanied by two civil wars (1642–1645 and 1648), spread throughout the country, and ended with the establishment of Cromwell's dictatorship. The American Civil War of 1861–65 between the Northern and Southern states, with armies numbering in the millions on either side, can also serve as an example of such a war.

No one wanted that kind of massive civil war in Russia in 1917. Therefore, one of the main arguments against a Bolshevik seizure of power was that the dictatorship of the proletariat would lead to a long and bloody civil war.

In answering his opponents Lenin acknowledged that any revolution entailed a risk of civil war and terror. But he also tried to demonstrate that in the Russia of 1917 that risk was minimal. As early as June 1917 Lenin wrote:

> If the "Jacobins" of the twentieth century, the workers and semi-proletarians, assumed power, they would proclaim as enemies of the people the capitalists who are making thousands of millions in profits from the imperialist war, *that is,* a war for the division of capitalist spoils and profits.
>
> The "Jacobins" of the twentieth century would not guillotine the capitalists—to follow a good example does not mean copying it. It would be enough to arrest fifty to a hundred financial magnates and bigwigs, the chief knights of embezzlement and of robbery by the banks. It would be enough to arrest them for a few weeks *to expose their frauds* and show all exploited people "who needs the war." Upon exposing the frauds of the banking barons, we could release them, placing the banks, the capitalist syndicates, and all the contractors "working" for the government under workers' control.[1] (Emphasis in original—R.M.)

In September 1917 Lenin commented, "Of all the methods of intimidation, that of scaring with civil war is perhaps the most widespread." As Lenin put it, the philistines try to frighten people with the idea that "civil war may sweep away all the gains of the revolution and drown in rivers of blood our young, still unstable freedom. . . ."[2]

Replying to this "scare tactic," Lenin wrote that since February 1917 the Russian revolution had provided a number of examples of "incipient civil war" both on the part of the proletariat and peasantry and on the part of the bourgeoisie. The Kornilov revolt was an obvious attempt to unleash civil war but it failed primarily because of the spontaneous alliance that developed between the proletariat, led by the Bolsheviks, the lower strata of the peasantry, and those workers who still supported the Mensheviks. Lenin drew the conclusion that the further progress of the revolution and the transfer of power to the Soviets and the working class could happen without a bloody civil war. The condition for this was the spontaneously formed alliance among the bottom layers of society. Lenin commented:

> The bourgeoisie's resistance to the transfer of the land to the peasants without compensation, to similar reforms in other realms of life, to a just peace and a break with imperialism, is, of course, inevitable. But for such resistance to reach the stage of civil war, *masses* of some kind are necessary, masses capable of *fighting* and vanquishing the Soviets. The bourgeoisie does *not* have these masses, and has nowhere to get them. The sooner and the more resolutely the Soviets take all power, the

sooner both Savage Divisions and Cossacks will split into an insignificant minority of politically-conscious Kornilov supporters and a huge majority of those in favour of a democratic and *socialist* (for it is with socialism that we shall then be dealing) alliance of workers and peasants.[3] (Emphasis in original—R.M.)

This prognosis was not realized. The problem was that the "alliance among the lower strata," which Lenin referred to as a guarantee against civil war, required certain specific policies and certain specific concessions, taking into account the interests of the social groups constituting the lower strata. The greater part of Russia's lower strata, however, were peasants, and their economic interests diverged fundamentally from those of the working class.

The Bolsheviks were able to make concessions to the peasantry, to follow a policy of compromise, in October 1917, when they took the main programmatic demands of their Decree on Land, not from their own program, but from the peasant-based land program of the SRs.

But the Bolsheviks did not manage to repeat this experiment in social compromise in the spring of 1918, when the main demand of the peasant who had received land was partial freedom to trade, at the minimum. This demand corresponded not only to the interests of the majority of Russia's petty bourgeois population but also to the existing situation. Direct exchange of products, centralized purchasing and distribution of all foodstuffs, and forced confiscation of all grain surpluses from the peasants all required an enormous apparatus which the Bolsheviks did not yet have and which it was no easy task to create. Moreover, trade is a self-regulating process, which would have relieved the Soviet government of a significant share of the concerns then weighing it down. But the Soviet government maintained the grain monopoly and tried to make it even more absolute and extend it to most other basic necessities. This turned the bulk of the peasants and former soldiers, as well as the Cossacks and urban petty bourgeois, against the Bolsheviks, and gave the counterrevolution the discontented masses it needed in order to unleash civil war.

It is instructive to compare the spring of 1918 with that of 1921 in this regard. In the spring of 1921 the devastating civil war that had swept over the entire country in repeated waves had just ended. There actually was no grain in the country, at any rate no surplus at all, even in those regions which had been most abundant in grain in the past.

In addition there were no kulaks. They had been dissolved into the general mass of the rural population after three years of *prodrazverstka* and repeated redivision of the land. Total grain production in 1920 was only 50 percent of prewar production, which did not even cover the most urgent needs of the village itself. The peasants and Cossacks returned to their homes once again, this time from the Red Army or one of the White armies, after two or three years of civil war. Once more they had many weapons, but there was very little grain. The villages were in ruins but so were the towns. Transport was not simply working poorly; it had in fact been destroyed. In most of the country the trains were not moving at all; everywhere along the tracks, broken-down railroad cars and locomotives were left standing. Industry, too, had been devastated and destroyed. Only a very few factories continued to operate. Even the small craft workshops, nationalized during the period of "war communism," could no longer function. There were not enough raw materials.

Trade had died out in many cities, even on the black markets, since there was hardly anything to trade with.

The attempt to persist with the policy of "surplus-grain appropriation" after the end of the civil war, maintaining the food detachments and forced requisitioning, provoked a wave of peasant revolts that swept over the entire country. Former Red Army soldiers, Red Cossacks, and sailors were among the rebels. Soviet power hovered at the brink. After winning its most difficult victory the Bolshevik government experienced its severest political crisis. Mass strikes by workers in Petrograd and the Kronstadt revolt showed that the Communist Party's last base of support was evaporating. Once again predictions were heard that the Bolsheviks could hold out for only a few more months, and these predictions were, unfortunately, not without foundation.

The situation was saved by the introduction of NEP, the suspension of grain requisitioning, and the introduction of a tax in kind. With some restrictions, free trade and private enterprise were permitted. This was a concession to the middle peasants, and to the peasantry as a whole, from which the working class only stood to gain. It was trade that became the "main link" by which Lenin hoped to "drag along the whole chain" and turn the ruined economy in the direction of revival and progress. The former speculators began unwillingly to help strengthen Soviet power; the roadblock detachments and food detachments were disbanded, and the concentration camp gates were opened to release hundreds of thousands of free trade "violators." In the cities the petty craftspeople and small cooperative workshops re-sumed operations. Middlemen appeared who opened the way to res-toration of free commodity circulation both locally and later through-out the Soviet Union. Within this system both cooperative and state trading organizations began to be formed, and they were obliged to compete with private trade. The blood began to circulate again in the body of the exhausted country, and the organism began to revive. Within a year or two the big state-owned factories and plants, one after another, likewise resumed operation.

The restoration of state industry was helped along by the tax which the government collected at that time from the peasants and from all private businessmen. Even the dreadful famine in the Volga region, which took millions of lives, did not induce the Bolsheviks to revert to the policy of "surplus grain allocation."

Now let us return to the spring of 1918. The situation was difficult that spring, but it was incomparably less difficult in every respect than the spring of 1921. There was less grain in the country than in the prewar years; nevertheless, there was some. There were surpluses from the harvests of 1916 and 1917. The enormous Russian army had been demobilized, and millions of sturdy peasant lads and older men had returned to their native villages. They were no longer a state re-sponsibility, to be fed and clothed. Instead they were engaging them-selves in the difficult work of farming, preparing to sow the land on the large estates which had become theirs. The transport system was still working, though intermittently. The railroads had not yet been de-stroyed. Freed of their burdensome war-related obligations, the railroads could have performed their peacetime tasks with relative suc-cess.

At the end of 1917 and in early 1918 almost all the industrial en-terprises were working more or less normally. Most of the plants pro-ducing for the defense effort until then could have been converted to the production of goods necessary to the economy. The urban popu-lation was not too large in 1918, and the resources still at Russia's dis-posal were quite sufficient to provide it with food.

The question naturally arises, Why could NEP not have been in-troduced in the spring of 1918 instead of in 1921? Such a policy shift would have been easier and more natural at that time. Once peace had been made and the army demobilized, the grain monopoly could also have been revoked, and compulsory purchases of grain at arbitrarily fixed prices could have been replaced by a tax in kind. The middle peasantry, which was starting to turn against the Bolsheviks, would once again have taken the side of the Soviet government, and the kulaks and rich peasants would have been neutralized. The discontent of the petty bourgeois masses and a section of the urban workers would have faded away. There would no longer have been a mass of discontented elements ready to fight against Soviet power, and thus the scattered outbreaks of civil war might not have developed into a long and destructive conflict. Neither would foreign intervention have been able to accomplish anything. As things were, the Entente units were not very large, had become demoralized, and were demanding they be sent home. Even if the revolt of the Czech Legion had nevertheless occurred, the separate centers of revolt would have died down quickly. The coalition with the Left SRs (especially after the Brest treaty) would gradually have been strengthened. And the possibility of a coalition with the left-wing Menshevik Internationalists would have emerged. (Even in 1917 Lenin frequently indicated the desirability of such a coalition within the framework of the Soviets.) As for the Right SRs and right-wing Mensheviks, their remaining influence on the masses would have been canceled out completely, and in all probability new political splits would have developed in these parties.

Why, then, was NEP not begun in the spring of 1918? One old Bolshevik, who took an active part in the events of that distant time, has answered this question roughly as follows.

The party, he says, did not have the forces to introduce and control NEP. In 1918 the uncontrolled natural force of free trade would have overwhelmed the still weak organs of Soviet power and toppled the system of proletarian dictatorship which was only beginning to take shape. It was easier to ban free trade than regulate it.

But we cannot agree with this answer. It is true that in the spring of 1918 the party did not have many forces. But for that very reason it could not assume such tasks as the organization of universal cooperation, nationalization of all enterprises, including the smallest workshops, and the organization of direct product exchange between town and country in place of trade. All of that required much more experience and many more forces than did supervision over relatively free trade. The party did not have sufficient forces and resources to create the countless food requisition detachments and roadblock detachments to put into effect the dictatorship of the Narkomprod; consequently free trade actually continued, as we have indicated, and without it Soviet power could not have lasted. In 1918 NEP existed illegally, and that was the salvation of the urban and rural populations. We have cited N. Kondratiev's testimony to this effect. We can also refer to the testimony of A. S. Izgoyev, another eyewitness. Being an opponent of the Bolsheviks, he allows himself quite a few exaggerations. But on the main issue, he is unquestionably correct when he writes:

> Life replied to the struggle of the socialists against the property principle with a spontaneous and irresistible, though distorted, affirmation of that principle in the form of the army of bag traders, many million strong. For the fact that the socialist experiments did not bring millions of Russian people to the disaster of death by starvation we must thank the bagmen, who risked their lives to feed their families and maintain the exchange of goods at a time when the Soviet government did everything it could to stop it. Many-millioned Russia with its strong muscles and sturdy legs took to the road and began to trade. After the banning of normal trade, replaced by hundreds of thousands of well-paid, ignorant, and dishonest, new bureaucrats, who knew nothing about trade, the bagmen alone gave the population of Russia's towns and factories a chance to survive the frightful spring and summer months of 1918.[4]

Certainly Izgoyev is not very flattering or very fair in the way he refers to the enormous and often quite heroic work of the Narkomprod bodies. But he is right in saying that the work of Narkomprod alone could not have saved Russia from death by famine.

Of course there was no malicious intent in Bolshevik policy. It was simply that the Bolsheviks, and Lenin as their leader, did not at that time arrive at the more correct solution to the economic problems of the post-revolutionary period. It took the hard experience of the civil war and the political crisis of 1921 to accomplish that.

But can we blame Lenin and the other Bolshevik leaders for this? We think that would be asking too much of revolutionaries who were the first to take the road of socialist revolution, and in such a country as Russia at that! The French writer and scholar Jean-François Revel was quite right to say the following in *Without Marx or Jesus,* which is highly debatable in many other respects:

> The purpose of revolution . . . is neither to titillate doctors of the law nor to fulfill prophecies. By definition, revolution signifies an event such as has never taken place before; an event that comes to fruition by ways that were hitherto unknown in history. When we use the word "revolu-

tion," we must necessarily speak of something that cannot be conceived or understood within the context of old ideas. The stuff of revolution, and its first success, must be the ability to innovate. It must be mobility with respect to the past, and speed with respect to creation.[5]

The problem is not that revolutionaries make mistakes, however serious they may be, but whether they can learn from their mistakes and draw the necessary lessons from them. Lenin knew how to do that, and it helped him find the correct solution in the truly critical situation in the spring of 1921. In his writings of 1921–1922 Lenin often returns to the 1918–1920 period and often refers to the mistakes that were made then. He also said many times that the entire socialist revolution in Russia was—to use the later words of Vladimir Mayakovsky—"a journey into the unknown." Without social experiments, without trial and error, there was no way to get by in such a revolution. Some opponents of Marxism cry out indignantly, how can you make experiments on society, on people, and on living social classes? But this is a false objection. All of human history, with its wars and revolutions, is the history of just such experiments. And were not the men who started World War I using humanity for their own, plainly criminal purposes? Why couldn't the Bolsheviks, who had taken up the noble aim of building a just socialist society, make a revolution to break out of the deadly grip of war, which was daily taking tens of thousands of human lives? They had a right to run a risk and, if they were true revolutionaries, they could not fail to take advantage of odds that favored them. Lenin was right to say that history would not forgive the Bolsheviks for delaying at the decisive and most favorable moment. The whole problem is to draw the correct lessons from the mistakes made in the course of the revolution. Lenin was able to do that in most cases. And in comparing the spring of 1918 with the spring of 1921 he indicated clearly enough what mistakes had been made in that difficult first spring under Soviet rule. We will conclude our essay with a long but highly appropriate excerpt from an article by Lenin written on the fourth anniversary of Soviet power.

The best way to celebrate the anniversary of a great revolution is to concentrate attention on its unsolved problems. It is particularly appropriate and necessary to celebrate the revolution in this way at a time when we are faced with fundamental problems that the revolution has not yet solved, and when we must master something new (from the point of view of what the revolution has accomplished up to now) for the solution of these problems.

What is new for our revolution at the present time is the need for a "reformist," gradual, cautious and roundabout approach to the solution of the fundamental problems of economic development. This "novelty" gives rise to a number of questions, perplexities, and doubts in both theory and practice.

A theoretical question. How can we explain the transition from a series of extremely revolutionary actions to extremely "reformist" actions in the same field at a time when the revolution as a whole is making victorious progress? Does it not imply a "surrender of positions," an "admission of defeat," or something of that sort? Of course, our enemies . . . say that it does. They would not be enemies if they did not shout something of the sort. . . .

But there is "perplexity" . . . among friends, too.

Restore large-scale industry, organize the direct exchange of its goods for the produce of small-peasant farming, and thus assist the socialization of the latter. For the purpose of restoring large-scale industry, borrow from the peasants a certain quantity of foodstuffs and raw materials by requisitioning—this was the plan [or method, system] that we followed for more than three years, up to the spring of 1921. This was a revolutionary approach to the problem—to break up the old social-economic system completely at one stroke and to substitute a new one for it.

Since the spring of 1921, instead of this approach, plan, method, or mode of action, we have been adopting . . . a totally different method, a reformist type of method: not to *break up* the old social-economic system—trade, petty production, petty proprietorship, capitalism—but to *revive* trade, petty proprietorship, capitalism, while cautiously and gradually getting the upper hand over them, or making it possible to subject them to state regulation *only to the extent* that they revive.

That is an entirely different approach to the problem.

Compared with the previous, revolutionary, approach, it is a reformist approach. . . . The question that arises is this. If, after trying revolutionary methods, you find they have failed and adopt reformist methods, does it not prove that you are declaring the revolution to have been a mistake in general? Does it not prove that you should not have started with the revolution but should have started with reforms and confined yourselves to them?

That is the conclusion which the Mensheviks and others like them have drawn. But this conclusion is either sophistry, a mere fraud perpetrated by case-hardened politicians, or it is the childishness of political tyros. The greatest, perhaps the only danger to the genuine revolutionary is that of exaggerated revolutionism, ignoring the limits and conditions in which revolutionary methods are appropriate and can be successfully employed. True revolutionaries have mostly come a cropper when they began to write "revolution" with a capital R, to elevate "revolution" to something almost divine, to lose their heads, to lose the ability to reflect, weigh, and ascertain in the coolest and most dispassionate manner at what moment, under what circumstances, and in which sphere of action you must act in a revolutionary manner, and at what moment, under what circumstances, and in which sphere you must turn to reformist action. True revolutionaries will perish (not that they will be defeated from outside, but that their work will suffer internal collapse) only if they abandon their sober outlook and take it into their heads that the "great, victorious, world" revolution can and must solve all problems in a revolutionary manner under all circumstances and in all spheres of action. If they do this, their doom is certain. . . .

From the theoretical point of view—foolish things are done in time of revolution just as at any other time, said Engels, and he was right. We must try to do as few foolish things as possible, and rectify those that are done as quickly as possible. . . .[6]

Lenin wrote all this in 1921. But the same ideas, in more expanded form, lie at the basis of the present essay. Unfortunately not everything that happened long ago, in the first four years of Soviet power, has ceased to be relevant today. It is impossible not to recognize that all of the political and economic crises in our country during the past fifty years (the 1928–1932 crisis, the 1953–1954 crisis, and the 1963–1964 crisis, as well as certain recent indications of crisis) have been linked primarily with mistakes of one kind or another in agricultural policy, a mistaken attitude toward a number of important problems of agricultural production and toward the workers in this sphere of production. This is why abundance in agricultural production still eludes us, why we have no surpluses of grain and meat. This is why we have to buy such surpluses from the capitalist countries. Of course the solution to our present economic problems cannot be what it was at Lenin's time. But it does not hurt to keep in mind certain aspects of NEP even today.

★ ★ ★

Author's Notes

All of the author's references to Marx and Engels *Sochineniia* (Collected Works) are to the 2nd Russian edition, 1955—1966. In some cases references have been added to English-language editions in which the quoted passages may be found.—*Trans.*

In references to citations from Lenin:

PSS = *Polnoe sobranie sochinenii* (Complete Collected Works)

CW = *Collected Works*

All author's references to Lenin's PSS are to the fifth edition, Moscow, 1958—1965. References have been added in each case to CW, the English-language version published in the 1960s by Progress Publishers, Moscow. The English wording of this edition has been followed except for some changes for style or occasionally because of inadequacy in the translation.—*Trans.*

Introduction

1. *World Politics,* April 1966, p. 452.
2. Marx and Engels, *Sochineniia,* v. 8, 122–23. [Literally the Latin phrase means "Here is Rhodes, leap here." Compare the explanation of this phrase in the Moscow Foreign Languages Publishing House 1955 edition of Marx and Engels *Selected Works in Two Volumes* (1:250–51).—*Trans.*]

One. Various Points of View

1. *Politics and Society in the USSR,* London: Weidenfeld 1970, pp. 48, 50.
2. "The Bolshevik Gamble," in *Russian Review,* October 1967, pp. 337–40. (reprinted in *The Russian Revolution: An Anthology,* ed. M. K. Dziewanowski, New York: T. Y. Crowell, 1970, p. 180–82).
3. *World Politics,* April 1966, p. 456.
4. William Z. Foster, *The Russian Revolution,* Chicago, 1921, p. 27.
5. Iosif [Joseph] Berger, *Krushenie pokoleniia,* Italy, 1973, p. 19. [This is a memoir of Stalin's prisons and camps, in which Berger spent seventeen years

(1935–1951). In 1956 he was allowed to leave the USSR. His book was first published in England under the title *Shipwreck of a Generation*. Compare the American edition, entitled *Nothing But the Truth*, New York: John Day Co., 1971, pp. 15–16.—*Trans.*]

6. Ivan A. Bunin, *Pod serpom i molotom* (Under the Hammer and Sickle), London, Canada, 1975, pp. 211–12.

7. Cited in the Paris Russian newspaper *Russkaia mysl'* (Russian Thought), no. 3011, August 8, 1974, p. 10.

8. Leon Trotsky, *Chto takoe SSSR i kuda on idet* (What Is the USSR and Where Is It Going?), manuscript, 1936, p. 4. [The author cites the facsimile edition of Trotsky's Russian manuscript—which was published in book form in Paris, 1972. There was no regularly printed Russian edition of this book, which is best known by its English title, *The Revolution Betrayed*. We have followed Max Eastman's version in the Pathfinder Press edition, New York, 1970, p. 5.—*Trans.*]

9. *Kritika burzhuaznoi istoriografii sovetskogo obshchestva* (A Critique of Bourgeois Historiography on Soviet Society), Moscow, 1972, p. 34.

10. Marx and Engels, *Sochineniia*, 13:7. [See *Selected Works in Two Volumes*, vol. 1, Moscow, 1955, p. 363.—*Trans.*]

11. *Istoricheskaia nauka i nekotorye problemy sovremennosti* (Historical Science and Certain Problems of Today's World), Moscow, 1969, pp. 211–12.

12. A. I. Herzen, *Sobranie sochinenii v 30 tomakh* (Collected Works in 30 vols.), 14: 46.

13. *Ibid.*, 6:36.

14. In an account of Napoleon's return to France from Egypt in 1799, the Soviet historian A. Manfred compares Bonaparte to a gambler playing against odds of a hundred to one and winning. But was this the only such adventure Napoleon undertook in that period?

15. Georgy V. Plekhanov, *Izbrannye filosofskie proizvedeniia* (Selected Philosophical Works), vol. 2, Moscow, 1956, p. 327.

16. *Ibid.*

17. I. M. Sechenov, *Izbrannye proizvedeniia* (Selected Works), Moscow, 1953, p. 114.

18. *Amerika*, no. 68, (1962): 31.

19. Cited by Nicola Chiaromonte in his *Paradoks istorii*, Rome, 1973, p. 30. [This is a Russian edition of Chiaromonte's *The Paradox of History: Stendhal, Tolstoy, Pasternak, and Others*, London: Weidenfeld, 1970; the quotation is on p. 24 of the English edition.—*Trans.*]

20. *Ibid.*, p. 58. (Cf. English ed., p. 43).

21. See B. F. Skinner, *Beyond Freedom and Dignity*, New York: Knopf, 1971.

22. Herzen, *Sobranie sochinenii*, 20 (bk. 1):440.

23. Roger Garaudy, *Krutoi povorot sotsializma*, Moscow: Progress Publishers (special edition), p. 11. [This is apparently a confidential Russian edition, available only to a "special" Soviet audience, of a critical work by Garaudy, the prominent French Marxist. First published in France in 1969 as *Le grand tournant du socialisme*, this was the book that led to Garaudy's expulsion from the French Communist Party. An authorized English edition is *The Turning Point of Socialism*, London: Fontana, 1970; the quotation is on p. 11 of the English edition as well.—*Trans.*]

24. Leonid Rendel, *Ob osobennostiakh istoricheskogo razvitiia Rossii* (On the Peculiarities of Russia's Historical Development), unpublished manuscript, p. 159. [As a graduate student in history in Moscow around 1956, Leonid Rendel helped found a dissident Marxist circle. The group was broken up and its members arrested in 1957. Rendel was sentenced to ten years detention for "anti-Soviet activity." Since his release in 1967, he has continued to be harassed by the authorities and his unauthorized writings are denied publication in the official Communist press.—*Trans.*]

25. *Kontinent,* no. 6 (1976):441.

26. Nevertheless a detailed and convincing analysis of Solzhenitsyn's book may be found in Boris Souvarine's lengthy article "Solzhenitsyn and Lenin" in the French journal *Est et Ouest,* no. 570 (January 1—15, 1976). [An English version of Souvarine's article appeared in *Dissent* magazine (New York) in 1977.—*Trans.*]

27. N. N. Sukhanov, *Zapiski o revoliutsii* (Notes on the Revolution), Berlin-Petrograd-Moscow, 1922, bk. 3, pp. 4—55 [An abridged edition of Sukhanov's multivolume work is *The Russian Revolution, 1917: A Personal Record,* London: Oxford University Press, 1955.—*Trans.*]

28. V. Valentinov [N. V. Vol'skii], *Maloznakomyi Lenin* (The Little-Known Lenin), Paris, 1972, p. 96.

29. *Russian Review,* January 1967, p. 12.

Two. On the February Bourgeois Democratic Revolution

1. In the Paris Russian publication *Vestnik RKhD* [Russkogo Khristianskogo Dvizheniia] (Bulletin of the Russian Christian Movement), nos. 112—13, pp. 106—7.

2. Cited by M. Vishniak in the article "19 fevralia 1861 goda" (February 19, 1861), in the émigré Menshevik periodical *Sotsialisticheskiĭ vestnik* (Socialist Courier), 1960, nos. 2—3.

3. D. Anin, *Revoliutsiia 1917 goda glazami ee rukovoditelei* (The 1917 Revolution Through the Eyes of Its Leaders), Rome, 1971, pp. 77—78.

4. Fyodor Dan, *Proiskhozhdenie bolshevizma,* New York, 1945, pp. 444—45. [Compare the English-language edition, *The Origins of Bolshevism,* New York: Harper, 1964.—*Trans.*]

5. I. I. Mints, *Istoriia Velikogo Oktiabria* (The History of Great October), 3 vols., Moscow, 1966, 1967, 1973.

6. V. Shulgin, *Dni* (Days), Leningrad, 1927, p. 124.

7. Georgii Adamovich, *V. A. Maklakov: Politik, iurist, chelovek* (V.A. Maklakov: Politician, Lawyer, Man), Paris, 1959, pp. 110—11.

8. *Perepiska Nikolaia i Aleksandry Romanovykh* (The Correspondence of Nicholas and Alexandra Romanov), vol. 4, Moscow: Gosizdat [the State Publishing House], 1926, p. 129.

9. *Ibid.,* vol. 3, Moscow, 1923, p. 167.

10. In the Paris Russian newspaper *Dni* (Days), May 22, 1932.

11. Cited in the book by N. Yakovlev *I avgusta 1914 g.* (August 1, 1914), Moscow, 1974, p. 156.

12. Iu. V. Lomonosov, *Vospominaniia o martovskoi revoliutsii 1917 goda* (Reminiscences of the March [i.e., February] Revolution of 1917), Stockholm and Berlin, 1921, p. 15.

13. A. Blok, "Poslednie dni starogo rezhima" (The Last Days of the Old Regime), in *Arkhiv russkoi revoliutsii* (Archives of the Russian Revolution), vol. 4, Berlin, 1922, pp. 22–23.

14. A. I. Denikin, *Ocherki russkoi smuty* (Outlines of the Russian Turmoil), vol. 1, pt. 1, Paris, 1922, pp. 38–39.

15. In the magazine *Proletarskaia revoliutsiia* (Proletarian Revolution), no. 1 (1923): 6.

16. Anin, *Revoliutsiia . . . ,* p. 49.

17. This book, whose chauvinist and promonarchist point of view caused a sensation among Soviet historians, was published in a large edition by the Molodaya Gvardiya (Young Guard) publishing house in Moscow. See above, note 11.

18. Yakovlev, *I avgusta 1914,* p. 121.

19. *Ibid.,* p. 205 and *passim.*

20. Attempts by some historians to argue that Russia's military effort was sabotaged by certain "Zionist" circles who had gained control of the Russian press and brought Rasputin under their influence—and through him, the tsarist court as a whole—are of course totally outside the sphere of genuine scholarship.

21. *Partiia bol'shevikov v fevral'skuiu revoliutsiiu v Rossii* (The Bolshevik Party During the February Revolution), Moscow, 1971, p. 138.

22. *Gosudarstvennaia Duma. Sessiia V* (The State Duma. Session V), the stenographic record, Petrograd, 1917, p. 1297.

23. *Proletarskaia revoliutsiia,* no. 1 (1923): p. 23.

24. *Ibid.,* p. 27.

25. *Ibid.,* p. 35.

26. Aleksandr Solzhenitsyn, "Pis'ma iz Ameriki" (Letters from America) in *Vestnik RKhD,* no. 116 (1975):127.

Three. On the October Socialist Revolution

1. *Istoriia grazhdanskoi voiny v SSSR* (History of the Civil War in the USSR), vol. 1, Moscow, 1937, p. 133.

2. V. I. Lenin, *Polnoe sobranie sochinenii* ("Complete Collected Works," 5th ed., hereafter cited as Lenin PSS), 34:55. (Corresponds to CW, 25:225.)

3. *Ibid.,* p. 119. (CW, 25:285.)

4. *Ibid.,* p. 121 (CW, 25:288–89.) (Emphasis in the original.)

5. *Ibid.,* p. 436. (CW, 26:235.)

6. A. Rumiantsev, *Problemy sovremennoi nauki ob obshchestve* (Problems of Contemporary Social Science), Moscow, 1969, p. 23.

7. *Programmy russkikh politicheskikh partii* (The Programs of Russia's Political Parties), Moscow, 1917, pp. 18–19.

8. *Izvestiia Vserossiiskogo Soveta Krest'ianskikh deputatov* (News of the All-Russia Soviet of Peasants' Deputies) (Petrograd), no. 88, August 19, 1917. This paper reflected the views of the right wing of the SR Party.

9. *Delo naroda* (The People's Cause), September 29, 1917.
10. Lenin, PSS, 35:27. (CW, 26:260.)
11. Dzhon Rid [John Reed], *Desiat' dnei, kotorye potriasli mir,* Moscow, 1959, p. 40. [The author cites the Russian edition of John Reed's *Ten Days That Shook the World.* Compare the American edition, New York: Vintage, 1960, p. 26.—*Trans.*]
12. Anin, *Revoliutsiia . . . ,* pp. 365, 367.
13. Reed, *Desiat' dnei . . . ,* p. 74. Vintage ed., p. 94.
14. Louis Fischer, *Zhizn' Lenina,* London, 1970, pp. 232–33. [The author cites the Russian edition of Fischer's *The Life of Lenin,* New York: Harper, 1964. Compare the English original, p. 154.—*Trans.*]
15. L. M. Spirin, *Klassy i partii v grazhdanskoi voine v Rossii* (Classes and Parties in the Russian Civil War), Moscow, 1968, pp. 82–83.
16. S. Piontkovskii, *Granzhdanskaia voina v Rossii. Khrestomatiia* (The Civil War in Russia: Readings), Moscow, 1927, pp. 206–7.
17. B. T. Kiriushin, *Puti Rossiiskoi revoliutsionnosti* (The Pathways of Russian Revolutionism), p. 197. This book was published outside the Soviet Union. The date and place of publication are unknown to me.—R.M.

Four. Spontaneity and Organization

1. *Iskra* (The Spark), 1905, no. 84. [The newspaper *Iskra* was founded by Lenin in 1900 as a means of organizing the illegal Russian Social Democratic Labor Party (RSDLP), especially through a Russia-wide network of agents to circulate and contribute to the paper. Lenin was *Iskra*'s most influential editor through the Second Congress of the RSDLP in July–August 1903, when the paper was made the central organ of the party. Not long after that congress, at which the Bolshevik-Menshevik split occurred, *Iskra* passed out of Lenin's control. By November 1903 it became and remained a vehicle for the views of the Mensheviks until it ceased publication in October 1905.—*Trans.*]
2. *Iskra,* 1905, no. 85.
3. Rosa Luxemburg, *Vseobshchaia zabastovka* (The General Strike), p. 55, 108. [The author gives no date or place of publication for the Russian edition he cites. The corresponding passages in an English version, under the title "The Mass Strike, the Political Party, and the Trade Unions" may be found in *Rosa Luxemburg Speaks,* New York: Pathfinder Press, 1970, pp. 188, 218.—*Trans.*]
4. Lenin, PSS, 34:217. (CW, 26:31.)
5. *Ibid.,* 9:259. (CW, 8:153.) (Emphasis in original.)
6. *Russkaia mysl',* no. 3011, August 8, 1974, p. 10.
7. V. Bazarov, "Pervye shagi russkoi revoliutsii. 1917" (The First Steps of the Russian Revolution, 1917), in *Letopis'* (Chronicle), nos. 2–4, p. 379.
8. N. N. Sukhanov, *Zapiski o revoliutsii* (Notes on the Revolution), Berlin-Petrograd-Moscow, 1922, bk. 1, p. 19.
9. *Delo naroda,* March 15, 1917.
10. O. A. Yermansky, *Iz perezhitogo* (From My Past), Moscow-Leningrad, 1927. pp. 141, 148.

11. Merle Fainsod, *How Russia Is Ruled,* Cambridge, Mass.: Harvard University Press, 1963, p. 60.

12. W. B. Walsh, *Russia and the Soviet Union,* Ann Arbor, Mich.: University of Michigan Press, 1958, p. 370.

13. Lenin, PSS, 36:6. (CW, 27:90.)

14. Shulgin, *Dni,* pp. 136–37.

15. *Kanun revoliutsii* (The Eve of Revolution), Petrograd, 1918, p. 104.

16. *Voprosy istorii KPSS* (the magazine "Problems of CPSU History"), no. 9 (1965):81.

17. *Ibid.*

18. Sukhanov, *Zapiski,* bk. 1, p. 50.

19. Leon Trotsky, *Istoriia russkoi revoliutsii. Tom 1: Fevral'skaia revoliutsiia* (History of the Russian Revolution. Vol. 1: The February Revolution), New York: Monad Press facsimile ed., 1976, pp. 178–79. [Trotsky's *History* was first published in Russian in three parts—vol. 1, cited above, in Berlin, 1931; and vol. 2 in two parts, both Berlin, 1933. The Monad Press facsimile edition includes the three parts in one binding, each part retaining the original page numbering. Trotsky used the title *Oktiabr'skaia revoliutsiia* (The October Revolution) for both parts of his second volume in Russian. But the English edition renders part one as "Vol. 2: The Attempted Counterrevolution" and part two as "Vol. 3: The Triumph of the Soviets." A useful English-language edition, is the 1977 Pluto Press (London) paperbound edition, which has the full three volumes in one binding. In all citations from Trotsky's *History,* we have followed Max Eastman's English rendering with some minor changes for style purposes.—*Trans.*]

20. *Bol'sheviki v fevral'skoi revoliutsii 1917 g.* (The Bolsheviks in the February Revolution of 1917), Moscow, 1971, p. 142.

21. M. P. Yakubovich, *Iz zhizni idei,* pt. 1. [The author cites only the unpublished Russian memoirs, which have since been published in English as "From the History of Ideas (Part I)" in *The Samizdat Register,* New York: Norton, 1977.—*Trans.*]

22. Lenin, PSS, 30:341. (CW, 23:264.) (Emphasis in original.)

23. *Ibid.,* pp. 328–29.

24. N. K. Krupskaya, *Vospominaniia o Lenine* (Reminiscences of Lenin), Moscow, 1957, p. 271. [Compare the English-language edition, Moscow, 1959, pp. 334–35.]

25. Lenin, PSS, 49:390. (CW, 35:288.)

26. *Voprosy istorii KPSS,* no. 2 (1977):53.

27. Lenin, PSS, 36:496. (CW, 27:511.); *ibid.,* 38:393. (CW, 26:188.)

28. *Ibid.,* 34:391. (CW, 26:188.)

29. *Ibid.,* pp. 412–13.

30. Jean-François Revel, *Ni Marks i ni Khristos,* Paris, 1975, pp. 27–28. [The author cites the Russian edition of Revel's work. We have used the wording from the English edition, *Without Marx or Jesus: The American Revolution Has Begun,* New York: Doubleday, 1971, p. 13; paperback edition, New York: Dell, 1974.—*Trans.*]

31. *Novaya Rus'* (New Russia), no. 27, October 12, 1917.

32. Anin, *Revoliutsiia . . . ,* p. 203.

33. *Izvestiia TsIK* (News of the Central Executive Committee), October 20, 1917.

34. *Voprosy istorii KPSS,* no. 9 (1972):86.

35. E. F. Yerykalov, *Oktiabr'skoe vooruzhennoe vosstanie v Petrograde* (The October Armed Insurrection in Petrograd), Leningrad, 1966, pp. 303–4, 434–35, 461–62.

36. Fischer, *Zhizn' Lenina,* pp. 374–75.

37. Trotsky, *Istoriia russkoi revoliutsii. Tom II: Oktiabr'skaia revoliutsiia, chast' vtoraia* (History of the Russian Revolution. Vol. 2: The October Revolution, pt. 2.), p. 253–54. [See note 19 to this chapter—*Trans.*]

38. *Oktiabr'skaia revoliutsiia. Memuary* (The October Revolution: Memoirs), Moscow-Leningrad, 1926, pp. 50, 52.

39. Joseph Stalin, *Sochineniia* (Works), 6:62.

40. N. V. Krylenko, "Smert' staroi armii" (The Death of the Old Army), in *Voenno-istoricheskii zhurnal* (Military-Historical Journal), 1964, p. 58.

41. Marx and Engels, *Sochineniia,* 8:80–81. [See *Selected Works in Three Volumes,* Moscow, vol. 1, 1969, pp. 361–62.]

42. *Ibid.,* 33:175. [See Marx, *Selected Correspondence,* Moscow, 1956, p. 320.]

43. Lenin, PSS, 14:378–79. (CW, 12:111.)

Five. Is a "Premature" Revolution Possible?

1. Marx and Engels, *ibid.,* 13:7. [See *Selected Works in Two Volumes,* Moscow, 1955, 1:363.]

2. *Ibid.*

3. *Ibid.,* 7:422–23. [See Engels, *The Peasant War in Germany,* Moscow, 1956, pp. 138–39.]

4. *Ibid.,* 28:490–91. [See Marx and Engels, *Selected Correspondence,* Moscow, 1956, p. 94.]

5. Herzen, *Sobranie sochinenii,* 20 (bk. 2):577.

6. Marx and Engels, *ibid.,* 38:150–51.

7. *Ibid.,* p. 158. [See Marx and Engels, *Selected Correspondence,* London, 1934, p. 492.]

8. *Ibid.,* pp. 163–64. [See Marx and Engels, *Selected Correspondence,* London, 1934, p. 493.]

Six. The Position of the Mensheviks and SRs

1. From the newspaper *Yedinstvo* (Unity), no. 9, April 9, 1917.

2. Georgy V. Plekhanov, *God na Rodine* (A Year in the Homeland), vol. 1, Paris, 1921, pp. 26, 28, 30.

3. L. Martov, *Sotsialisty-revoliutsionery i proletariat* (The Socialist Revolutionaries and the Proletariat), Petrograd, 1917.

4. *Vserossiiskaia konferentsiia men'shevistskikh organizatsii RSDRP* (All-Russia Conference of the Menshevik Organizations of the Russian Social Democratic Labor Party), Petrograd, 1917, p. 46.

5. *Sotsialisty o tekushchem momente* (The Socialists on the Present Situa-

tion), Moscow, 1917, p. 268. [The congress was in Petrograd, August 19–26.—*Trans.*]

6. *Programmy russkikh politicheskikh partii.*

7. *Delo naroda,* September 1, 1917.

8. Leon Trotsky, *Fevral' skaia revoliutsiia,* pp. 256–57. [See note 19 to chapter 4 above.—*Trans.*]

9. Yakubovich, *Iz zhizni idei,* pp. 21–24. [See *Samizdat Register,* p. 163, as cited in note 21 to chapter 4, above.—*Trans.*]

10. *Ibid.,* pp. 59–60. [See *Samizdat Register,* pp. 186–87.—*Trans.*]

11. Central State Archive of the October Revolution, collection 579, shelf 1, folder 854-a, sheet 3–4. See also G. Z. Mukhin, *Sotsialisticheskaia revoliutsiia i gosudarstvo* (The Socialist Revolution and the State) [n.p., n.d.] p. 100.

12. *Pervyi Vserossiiskii s"ezd Sovetov. Stenograficheskii otchet* (First All-Russia Congress of Soviets: Stenographic Record), vol. 1, Moscow-Leningrad, 1930, p. xxiv.

13. *Proletarskaia revoliutsiia,* no. 3, (1922):29.

14. *Ibid.,* p. 30.

15. N. Zhordania, *Moia zhizn'* (My Life), pp. 77–78.

16. *Novaia zhizn'* (New Life), September 29, 1917.

17. *Yedinstvo,* October 4, 1917.

18. *Delo naroda,* October 4, 1917.

19. *Yedinstvo,* October 28 (November 10, New Style), 1917. See also Plekhanov's *God na Rodine,* vol. 2, Paris, 1921, pp. 244–48. This is the same letter that Solzhenitsyn cites in *Gulag Archipelago,* vol. 1. However, Solzhenitsyn, unlike Plekhanov, considers the socialist revolution not only to have been premature but unnecessary in general for Russia and the Russian people.

20. Plekhanov, *God na Rodine,* 1:218.

21. Leon Trotsky, *Voina i revoliutsiia* (War and Revolution), 2d ed., 1:106.

22. *Ibid.,* pp. 99–100.

23. Trotsky, *Oktiabr'skaia revoliutsiia,* pt. 1, p. 346. [See note 19 to chapter 4.—*Trans.*]

24. "Dve kontseptsii" (Two Conceptions), in *Biulleten' oppozitsii* (The Bulletin of the Opposition), nos. 12–13, June–July 1930, pp. 34–35. [Reprinted in Trotsky's *The Permanent Revolution.* See Pathfinder Press edition, New York, 1972, pp. 154–55.—*Trans.*]

Seven. The Position of the Bolsheviks

1. Lenin, PSS, 31:114. (CW, 24:22.)

2. *Ibid.,* p. 161. (CW, 24:67.)

3. *Ibid.,* p. 116. (CW, 24:23–24.)

4. *VKP(b) v rezoliutsiiakh . . .* (The CPSU in Resolutions . . .), vol. 1, Moscow, 1936, pp. 236, 343.

5. *Izvestiia* (News of the Central Executive Committee of the Petrograd Soviet), no. 63, May 11, 1917.

6. Lenin, PSS, 32:121–22. (CW, 24:440.)

7. *Ibid.,* 34:115–16. (CW, 25:281.)

8. *Ibid.,* pp. 192–93. (CW, 25:385, 386.)

9. *Ibid.,* p. 295. (CW, 26:94.)
10. *Ibid.,* 32:31. (CW, 24:360.)
11. *Ibid.,* 34:295. (CW, 26:95.)
12. *Ibid.,* p. 204. (CW, 25:370.)
13. *Ibid.,* 45:381. (CW, 33:480.)
14. Marx and Engels, *Sochineniia,* 18:57.
15. *Ibid.,* 36:363–64.
16. *Ibid.,* 20:294. [See Engels, "Socialism: Utopian and Scientific," in Marx and Engels, *Selected Works in Two Volumes,* Moscow, 1958, 2:153.—*Trans.*]
17. *Ibid.,* 19:19–20 and *passim.*
18. Lenin, PSS, 17:127. (CW, 15:138.)
19. *Ibid.,* 32:196–97. (CW, 24:514.)
20. *Ibid.,* 34:181. (CW, 25:348.)
21. S. Grigoryev, *Kakikh poriadkov dobivaiutsia sotsialisty* (What Kind of System Socialists Are Trying to Achieve), Moscow, 1917, pp. 13–14.
22. Lenin, PSS, 33:97. (CW, 25:470.)
23. *Ibid.,* pp. 100–101. (CW, 25:473–74.)

Eight. The First Few Weeks

1. *Izvestiia VTsIK* (Bulletin of the All-Russia Central Executive Committee of the Soviet), February 19, 1918.
2. Lenin, PSS, 35:63. (CW, 26:294.)
3. *Dekrety Sovetskoi vlasti* (Decrees of the Soviet Government), 1:172–73.
4. Mints, *Istoriia . . . ,* vol. 3, Moscow, 1973, p. 828.
5. P. G. Sofinov, *Ocherki istorii VChk* (Essays in the History of the Cheka), Moscow, 1960, p. 18.
6. *Novaia zhizn'* no. 158 (1917).
7. *Oktiabr'skii perevorot. Fakty i dokumenty* (The October Revolution: Facts and Documents), compiled by A. L. Popov, Petrograd, 1918, p. 244.
8. Mints, *Istoriia . . . ,* vol. 3, p. 861.
9. N. I. Podvoisky, *God 1917* (The Year 1917), Moscow, 1958, pp. 184–85.
10. *Leninskii sbornik* (Lenin Miscellany), xviii, p. 75.

Nine. The Constituent Assembly

1. *Arkhiv russkoi revoliutsii,* vol. 13, Berlin, 1924. Cited in *Oktiabr'skaia revoliutsiia* (The October Revolution), Moscow-Leningrad, 1926, pp. 332–33.
2. Lenin, PSS, 31:197. (CW, 24:99.)
3. *Novaya Rus',* October 8, 1917.
4. Lenin, PSS, 35:11. (CW, 26:247.)
5. *Ibid.,* p. 28. (CW, 26:262.)
6. *Oktiabr'skaia revoliutsiia. Memuary,* pp. 336, 337, 338.
7. K. V. Gusev, *Partiia eserov* (The SR Party), Moscow, 1975, pp. 167–68.
8. *Dekrety Sovetskoi vlasti,* vol. 1, Moscow, 1957, pp. 25–26.

9. Lenin, PSS, 35:166. (CW, 26:383.)
10. *Vtoroi s"ezd RSDRP, protokoly* (Minutes of the Second Congress of the Russian Social Democratic Labor Party), Moscow, 1959, p. 182.

Ten. The Economic Situation

1. *S"ezdy Sovetov v dokumentakh, 1917–1936* (Congresses of Soviets in Documents, 1917–1936), 1:46–47.
2. *Tretii Vserossiiskii s"ezd Sovetov* . . . (Third All-Russia Congress of Soviets . . .), Petrograd, 1918, p. 87.
3. *Istoriia sotsialisticheskoi ekonomiki SSSR* (History of the Socialist Economy of the USSR), vol. 1, Moscow, 1976, p. 194–95.
4. Lenin, PSS, 35:312. (CW, p. 503.)
5. *Dekrety Sovetskoi vlasti*, vol. 1, Moscow, 1957, pp. 453–54.
6. *Istoriia proletariata v SSSR* (History of the Proletariat in the USSR), no. 4 (16), Moscow, 1933, p. 127.
7. Iu. K. Strizhkov, *Prodovol'stvennye otriady v gody grazhdanskioi voiny i inostrannoi interventsii* (The Food-Requisitioning Detachments During the Years of Civil War and Foreign Intervention), Moscow, 1973, p. 45.
8. Lenin, PSS, 35:174–75. (CW, 26:391–93.)
9. *Dekrety Sovetskoi vlasti*, vol. 1, pp. 293–300 and *passim*.
10. *Narodnoe khoziaistvo SSSR. Statisticheskii ezhegodnik* (The Economy of the USSR: Statistical Yearbook), Moscow, 1972, p. 9.

Eleven. The Program of Economic Construction

1. Lenin, PSS, 35:269. (CW, 26:455.)
2. *Ibid.*, 36:172–73. (CW, 27:242.)
3. *Otchet Narkomprosa IX s"ezdu Sovetov* (Report of the People's Commissar of Enlightenment to the Ninth Congress of Soviets), Moscow, 1921, p. 4.
4. Lenin, PSS, 44:151. (CW, 33:58.)
5. *Kommunist* (The Communist), organ of the "Left Communist" faction, March 8, 1918.
6. Lenin, PSS, 36:48, 65–66. (CW, 27:131, 147–48.)
7. *Ibid.*, 35:250–51. (CW, 26:449.)
8. *Protokoly zasedanii VTsIK, IV sozyv, 1918* (Minutes of the Sessions of the Fourth All-Russia Central Executive Committee, 1918), pp. 112–23.
9. Lenin, PSS, 36:74. (CW, 27:156.)
10. *Ibid.*, 44:199, 197. (CW, 33:88, 87.)
11. *Voprosy filosofii* (Problems of Philosophy), no. 6 (1976):27.
12. Lenin, PSS, 33:101–2. (CW, 25:473–74.)
13. *Ibid.*, 43:237. (CW, 32:341.)
14. *Voprosy istorii KPSS*, no. 11 (1975):6–7.
15. *Izvestiia Narodnogo komissariata po prodovol'stviiu* (News of the People's Commissariat of Food Supply), Moscow, no. 1 (1918):9.

16. *Dekrety Sovetskoi vlasti,* 2 (Moscow, 1959):29–30.
17. O. Kuperman, *Sotsial'no-ekonomicheskie formy promyshlennosti v SSSR* (The Social and Economic Forms of Industry in the USSR), Moscow-Leningrad, 1929, p. 97.
18. *Istoriia sotsialisticheskoi ekonomiki v SSSR* (History of the Socialist Economy in the USSR), 1 (Moscow, 1976):203.
19. N. D. Kondratiev, *Rynok khlebov* (The Grain Market), Moscow, 1922, pp. 197, 198.
20. N. A. Orlov, *Prodovol'stvennoe delo v Rossii* (The Food Supply System in Russia), Moscow, 1919, p. 19.
21. Kondratiev, *Rynok khlebov,* p. 201. (Kondratiev was falsely accused in 1929–1930 of organizing a mythical "Working Peasants' Party." He died a victim of government repression.—R.M.)
22. E. Ambartsumov, *Vverkh k vershine* (Toward the Summit), Moscow, 1974, p. 61.
23. *Dekrety Sovetskoi vlasti,* 2:187.
24. Lenin, PSS, 36:217–18. (CW, 27:318–19.)

Twelve. The Masses Turn Away

1. Lenin, PSS, 40:16–17. (CW, 30:268.)
2. N. V. Ruban, *Oktiabr'skaia revoliutsiia i krakh men'shevizma* (The October Revolution and the Fall of Menshevism), Moscow, 1972, p. 355.
3. *Novyi luch* (The New Ray), Petrograd, December 1, 1917.
4. Spirin, *Klassy i partii . . .* , p. 174.
5. Lenin, PSS, 39:299. (CW, 30:134.)
6. *Ibid.,* p. 40. (CW, 29:465.)
7. Fischer, *Zhizn' Lenina,* pp. 318—19. [Compare the English edition, p. 213. See note 14 of Chapter 3 above.—*Trans.*]
8. N. Ustrialov, *Pod znakom revoliutsii,* Harbin, 1925, p. 80.
9. Joseph Stalin, *Sochineniia,* 4:116.
10. *Ibid.,* pp. 123–24.
11. V. V. Anikeev, *Deiatel'nost' TsK RSDRP(b)-RKP(b) v 1917–1918 gg.* (The Activity of the Central Committee of the Bolshevik Party in 1917–1918), Moscow, 1974, p. 286.
12. *Ibid.,* p. 295.
13. Ivan Maisky, *Demokraticheskaia kontrrevoliutsiia* (The Democratic Counterrevolution), Moscow, 1920.
14. Lenin, PSS, 38:388. (CW, 29:390–91.)
15. *Dekrety Sovetskoi vlasti,* 2(Moscow, 1959):261–62.
16. Lenin, PSS, 50:82–83. (CW, 44:86.) (Emphasis in original.)
17. *Pravda,* June 1, 1918.
18. Konstantin Paustovsky, *Sobranie sochinenii* (Collected Works), 3 (Moscow, 1957):629–30.
19. Lenin, PSS, 36:316. (CW, 27:356.)
20. *Ibid.,* pp. 503–504. (CW, 27:519.)
21. *Sobranie uzakonenii i rasporiazhenii rabochego i krest'ianskogo pravitel'stva* (Collection of the Legislation and Regulations Issued by the Workers' and Peasants' Government), no. 44(1918):433.

22. Lenin, PSS, 50:106. (CW, 35:336.)
23. *Dekrety Sovetskoi vlasti,* 2:430–31.
24. N. Kondratiev, *Rynok khlebov,* p. 124.

Thirteen. The Poor Peasants' Committees

1. Strizhkov, *Prodovol'stvennye otriady.* . . .
2. *Voprosy istorii KPSS,* no. 7 (1975):97.
3. Lenin, PSS, 37:354. (CW, 28:340.)
4. Ambartsumov, *Vverkh k vershine,* p. 108.
5. *Istoricheskaia entsiklopediia* (Historical Encyclopedia), 8, (Moscow, 1965):519.
6. K. V. Gusev, *Krakh partii levykh eserov* (The Collapse of the Left SR Party), Moscow, 1963, p. 90.
7. Spirin, *Klassy i partii* . . . , p. 163.
8. "Pravda o chekhoslovatskom korpuse" (The Truth About the Czech Legion), in the collection *Marksizm-leninizm—edinoe internatsional'noe uchenie* (Marxism-Leninism—A Single International Doctrine), Moscow, 1968, issue 1, p. 428.
9. V. Maksakov and A. Turunov, *Khronika grazhdanskoi voiny v Sibiri. Sbornik dokumentov* (Chronicle of the Civil War in Siberia: A Documentary Collection), Moscow, 1926.
10. Lenin, PSS, 39:401; and 40:16. (CW, 30:219; and 30:268.)

Some Conclusions

1. Lenin, PSS, 32:306–7. (CW, 25:57–58.)
2. *Ibid.,* 34:214–15. (CW, 26:214–15.) Lenin cites an article from the right-wing newspaper *Rech'* (Speech), no. 210.—R.M.
3. *Ibid.,* p. 223. (CW, 26:37.)
4. *Iz glubiny. Sbornik statei o russkoi revoliutsii.* (From the Depths: A Collection of Articles on the Russian Revolution), Paris, 1967, pp. 199–200.
5. Revel, *Ni Marks i ni Khristos,* p. 134. [Compare the English edition, p. 123. See chapter 4, note 30 above.—*Trans.*]
6. Lenin, PSS, 44:221–23. (CW, 33:109–11.)

Glossary

Alekseev, Mikhail V. (1857–1918)—tsarist general, chief of general staff, 1915–1916; fought against Soviet government in civil war, with Denikin.

Alexander I (1777–1825)—tsar of Russia, 1801–1825; led the Russian armies in the wars against Napoleon.

Alexandra Fyodorovna Romanov (1872–1918)—tsarina, wife of Nicholas II; a member of the German princely house of Hesse, she was raised in London; married Nicholas in 1894; executed with the rest of the family.

Anarcho-Communists—a small political group in Russia at the time of the revolution, holding views intermediate between anarchism and communism.

Antonov-Ovseenko, Vladimir A. (1883–1939)—member of the RSDLP from 1903, joined the Bolsheviks in May 1917; played a leading role in the Military Revolutionary Committee and the October insurrection; prominent in the Red Army in the civil war; in the 1920s, a leader of the Left Opposition; capitulated to Stalin in 1928; appointed Soviet consul to Spain in 1936 during the Spanish civil war; called back to Moscow in 1937 and soon arrested; shot after refusing to sign a false confession to be used in a show trial.

April Theses—See Lenin's article containing the Theses ("The Tasks of the Proletariat in the Present Revolution," CW, 24:19–26). In particular Lenin opposed any support to the Provisional Government, advocating instead a republic of Soviets. The Theses included a number of transitional and tactical proposals toward this end.

Armand, Inessa (1875–1920)—Bolshevik; close associate of Lenin during World War I; held responsible positions in the Soviet government.

Arshin—Russian unit of length equivalent to 28 inches.

Avksentiev, Nikolai D. (1878–1943)—Right SR; minister of the interior in Provisional Government, July–August; chairman of the Central Executive Committee of Peasants' Soviets; helped organize an anti-Soviet government in Siberia; emigrated in 1918; active in opposition to the Soviet Union as an émigré.

Babeuf, François (pseudonym, Gracchus) (1760–1797)—French revolutionist who called for economic as well as political equality; organized a secret society in 1795–1796 which advocated egalitarian communism and came to be called the "Conspiracy of Equals." The organization was betrayed to the police and Babeuf was executed after a long trial.

Bagmen, or *Bag Traders*—the Russian word (singular, *meshochnik*) is derived from *meshok* meaning "sack, bag." These were individuals who traveled about the countryside buying up food from the peasants and carrying it in sacks to the towns for sale at very high prices; also, peasants who brought their grain to the towns to sell in the same way. The practice was called *meshochnichestvo* ("bag trading").

Baltic fleet—the sailors of the Baltic fleet stationed near Petrograd, particularly at the naval fortress of Kronstadt, were famous for their revolutionary militancy in 1917 and in the civil war.

Battleship Potemkin—the sailors of this ship of Russia's Black Sea fleet mutinied in June 1905 in the midst of strikes and street fighting in Odessa; they offered their support to Odessa's fighting workers, but were forced to flee to Romania when their mutiny failed to spread. A celebrated film by Sergei Eisenstein deals with the event.

Bebel, August (1840–1913)—a founder and central leader of the German Social Democratic Party; worked closely with Marx and Engels; leading figure in the Second International before World War I.

Bellers, John (1654–1725)—British economist, Quaker, social reformer; made a number of proposals for a society that would be free of poverty and inequality of wealth.

Beneš, Eduard (1884–1948)—Czechoslovak nationalist leader; close associate of Masaryk, whom he succeeded as president of Czechoslovakia, 1935–1938; resigned and emigrated to the United States after Munich crisis; after World War II, reelected president of Czechoslovakia, 1946–1948; resigned in June 1948, shortly after Communists took power.

Berdyaev, Nikolai A. (1874–1948)—advocated a philosophy of mysticism and "creativity" after 1905, having been a Social Democrat before that; expelled from Soviet Russia in 1922; lived as an émigré in France; achieved fame as an opponent of Marxism and revolution and an exponent of the Russian idealist tradition.

Black Hundreds—extreme reactionary groups in Russia from about 1905 to 1917 (forerunners of fascism). They were originally organized with the tsarist authorities' approval and complicity to assassinate radicals and carry out pogroms against Jews.

Blanqui, Louis Auguste (1805–1881)—French revolutionary; led militant secret organizations; took part in revolutions of 1830, 1848, and 1871; a utopian communist.

Bolsheviks and *Mensheviks*—the Bolsheviks were originally a faction of the Russian Social Democratic Labor Party (RSDLP), formed at its Second Congress in 1903. The Russian term meant "majority supporters," from the fact that the Bolsheviks, led by Lenin, won a crucial vote against the Mensheviks ("minority supporters") during that congress. The Bolsheviks were the more radical wing and favored an independent policy by the working-class, which was to take the leadership of the democratic revolution in a bloc with the peasantry—against the liberals as well as the monarchy. The Mensheviks favored cooperation with the liberals on the grounds that Russia would have to go through a relatively long stage of capitalist development. By 1917 both factions actually functioned as separate parties.

Bonch-Bruevich, Vladimir D. (1873–1955)—founding member of RSDLP, later close associate of Lenin; administrative officer in Soviet government, 1917–1920; held responsible post in the Soviet Union until his death.

Brest-Litovsk Treaty—separate peace treaty between Soviet Russia and the Central Powers (Germany, Austria-Hungary, and their allies) signed on March 3, 1918; among the terms of the treaty were that Poland, Lithuania, the Baltic states, and parts of Byelorussia, and Ukraine be placed under German control, that Soviet troops be withdrawn from Finland and Ukraine, and that Soviet Russia pay a large indemnity and demobilize its army. After the signing of the treaty the Central Powers occupied all of Ukraine and set up a puppet government there.

Bunin, Ivan Alekseevich (1870–1953)—Russian poet and prose writer; awarded Nobel Prize for literature in 1933; opposed Russian revolution; lived in exile in France from 1919 on.

Cadet Party, or *Cadets* (abbreviation for Constitutional Democrats)—

liberal capitalist party, founded in 1905, which favored a constitutional monarchy or republic for Russia and was the party of the middle bourgeoisie, bourgeois intellectuals, and progressive landowners; it was headed by Miliukov (q.v.).

Canton commune—uprising in Canton, China, December 11–13, 1927, led by Chinese Communists and representatives of the Comintern; the insurgents initially won control of the city and announced a revolutionary Soviet government; the uprising faced tremendous odds (5,000 rebels against 50,000 government troops), had not been prepared, and had little time to win support from workers and peasants; it came in the wake of a series of defeats of the Chinese Communists by Chiang Kai-shek in 1927; the hasty uprising was apparently ordered by Stalin with the aim of bolstering his position against opposition critics in the Russian Communist Party who blamed his policies for the defeats in China.

Chaikovsky, Nikolai V. (1850–1926)—Narodnik leader of the 1870s and 1880s; prominent as an émigré; became leader of the People's Socialists; returned to Russia in 1917; held patriotic, defensist positions; opposed the October revolution; headed an anti-Soviet government in northern Russia during the civil war; emigrated in 1919.

Cheka—the first Soviet state-security organization, 1917–1922; the word is derived from the Russian initials "Ch" and "K" in Chrezvychaynaya Kommissia (Extraordinary Commission).

Chernov, Viktor M. (1876–1952)—SR leader and theoretician; minister of agriculture in coalition cabinets of the Provisional Government, May—September; headed an anti-Bolshevik government in Samara in 1918; emigrated in 1920.

Chicherin, Georgy V. (1872–1936)—Soviet diplomat; served in the tsarist diplomatic service; supported SRs in 1905–1907 revolution; forced to emigrate from Russia; returned in January 1918, joined Bolsheviks; commissar of foreign affairs, 1918–1930.

Chkheidze, Nikolai S. (1864–1926)—Menshevik head of Social Democratic group in the Duma; first president of the Petrograd Soviet; president of the Constituent Assembly of Georgia in 1918; emigrated in 1921.

Comintern—The Communist, or Third, International, founded in Moscow in 1919, was supported by socialist and communist groups who had opposed World War I and who favored more radical and revolutionary methods than those followed by the Second, or Social Democratic, International. The Russian Bolsheviks exercised a dominant influence in the Comintern from the start. Under Stalin, in the late 1920s and the 1930s, the Comintern tended to be an arm of Soviet diplomacy rather than an alliance of revolutionary parties of different countries. Stalin dissolved the Comintern in 1943, during the Soviet government's "anti-Hitler coalition" with the United States and Britain against Nazi Germany and Japan.

Communards—in the *Paris Commune of 1871*—revolt of the people of Paris at the end of the Franco-Prussian war, March 18—May 28, 1871; the Communards (supporters of the Commune) established their own highly democratic government, which projected radical social reforms. Considered by Marxists the first workers' government, the Commune was crushed by troops of the French government based at Versailles.

Compromisers—term used for the moderate socialist parties, especially the SRS and Mensheviks, who held back from radical or socialist measures in order to maintain a coalition with the Cadets and other liberals in the Provisional Government.

Constituent Assembly—nationwide representative body to decide on the new governmental system after the overthrow of the monarchy. See chapter 9 for a detailed discussion of the conflicting policies in 1917—1918 in regard to such an assembly.

Council of Ministers—topmost executive body of the tsarist government, responsible only to the tsar and presided over by him.

CPSU—Communist Party of the Soviet Union—traces its origins back to the formation in 1903 of the Bolshevik faction of the Russian Social Democratic Labor Party (RSDLP). (*See also* Bolsheviks and Mensheviks.) In 1917 the Bolsheviks called their party the RSDLP (Bolshevik). In 1918 the name was changed to Russian Communist Party (Bolshevik). In 1925, after the formation of the Union of Soviet Socialist Republics (USSR), the party became the All-Union Communist Party (Bolshevik). In 1952 "Bolshevik" was dropped and the present name adopted.

Crises of 1928–1932; 1953–1954; 1963–1964—the period 1928–1932 was that of forced collectivization, with its resulting drastic losses in agricultural production and famine, and the period of crash industrialization, with the resulting dislocations in industrial production; 1953–1954 was marked by agricultural difficulties resulting from Stalin's policies in the last years of his rule; his successors instituted a series of reforms in agricultural policy in an attempt to overcome the crisis. In particular a campaign was begun to cultivate virgin lands in Kazakhstan and Siberia; 1963–1964 was again a period of agricultural crisis, this time resulting from Khrushchev's policies; in 1963 there was a particularly poor harvest; the discontent produced by these difficulties contributed to the ouster of Khrushchev in October 1964.

Dan, Fyodor I. (1871–1947)—early leader of the RSDLP, Menshevik; member of first Executive Committee of the Petrograd Soviet in 1917; worked in a Soviet commissariat after October; left USSR in 1922; active in the émigré Menshevik group.

December armed uprising—see Revolution of 1905–1907.

December 1905—see Revolution of 1905–1907.

Decembrist revolt of 1825—revolt by Russian officers, who had formed secret revolutionary societies in the wake of the Napoleonic wars. It was timed to coincide with the coronation of a new tsar, Nicholas I, in December 1825; its aim was a constitutional government and land reform. The revolt was crushed within a few days.

Decree on Peace and *Decree on Land*—the first two decrees of the Soviet government, written by Lenin, and adopted by the Second All-Russia Congress of Soviets on October 26, 1917. The Decree on Peace called for a just, democratic peace without annexations or indemnities, without making this a condition for the opening of peace negotiations. It urged the speediest possible peace negotiations and an armistice of at least three months in the meantime. It also called for an end to secret diplomacy and announced the intention of the Soviet government to publish the secret treaties agreed to by the previous regimes. The content of the Decree on Land is described in chapter 8. (The wording of both decrees may be found in Lenin, CW, 26:249–61.)

Defeatists—see Defensists.

Defensists, internationalists, defeatists—Among socialists there were three main positions on World War I: defensists supported participation by their own country in the war on the grounds of "defense of the fatherland"; internationalists opposed the war on the basis of the traditional socialist position that the workers of different countries were brothers and should not kill each other for the benefit of the ruling capitalist classes; defeatists (who were also internationalists) favored the defeat of 'their own" capitalist government as a lesser evil, since victory would strengthen that government. (Some internationalists called for the ruling governments to negotiate peace; defeatists, notably the Bolsheviks, called on the workers to "turn the imperialist war into a civil war.")

Democratic Conference and *Council of the Republic* (or *Pre-Parliament*)—The Democratic Conference was a conference called by the Menshevik-SR leadership of the VTsIK in September 1917 to consider the question of governmental power (in the wake of the Kornilov revolt and its suppression). It was held September 14—22 in Petrograd and called for the establishment of a Pre-Parliament (or caretaker Council of the Republic) to act as a deliberative and consultative body under the Provisional Government until the convening of a Constituent Assembly. The Pre-Parliament convened on October 7 and was still in session at the time of the October revolution; it was dispersed during the October revolution (on October 25).

Denikin, Anton I. (1872–1947)—tsarist general in 1917; one of the chief White leaders in the civil war, 1918–1920; became head of the *Volunteer Army,* to which many former tsarist officers rallied, based in the Kuban and Northern Caucasus regions (southeastern European Russia); in 1919, led a major drive to capture Moscow, but was defeated; resigned as head of White army and, in 1920, emigrated.

Deutsch, Lev G. (1855–1941)—a founder, with Plekhanov, of the Emancipation of Labor Group; RSDLP leader; became a Menshevik; defensist in World War I; an editor of Plekhanov's *Yedinstvo* in 1917; left politics after the October revolution; edited Plekhanov's literary legacy and wrote on the history of the Russian radical movement.

Directory (Council of Five)—faced with the crisis of Kornilov's revolt, Kerensky proposed the establishment of a Directory, a cabinet with only five ministers, having exceptional powers. This was a step toward the assumption of dictatorial powers by a single individual. The Central Executive Committee of the Soviets opposed the idea at first, but later accepted it. The Directory was formed on September 1.

Dual power—the existence of two bodies claiming to exercise governmental authority within a single state; a situation that usually leads to, or accompanies, civil war.

Dukhonin, Nikolai N. (1876–1917)—tsarist general; made chief of staff under Kerensky after the arrest of Kornilov, September 10, 1917; assumed role of commander in chief of the Russian armies on November 3, after Kerensky went into hiding; removed from his post by the Soviet government for refusal to follow orders; arrested November 20, 1917; killed by angry soldiers.

Duma (officially, the State Duma)—parliamentary body granted by Nicholas II in the midst of the 1905 revolution. It had limited powers, was based on a very restricted suffrage, and could be dissolved unilaterally by the tsar. Four Dumas were elected, one in 1906, two in 1907, the last in 1912 (it was still in existence when revolution broke out in February 1917). The First Duma was dissolved in July 1906, ten weeks after it was convened.

Durnovo, Pyotr N. (1845–1915)—tsarist official and rightist politician; minister of interior, 1905–1906, in charge of harsh measures to suppress revolution; member of the tsar's State Council from 1906 on.

Dybenko, Pavel Ye. (1889–1938)—Bolshevik, head of Tsentrobalt, the central organization of the revolutionary Baltic sailors in 1917; member of the Military Revolutionary Committee that made the October revolution; played a key role in the civil war, 1918–1920; Red Army commander from 1928 until his arrest and execution in Stalin's purge of the military in 1938.

Dzerzhinsky, Felix E. (1877–1926)—Polish revolutionary, member of RSDLP Central Committee from 1906; after the October revolution, president of the Cheka; after the civil war, a close supporter of Stalin.

Entente—the alliance between Russia, France, and England against Germany and Austria-Hungary, especially during World War I.

February revolution—the overthrow of Tsar Nicholas II, and of the Romanov monarchy, came as the result of mass demonstrations by workers in Petrograd, which were joined by the soldiers of the Petrograd garrison. Demonstrations began on February 23, 1917, going by the Russian calendar; by the Western calendar the date was March 8 (International Women's Day—women workers began the demonstrations); thus, Western writers sometimes refer to this as the March revolution. Demonstrations continued through February 27, by which time all power in the city was in the hands of the rebel workers and soldiers. A Petrograd Soviet of Workers' Deputies and a Provisional Committee of the State Duma were formed on that day, as new (and rival) seats of authority. Marxists often call the February revolution a bourgeois revolution because the Provisional Government which issued from it was dominated by political parties representing the interests of Russia's capitalist class.

Fifth All-Russia Congress of Soviets—held in Moscow, July 4–10, 1918.

Fighting outside Petrograd—after the October revolution Kerensky tried to bring Cossack troops under General Krasnov against Petrograd; stopped by Soviet forces after heavy fighting at Pulkovo Heights outside Petrograd, on October 30, 1917; Krasnov's troops declined to fight any more; the general was arrested and Kerensky went into hiding. (See p. 178 of text.)

Finland Station—railroad station in Petrograd where Lenin arrived from exile on April 3 and gave his first, brief speech to the revolutionary public.

First All-Russia Congress of Soviets—held in Petrograd June 3–24, 1917.

Fourier, Charles (1772–1837)—French socialist and reformer; advocated organization of society into cooperative units called *phalansteries,* each meeting all the social and industrial needs of its members.

Frederiks, Count Vladimir (1838–1922)—Finnish nobleman who was the tsar's minister of court, in charge of protocol.

General Army Committee—the overall army committee uniting all the committees elected by soldiers in the various military units after the February revolution.

Glebov-Avilov, Nikolai P. (1887–1942)—joined Bolsheviks in 1904; trade union leader in Petrograd in 1917; commissar of posts and telegraph in first Soviet government; later a party leader in Leningrad; joined opposition to Stalin in 1925 but capitulated in 1928.

Goremykin, Ivan L. (1839–1917)—tsarist official, premier briefly in summer of 1905 and again in the first period of World War I, 1914–1916.

Gotz, Abram R. (1882–1940)—a leader of the SR Party, and of the Right SRs in 1917 and after; elected chairman of the VTsIK in June 1917; opposed the October revolution; arrested in 1920 and tried by the Soviet government in 1922; subsequently amnestied, worked in Siberia, 1925–1936; arrested again in connection with the Moscow show trials.

Guchkov, Aleksandr I. (1862–1936)—prominent Moscow industrialist, a founder and leader of the Octobrist Party; became first minister of war in the Provisional Government, March–May 1917; emigrated in 1918.

Hectare—a unit of land measure equivalent to 2.47 acres.

Herzen, Aleksandr I. (1812–1870)—liberal-socialist critic and editor; after Siberian exile as a young man and participation in the ferment among Russian intellectuals of the 1840s, emigrated in 1847; lived in France and England; founded the first free Russian press abroad; published the journal *Kolokol* (The Bell) attacking tsarism and exerted significant influence on the Russian radical and Narodnik movements which emerged in the 1860s.

Internationalists—see Defensists.

Ivan the Terrible—see Peter the Great.

Izgoyev, Aleksandr S. (1872–c.1939)—right-wing Cadet author; expelled from Soviet Union in 1922.

Izvestia (News)—daily newspaper of the Petrograd Soviet; began publication on February 28, 1917; after the election of the first VTsIK, became the organ of both the VTsIK and the Petrograd Soviet; controlled by the Mensheviks and SRs from February until the October revolution; then became the official organ of the Soviet government.

January 1905 demonstration—see Revolution of 1905–1907.

"July Congress"—see Sixth Congress of the Bolshevik Party.

July demonstrations—spontaneous, semi-insurrectional outpouring of armed workers, sailors, and soldiers in opposition to the war and the policies of the Provisional Government (July 3 and 4); followed by government attempt to stamp out Bolshevism.

June demonstration—the SR and Menshevik leaders of the First All-Russia Congress of Soviets called a demonstration for June 18, 1917, to show support for the Provisional Government and its preparations for an offensive against the Germans and Austrians. The Bolsheviks organized mass participation by discontented workers and soldiers in this demonstration, which proved to be overwhelmingly hostile to the policies of the Provisional Government; most of the 500,000 demonstrators carried banners with Bolshevik slogans, including "End the War" and "All Power to the Soviets."

June offensive—offensive launched by the Provisional Government, with Kerensky as minister of war, against the Austrian and German lines. It began on June 18 and was successful at first, but the Germans soon turned it back, made a major breakthrough, and caused the Russians to retreat in disorder, with casualties of about 60,000 in twenty days, June 18–July 6.

Kaledin, Aleksei M. (1861–1918)—tsarist general; leader of the Don

Cossacks, among whom he organized a counterrevolutionary revolt after the October revolution; defeated in January 1918, he shot himself.

Kamkov, Boris D. (1885–1938), SR leader; during World War I, an internationalist; in left wing of SRs during 1917; member of Central Committee of Left SR Party; helped organize the Left SR revolt of July 1918; sentenced to three years in prison; later worked as a statistician; a defendant in Stalin's show trial in Moscow in 1938; executed.

Kautsky, Karl (1854–1938), leading Marxist theoretician; influential figure in the Social Democratic parties of Austria and Germany; after Engels' death in 1895, generally regarded as the most authoritative Marxist in the Second International; in World War I, took a pacifist but not defeatist position; became foreign secretary of the German Social Democratic government briefly after 1918; moved to Vienna in 1924; opposed the October revolution and wrote a number of works attacking it.

Kerensky, Aleksandr F. (1881–1970)—prominent as a radical lawyer before World War I; Trudovik deputy in the Duma, 1912–1917; joined the SRs in 1917; first socialist to join the Provisional Government, in which he played an increasingly important role through 1917, becoming premier and "supreme commander in chief" in September; deposed by the October revolution; fled from Russia, and lived in exile in France and the United States.

Kolchak, Aleksandr V. (1874–1920)—tsarist admiral; headed anti-Bolshevik military dictatorship in Siberia, 1918–1920; defeated and executed by the Bolsheviks.

Kolegaev, Andrei L. (1887–1937)—Left SR leader; commissar of agriculture in Bolshevik–Left SR coalition government; broke with Left SRs after their July 1918 uprising; joined Bolsheviks; held responsible posts in civil war and after; arrested and killed in Stalin's purges.

Kondratiev, Nikolai D. (1892–193?)—Russian economist; professor at the Soviet Agricultural Academy and head of the Business Research Institute of Moscow after the October revolution. His theory of fifty-year, self-adjusting economic cycles provoked wide controversy in the 1920s. In 1930 he was arrested on fabricated charges; died in prison.

Kornilov, Lavr G. (1870–1918)—tsarist general, in command of Petrograd district after February; commanded Russian forces against Austria in June; made commander in chief by Kerensky on July 18; led revolt against Kerensky, August 25–September 1, but was defeated and arrested; escaped after October; led a White army in the Don and Kuban area, killed in battle.

Krasnov, Pyotr N. (1869–1947)—tsarist general; tried to suppress the October revolution in Petrograd at Kerensky's request; led rebellion against Soviet rule in Don Cossack region, 1918–1919; resigned and went into exile in Germany.

Krivoshein, Aleksandr V. (1857–1921)—tsarist official; close collaborator with Stolypin in agrarian policies; minister of agriculture, 1908–1915; resigned from tsarist government in 1915; actively opposed October revolution, heading a White government in the Crimea in 1920; fled to France after the Soviet victory in the civil war.

Kronstadt revolt—The Kronstadt naval base in the Gulf of Finland, dominating the harbor of Petrograd, was the site in March 1921 of a revolt by sailors of the Black Sea fleet against the Bolshevik regime. The rebels called for "free Soviets," not dominated by political parties, and opposed many features of war communism, such as the ban on trade and the requisitioning of grain. The Bolsheviks suppressed the uprising, but in its wake granted the concessions embodied in the New Economic Policy (NEP).

Krupskaya, Nadezhda K. (1869–1939)—participated in Marxist workers organization in St. Petersburg in early 1890s; married Lenin, 1896; worked with him in leading bodies of the RSDLP and Bolshevik Party; after October 1917 held prominent Soviet posts, especially in education.

Krylenko, Nikolai V. (1885–1938)—active as a Bolshevik from 1904; first people's commissar of war, 1917–1918; chief state prosecutor for major political trials, 1918–1931; commissar of justice of the RSFSR, 1931–1936; arrested in 1937 and shot without trial.

Kulak, middle peasant, poor peasant—Russian Marxist terms specifying class differentiation in the countryside. The kulak (literally, a "fist") was a wealthy peasant who rented land from others, employed hired agricultural labor, and produced on a relatively large scale for the market. The middle peasant (*seredniak*) had average-size holdings, mostly worked by family labor, and sold some surplus on the market. The poor peasant (*bedniak*) did not have enough land to feed his family and usually had to borrow or hire himself out.

Kutuzov, Mikhail I. (1754–1813)—Russian general, commanded the Russian armies in the wars against Napoleon.

Labor standard—(in Russian, *trudovaia norma*) the amount of land that could be tilled by a peasant family without hiring outside labor; contrasted with the consumption standard (in Russian, *potrebitelskaia norma*), the minimum amount of land needed by a peasant family to feed all its members.

Lafargue, Paul (1842–1911)—French socialist leader and theoretician; worked closely with Marx and Engels; married Karl Marx's daughter Laura; author of numerous books and pamphlets on political, economic, philosophical, social, and literary topics from a historical materialist standpoint.

Lake Baskunchak—lake with extensive salt deposits, near the Caspian Sea, northeast of Astrakhan; it furnishes as much as one-fourth of all Soviet salt production. The salt extraction processes were mechanized under the Soviet regime in 1930.

Lander, Karl I. (1883–1937)—active as a Bolshevik from 1905; commissar of state control, 1918–1919; held responsible Soviet government posts, 1920–1925.

Lieber, Mikhail I. (1880–1937)—right-wing Menshevik leader; defensist during World War I; member of first VTsIK; held minor posts in Soviet economic administration in the 1920s; executed in Stalin's purges.

Lobov, Semyon S. (1888–1937)—joined Bolsheviks in 1913; active in Petrograd party organizations; Left Communist at time of Brest treaty; held leading posts in the Cheka, 1918–1920; and various Soviet government posts thereafter; died a victim of Stalin's purges.

Lomov-Oppokov, Georgy I. (1888–1938)—joined Bolsheviks in 1903; party leader in Moscow in 1917; commissar of justice in first Soviet government; later an official in Soviet economic institutions; died in prison, a victim of Stalin's purges.

Lunacharsky, Anatoly V. (1875–1933)—joined Bolsheviks in 1904; left them in 1908 over philosophical and tactical differences; rejoined Bolsheviks in 1917; commissar of education, 1917–1929; held prominent Soviet government posts; he was also a dramatist and wrote widely on art, culture, history, and politics.

Luxemburg, Rosa (1871–1919)—leader of the left wing in the German Social Democratic Party; jailed in Germany for most of World War I because of her antiwar activity; helped form the Spartacus League, which in 1918 became the Communist Party of Germany; assassinated during an insurrectional strike in Berlin in January 1919.

Lvov, Prince Georgy E. (1861–1925)—Cadet leader; premier of the

Provisional Government, February–July 1917; after the October revolution emigrated to France, where from 1918 to 1920 he headed an anti-Soviet émigré organization.

Lyons—armed uprisings by weavers in November–December 1831 and April 1834, with the aim of establishing a republic with democratic rights as well as protesting harsh conditions in the weaving industry and the banning of workers' associations; first revolt suppressed by government troops after two weeks, second within a week; regarded by Marxists as among the first instances of revolutionary action by workers in the modern era.

Maisky, Ivan M. (1884–   ), Soviet historian and diplomat; leading Menshevik at the time of the revolution; after October, held a post in an anti-Bolshevik government; joined Soviet side in 1919; held important Soviet diplomatic posts in the 1920s; Soviet ambassador to London, 1932–1943; deputy commissar of foreign affairs, 1943–1946; his memoirs published in the post-Stalin era revealed many facts suppressed earlier.

Maklakov, Vasily A. (1869–1957)—prominent lawyer and a leader of the Cadet Party; member of the Duma 1907–1917; made ambassador to France by the Provisional Government; opposed October, and remained in exile after 1917.

Martov, L. (pseudonym of Yuly Osipovich Tsederbaum—1873–1923)—a leader of the early RSDLP; an editor of *Iskra;* one of the central Menshevik leaders from 1903 on; headed the Menshevik Internationalists, 1914–1918; opposed the October revolution; emigrated in 1921; active in the émigré Menshevik group.

Masaryk, Tomáš (1850–1937), Czechoslovak nationalist leader, writer and philosopher; became president of the revolutionary Czechoslovak National Council during World War I; with the winning of Czechoslovak national independence he became the president of Czechoslovakia, 1918–1935.

Mayakovsky, Vladimir V. (1893–1930)—Russian Futurist poet; enthusiastically supported the October revolution and Soviet regime; considered the "poet of the revolution"; had difficulties with the literary bureaucracy in the later 1920s; committed suicide.

Menshevik Defensists—those Mensheviks who supported the war with the argument that the homeland had to be defended; opposed to the Menshevik Internationalists. See also *Defensists, defeatists, internationalists.*

Menshevik Internationalists—during World War I and the Russian revolution, a group of left Mensheviks led by Martov; they were in agreement with the Bolsheviks on a number of issues in 1917.

Mensheviks—see Bolsheviks.

Michael Alexandrovich, Grand Duke (1878–1918)—brother of Nicholas II, to whom Nicholas abdicated but who, on March 3, 1917, declined the throne; executed.

Middle peasant—see Kulak.

Military coup in Omsk—in November 1918 the anti-Bolshevik government of Siberia, the Directory, consisting of SRs and liberals, was overthrown and Kolchak (q.v.) installed as dictator.

Military Revolutionary Committee—established by the Petrograd Soviet in early October 1917 (after the Bolsheviks had won a majority in the Soviet). It asserted that no troop movements could be made in the capital without its permission. The insurrection of October 24–25 giving all power to the Soviets was organized through this body. See also October revolution.

Miliukov, Pavel N. (1859–1943)—Russian historian and politician; central leader of the Cadet Party; foreign minister of the first Provisional Government, February–April; cooperated with Whites in civil war; later a leader of anti-Soviet émigrés; edited a Russian paper in Paris, 1921–1940.

Miliutin, Vladimir P. (1884–1937)—member of RSDLP, at first a Menshevik; joined Bolsheviks in 1910; commissar of agriculture in first Soviet government; deputy chairman of Vesenkha, 1918–1921; worked for Comintern, 1922–1924; held important posts in 1920s and 1930s; died a victim of Stalin's purges.

"Model Peasant Mandate on the Land" (*obshchii krest'ianskii nakaz*), also called the "model decree"—a general summary of mandates, or sets of instruction (*nakazy*), brought by peasant deputies from 242 localities to the First All-Russia Congress of Peasants' Deputies, held in Petrograd May 4–28. The mandates reflected the main demands of the peasants in the deputies' home areas.

More, Sir Thomas (1478–1535)—English statesman, Lord Chancellor, 1529–1532; humanist writer; his *Utopia* was one of the earliest descriptions of an ideal communistic society.

Morelly—eighteenth-century French writer who published his works anonymously; nothing certain is known of his life; his writings, in the form of legal codes, advocated abolition of private property, centralized accounting and distribution, and work according to one's ability.

Morozov, Nikolai (1854–1946)—Narodnik leader of the 1870s and 1880s; later prominent as a scientist; active supporter of the tsarist war effort, 1914–1917; director of a Soviet scientific institute, 1918–1946.

Muenzenburg, Willi (1889–1940)—German socialist worker, secretary of International Socialist Youth League, 1914–1921; later, secretary of Communist Youth International; prominent in the German Communist Party and Comintern as a propagandist; died under suspicious circumstances in France after expulsion from the Communist Party in 1938 for refusing to go to Moscow during the great purges.

Nabokov, Vladimir D. (1869–1922)—a leader of the Cadets; member of the Provisional Government in 1917; member of an anti-Soviet government in the Crimea in 1919; emigrated in 1920; killed by an émigré monarchist.

Narkomprod—the Soviet acronym for the People's Commissariat of Food Supply (Narodnyi Kommisariat Prodovolstviia).

Narodniks—general name, from the 1870s on, for Russian socialists who "went to the people" (the *narod*), primarily to live among the peasants and spread socialist ideas with the hope of rousing the peasants to overthrow the monarchy and transform Russia. Unlike the Marxists, the Narodniks held that Russia could go directly to a socialism based on communal land ownership in the villages without passing through an industrial capitalist stage. In the period from 1905 to 1917 the term was also used for parties or groups which generally identified with this tradition of "peasant socialism," in particular the SRs, Trudoviks and Narodnye Sotsialisty (People's Socialists).

Natanson, Mark A. (1850–1919), Narodnik from the 1860s, joined the SR Party; internationalist in World War I; commissar in the Left SR-Bolshevik coalition government, 1917–1918.

NEP—abbreviation for the New Economic Policy, instituted by the Soviet government under Lenin in 1921; its main feature was that peasants were allowed to trade on the market and were taxed a certain amount of grain or other produce instead of having it requisitioned by the state. Grain requisitioning was the policy under "war communism" during the civil war of 1918–1920. NEP ended with the beginning of Stalin's forced collectivization and industrialization in 1929–1930.

Nevsky Prospect—main avenue of Petrograd and its fashionable shopping district.

Nicholas II (1868–1918)—last tsar of the Romanov dynasty, which had ruled Russia for three hundred years. Became tsar in 1894.

Nogin, Viktor P. (1879–1924)—a leading Bolshevik; became chairman of the Moscow Soviet in 1917; commissar of commerce and industry in the first Soviet government; resigned in November 1917; later in charge of textile industry.

October revolution—also called the Bolshevik revolution. The overthrow of the Provisional Government by the Military Revolutionary Committee of the Petrograd Soviet. This occurred on October 24–25 by the Russian calendar (November 6–7 by the Western; thus the revolution is sometimes referred to in the West as the November revolution). The seizure of power coincided with the opening of the Second All-Russia Congress of Soviets, in which the Bolsheviks and their allies, the Left SRs, had the overwhelming majority. That congress at once proclaimed that all power from then on belonged to the Soviets. Marxists refer to this as a socialist revolution because the Bolshevik Party, which dominated the new Soviet government, represented the interests of Russia's working class and soon introduced measures aimed at replacing the capitalist market economy with a nationalized socialist economy.

Octobrists—a party named for its support of Nicholas II's manifesto of October 1905 establishing the Duma. It favored the monarchy, and was the party of the large commercial, industrial, and landowning bourgeoisie; it was headed by a Moscow industrialist, Guchkov.

Okhrana—the tsarist political police, 1855–1917; short for *Okhrannoe otdelenie* (the "division for protection of public security and order" under the tsarist Department of Police).

Order No. 1—the first official administrative pronouncement of the Petrograd Soviet, authorizing the formation of soldiers' committees (which would replace officers in control over weapons) and the election of soldiers' representatives to the Soviet, abolishing humiliating forms of discipline, etc.

Osinsky, N., pseud.; real name, *Valerian V. Obolensky* (1887–1938)—joined Bolsheviks in 1907; active in party work in Moscow and elsewhere; helped write platform of the Left Communists in the spring of 1918; held responsible positions in the Soviet government, although he belonged to the Democratic Centralist, and later the Trotskyist, opposition; defendant in Stalin's major show trial of 1938; executed.

Owen, Robert (1771–1858)—successful Welsh textile manufacturer; attempted to improve conditions for workers in his mills at New Lanark after 1814; founded several cooperative communities, including one at New Harmony, Indiana; wrote a number of works on his utopian socialist ideas.

Paul, Emperor—see Peter the Great

People's Socialists (Narodnye Sotsialisty)—Russian political party, formed in 1906 from a moderate wing of the SR Party; held a political position roughly between the reformist socialists and the liberal Cadets; participated in the Dumas; merged with Trudoviks in June 1917.

Peter and Paul fortress—formidable prison-fortress in Petrograd on an island in the Neva River overlooking the Winter Palace.

Peter the Great, Ivan the Terrible, Emperor Paul—tsars of Russia. *Peter I* ("the Great") ruled from 1682 to 1725, engaged in many wars, famed for introducing Western techniques into Russia, establishing the capital of St. Petersburg, and making Russia one of the powers of Europe. *Ivan IV* ("the Terrible") ruled from 1547 to 1584, broke the power of the feudal lords (boyars) by brutal methods, and extended Russia's rule over the Tatar khanate on the Volga and Siberia. *Paul I* had a reputation as an erratic and despotic ruler; his reign, from 1796 to 1801, ended with his assassination in a palace coup.

Petrograd—the capital of Russia from 1712 to 1917; called St. Petersburg before 1914; renamed Leningrad in 1924.

Petrovsky, Grigory I. (1877–1958)—leading Bolshevik; deputy in the Duma, arrested in 1914; after October revolution, people's commissar of the interior, 1917–1919; subsequently held many important party and government posts.

Plekhanov, Georgy V. (1857–1918)—founder of Russian Marxism; active in the Narodnik movement of the 1870s; opposed the policy of terrorism aimed at liberalizing Russia by assassinating the tsar; emigrated in 1880; founded the Emancipation of Labor Group in 1883, which translated Marxist writings and propagandized in favor of the building of a mass, Social Democratic working-class movement. When the RSDLP was formed, 1899–1903, Plekhanov collaborated with Lenin, but after the 1903 congress broke with him and sided with the Mensheviks. Later he maintained an independent position, and briefly allied himself with Lenin around 1912; during World War I, he adopted an extreme patriotic and conservative stand. In the 1917 revolution, he headed a group which published the newspaper *Yedinstvo* (Unity), standing to the right even of the Mensheviks on most questions.

Podvoisky, Nikolai I. (1880–1948), joined RSDLP in 1901; active

Bolshevik from 1904 on; headed military organization of Bolsheviks in Petrograd in 1917; member of Military Revolutionary Committee; took part in seizure of Winter Palace in October revolution; held military posts in civil war and important government posts afterward.

Pood—Russian unit of dry measure, equivalent to 36.11 pounds.

Poor peasant—see Kulak.

Potresov, Aleksandr N. (1869–1934)—member of St. Petersburg Marxist workers' league in mid-1890s; leading figure in the RSDLP; sided with Mensheviks; during World War I, a defensist and leader of the Menshevik right wing; emigrated after October revolution.

Prodamet—a monopolistic "syndicate" in the Russian metal industry; abbreviation for Society for Marketing Russian Metallurgical Products.

Prodrazverstka—"surplus-grain appropriation," a central feature of "war communism"; a form of grain requisitioning introduced by the Soviet authorities in late 1918 and early 1919; under this system surplus grain or other produce was to be delivered at fixed prices by each peasant household in amounts "allocated" by the authorities; the produce was taken by the food-requisitioning detachments. The system was replaced by the tax in kind in 1921, under the New Economic Policy, or NEP.

Produgol—a monopolistic "syndicate" in the Russian coal industry; abbreviation for the Russian Society for Trade in Mineral Fuel of the Donets Basin; founded in 1906.

Progressists—a political party in the third and fourth Dumas, representing the large bourgeoisie and landowners and holding an intermediate position between the more liberal Cadets and more conservative Octobrists. Prince G. E. Lvov, premier of the first Provisional Government, was one of its founders.

Progressive Bloc—from 1915 to 1917 an alliance of most of the deputies in the Duma, who called for a "government of public confidence," which would prosecute the war more effectively and strengthen the authorities in the face of popular unrest. Only the Social Democrats and Trudoviks—on the left—and the ultra-right Black Hundred deputies did not belong to it.

Protopopov, Aleksandr D. (1866–1918)—a leader of the Progressive Bloc in the Duma in 1915–1916; subsequently broke with the liberals, ingratiated himself with the court, and was made minister of the interior in September 1916; arrested during the February revolution and later executed.

Provisional Government—a government proposed on February 28,

1917, by the Provisional Committee of the Duma. It announced its formal assumption of office on March 3, accompanied by an expression of support from the Petrograd Soviet. Tsar Nicholas had formally abdicated on March 2. The first cabinet of the Provisional Government was composed of Cadets, Octobrists, and individuals allied with those parties, the only socialist member being Kerensky. Subsequently, in May, a coalition cabinet of liberals and socialists was formed, and a second coalition cabinet in July. After the Kornilov revolt was suppressed in September, the last cabinet of the Provisional Government was formed. It was overthrown by the October revolution.

Pugachev, Yemelian I. (1726–1775)—leader of extensive peasant revolt of 1773–1774 in the Volga region during the reign of Catherine II. The revolt was crushed and Pugachev publicly executed in Moscow.

Rahya, Eino (1885–1936)—Lenin's Finnish bodyguard, who organized his clandestine move to Finland in August 1917; helped maintain contact between Lenin and the Bolshevik Central Committee between August and the October insurrection; served in the Red Army in the civil war and after; retired in 1932.

Raskolnikov, Fyodor F. (1892–1939)—Bolshevik, head of the Kronstadt party committee in 1917 and a leader of the militant Baltic sailors; played an important role in the October revolution and the civil war; assigned to diplomatic work in the 1920s and 1930s; in the summer of 1939, sought political asylum in France and wrote an open letter denouncing Stalin for the Moscow trials; died in September 1939 under mysterious circumstances.

Rasputin, Grigory Ye. (1872–1916)—peasant "holy man" from Siberia, who gained influence over the tsar's family by his supposedly miraculous powers to stop the bleeding of the hemophilic heir-apparent, Alexis. His influence in the court, and hence over the country's politics, became a public scandal; assassinated by men high in the court circles.

Razin, Stepan T. (*Stenka*) (1630?–1671)—leader of peasant and Cossack revolt of 1670–71 in the Volga region. After initial success Razin's army was routed; he was captured and executed. Celebrated in folk songs and legends.

Red Army—new army organized by the Soviet government, beginning in January 1918; by April 1918 it had only 100,000 men, compared to the tsarist army of 10 million at its height. By the end of the civil war in 1921 it numbered about 5 million.

Revolution of 1905 – 1907—began with a march of workers in St. Petersburg to the tsar's palace with a peaceful petition. The crowd was fired upon by government troops. This event, known as "Bloody Sunday" (January 9), provoked a general strike in St. Petersburg. Strikes, ferment, and peasant revolts spread throughout the country. A nationwide general strike broke out in October 1905, as a result of which Nicholas announced he would grant a constitution and elections to form a Duma. Workers began to form their own councils (Soviets) and in December the workers of Moscow (led by Bolsheviks and SRs) attempted an armed insurrection to overthrow the monarchy but were suppressed, the government resorting to punitive military expeditions and mass executions. Unrest and strikes continued through 1906 (when peasant revolts spread even farther than in 1905) and into 1907. The revolutionary movement was finally suppressed in the latter half of 1907.

Rodzianko, Mikhail V. (1859 – 1924)—large landowner and leader of the Octobrist Party; president of the fourth Duma; opposed the October revolution and supported the Whites in the civil war; emigrated to Yugoslavia in 1920.

Romanov, Alexis (1904 – 1918)—the hemophilic heir-apparent of Nicholas II and Alexandra Fyodorovna; executed with the rest of the family.

RSDLP. See Russian Social Democratic Labor Party.

RSFSR—Russian Soviet Federated Socialist Republic; the official name of Soviet Russia from 1917 to 1922, when the USSR was formed; now the name of the largest republic of the Soviet Union, the Russian Republic.

Rumiantsev, Pyotr A. (1725 – 1796)—Russian general, famous for his campaigns against the Turks in the Russo-Turkish war of 1768 – 1774.

Rural district (volost), *county* (uyezd)—The following equivalents for Russian administrative units have been used: rural district, or district, for *volost;* county for *uyezd;* territory for *krai;* region for *okrug;* and province for *gubernia.*

Russian Social Democratic Labor Party (RSDLP)—affiliate of Second International, suppressed after founding congress in 1898, reorganized at Second Congress in 1903, where Bolshevik-Menshevik split occurred. Also see notes above on CPSU, Bolsheviks, and Mensheviks.

Russo-Japanese war—1904 – 1905; resulted from rivalry between Russia and Japan in Korea and Manchuria; a series of Japanese victories ended in a peace treaty in September 1905, with Russia ceding certain territories and privileges to Japan.

Rykov, Aleksei I. (1881–1938)—a leading member of the Bolshevik Party; after Lenin's death became chairman of Sovnarkom, 1924–1930; leader of Right Opposition to Stalin, recanted in 1929; restored to minor posts; executed after third major show trial of Stalin's great purges.

Sechenov, Ivan M. (1829–1905)—Russian physiologist and scientific materialist; propounded a theory of psychology based on reflexes, similar to the one more fully elaborated by Ivan Pavlov in the twentieth century.

Second All-Russia Congress of Soviets—held in Petrograd, October 25–26, 1917. It approved the transfer of power to the Soviets, adopted the decrees on peace and land, formed a new government (the Council of People's Commissars—all Bolsheviks), and elected a new VTsIK, which had a Bolshevik majority.

Seventh (April) All-Russia Conference of the Bolshevik Party—held in Petrograd April 24–29, 1917; after sharp debate adopted Lenin's positions on the war, the Provisional Government, the prospect of socialist revolution, etc. Lenin won a similar victory over the Bolsheviks, who disagreed with his April Theses at the Petrograd city conference of the Bolshevik Party, April 14–22, 1917.

Seventh (Extraordinary) Congress of the Bolshevik Party—held in Petrograd March 6–8, 1918, to decide the disputed question of the Brest-Litovsk peace treaty; the majority voted for Lenin's position on the necessity for the Brest treaty and against the "Left Communists," who called for a revolutionary war.

Shliapnikov, Aleksandr G. (1884–1937)—Bolshevik leader, organized Russian Bureau in Petrograd during World War I; member of Executive Committee of the Petrograd Soviet in 1917; later commissar of labor and other posts in the Soviet government; leader of the Workers' Opposition group in the Bolshevik Party, 1921; expelled from party in Stalin's 1933 purge; disappeared at the height of the great purges in 1937–1938, presumably arrested and shot.

Shteinberg, I. A.—Left SR; commissar of justice in the Bolshevik–Left SR coalition government.

Shulgin, Vasily V. (1878–1965)—monarchist, emigrated from Russia after the October revolution; returned to Soviet Union at end of World War II; sent to labor camp; amnestied in 1956; Soviet press published

his articles supporting the Soviet government from a Russian nationalist standpoint, 1960–1961.

Sixth Congress of the Bolshevik Party—held in Petrograd July
26–August 3, 1917; passed a resolution calling for the proletariat to
take power, in alliance with the poor peasantry, by means of armed insurrection.

Skobelev, Mikhail D. (1843–1882)—Russian general, famous for his
role in Russia's expansion into Central Asia in the 1870s and his victories in the Russo-Turkish war of 1877–1878.

Skvortsov-Stepanov, Ivan I. (1870–1928)—joined RSDLP in 1896;
active as a Bolshevik in Moscow, 1904–1917; first Soviet commissar
of finance; held important Soviet government posts; editor of major
Soviet newspapers, 1925–1928; author of works on economics, revolutionary history; editor of Marx's *Capital* in Russian.

Smolny Institute—former school for daughters of the nobility on the
eastern edge of Petrograd; meeting place of the Petrograd Soviet and
the VTsIK, which were moved from the Tauride Palace in July 1917.

Social Democracy—the name used by the international socialist movement and many national parties in the decades before World War I,
the Russian revolution, and formation of the Comintern. The German
Social Democratic Party, for example, was the largest and most influential party in the Second International, and the Russian Social Democratic Labor Party was modeled after it in certain ways.

Sokolov, Nikolai D.—radical lawyer who defended workers in many
labor cases; as chairman of one of the first sessions of the Petrograd
Soviet, he is reported to have written down soldiers' demands as they
dictated them and codified them into Order No. 1.

Sorge, Friedrich Albert (1828–1906)—took part in the 1848–1849
revolution in Germany together with Marx and Engels; emigrated to
the United States; became a leader of the First International; active in
the American labor movement.

Soviet—originally, a representative body of the revolutionary populace
in Russia (the Russian word meaning "council"). The first Soviet of
Workers' Deputies appeared in St. Petersburg in the 1905 revolution.
When the February revolution broke out in 1917 soldiers as well as
workers formed Soviets; these were soon merged as the *Petrograd Soviet of Workers' and Soldiers' Deputies*. On the model of the Petrograd Soviet, workers' and soldiers' Soviets were established
throughout the country, followed by the formation, mainly on SR ini-

tiative, of Soviets of Peasants' Deputies in the rural areas. From the first, the Soviets began to assume administrative functions, since the workers and soldiers refused to recognize orders unless authorized by a Soviet. In the present-day USSR, the Soviets have little real influence, although the one-party government still derives its formal powers from the election of its (chosen) candidates to local, regional, and nationwide Soviets.

Sovnarkom—Council of People's Commissars (acronym for Soviet Narodnykh Kommisarov); the equivalent of the cabinet of the early Soviet government or of the present Council of Ministers in the USSR.

Spartacus (died 71 B.C.), Roman slave and gladiator, led a major slave revolt, 73–71 B.C. His name is often used by socialists as a symbol of revolt against oppression.

Spiridonova, Maria A. (1884–1941)—SR leader; shot tsarist official in charge of suppressing a peasant revolt during the 1905–1907 revolution; spent many years at hard labor; emerged as a leader of the Left SRs in 1917; after the Left SR revolt of July 1918, was arrested; later amnestied, quit politics; arrested again during Stalin's purges; died in the camps.

SR—Socialist Revolutionary, member of the Socialist Revolutionary Party, founded in 1902, from among several Narodnik groups. The party oriented mainly toward the peasants rather than the workers, and had a strong following among radical intellectuals. It was the largest party in Russia in 1917 and, together with the Mensheviks, was the main influence in the Soviets until September 1917. During 1917 distinct Right and Left wings developed. The *Left SRs* constituted themselves a separate party in November 1917 and joined the Bolsheviks in a coalition Soviet government until March 1918, when they withdrew in opposition to the Brest treaty. In July 1918 the Left SRs began an armed revolt against the Bolshevik-led Soviet government and were suppressed.

SR-Maximalists—extreme left-wing group that split from the SRs in 1905 and held views close to anarchism.

Stanitsas—the large, distinctively organized villages of the Cossacks.

Stavka—the General Headquarters of the Russian army in World War I, located in Mogilev in west-central Russia.

Steklov, Yuri M. (1873–1941)—Bolshevik until February 1917, when he became a defensist; later held prominent posts in the Soviet government; wrote on history of socialism; victim of Stalin's purges of the late 1930s.

Stolypin, Pyotr A. (1862–1911)—tsarist official, made premier in 1906; presided over suppression of revolutionary movement; introduced agrarian reforms aimed at encouraging the growth of a small prosperous layer of peasant farmers who would be loyal to the government; assassinated by a police agent posing as an SR terrorist.

Stürmer, Boris V. (1848–1917)—premier of Russia for most of 1916, forced to resign in November after being denounced in the Duma as pro-German.

Sukhanov, Nikolai N. (1882–1940)—author of the detailed "Notes on the 1917 Revolution"; although a Menshevik, he supported the October revolution; under Stalin in 1931 he was arrested and tried with other Mensheviks on fabricated charges; died in prison or a labor camp.

Sukharevka—large marketplace in Moscow.

Surplus-grain appropriation—see prodrazvertska.

Suvorov, Aleksandr V. (1729–1800)—Russian general, famous for his campaigns against the Turks, the Poles, and Napoleon's armies.

Sverdlov, Yakov M. (1885–1919)—active in the underground Bolshevik Party from 1902, elected to the Central Committee, of which he became a secretary, in 1917; played a central role in the October revolution and became chairman of the Central Executive Committee of the Soviets (hence, titular head of state) in 1918.

Tauride Palace—palace in Petrograd (originally built by Catherine II for Count Potemkin, one of her favored officials); the Duma met there, as did the Petrograd Soviet in the first few months after the February revolution.

Teodorovich, Ivan A. (1875–1937)—member of RSDLP from 1902; Bolshevik; first commissar of food supply, but resigned in December 1917; fought on the Bolshevik side in the civil war, 1919–1920; held posts in the commissariat of agriculture, 1920–1928; general secretary of the Peasant International, 1928–1930.

Tereshchenko, Mikhail I. (1886–1956)—Cadet leader, member of Provisional Government; minister of finance, March–May; minister of foreign affairs, May–October; arrested during October revolution; escaped to France; helped organize anti-Soviet side in civil war, 1918–1920; active as a financier in France thereafter.

Third Congress of the RSDLP—held in London April 12–27 (Old Style), 1905; its resolutions, drafted by Lenin, defined the party's attitude toward the peasant movement, the liberals, and the possibility of Social Democratic participation in a revolutionary government, a "dictatorship of the proletariat and peasantry." Lenin's *Two Tactics of Social Democracy in the Democratic Revolution* (written June–July 1905) spelled out these positions in more detail and criticized the Menshevik tactics of compromise and collaboration with the liberals.

Tolstoy, Leo N. (1828–1910)—the great Russian novelist and religious and philosophical writer. Expounded his theory of the relation between leaders and masses in the novel *War and Peace.*

"To the Citizens of Russia!"—proclamation written by Lenin and issued on the morning of October 25, 1917, shortly before the last stronghold of the Provisional Government was taken. It announced that power was transferred to the Soviets and the aims for which this was done. (See Lenin, CW, 26:236; see frontispiece for Russian text.)

Triple Alliance—the diplomatic bloc of Germany, Austria-Hungary, and Italy, in the years before World War I; opposed to the Entente, or Triple Entente, of England, France, and Russia. The term was still used for Germany and its allies even though Italy left the Triple Alliance in 1915.

Trotsky, Leon D. (1879–1940)—a leading figure in the RSDLP and later in the Communist movement; chairman of the St. Petersburg Soviet in 1905; held a position apart from both Bolsheviks and Mensheviks, 1904–1917; joined the Bolsheviks in 1917 and played a key role in the October revolution; commissar of war in the Soviet government, 1918–1925; leader of the Left Opposition in the Soviet Communist Party in the mid-1920s; expelled from the USSR by Stalin in 1929; became chief opponent of Stalinism in the international Communist movement; founded the Fourth International, 1938; assassinated by a Stalinist agent in Mexico.

Trudoviks—Russian political party, second largest grouping in the first Duma (1906), identifying with the Narodnik tradition and favoring land distribution on a labor standard (*trudovaia norma;* whence the name *trudovik*); enjoyed support among the peasants and radical urban middle class. In the Duma the Trudoviks sided at first with the Cadets, later voted with the Social Democrats on many issues, but did not consider themselves socialists. During World War I, they were mostly defensist; Kerensky was a Trudovik leader in the Duma, 1912–17, before joining the SRs.

Tsereteli, Irakly G. (1882–1959)—Menshevik; member of Executive Committee of Petrograd Soviet; minister of posts and telegraph in the first coalition cabinet of the Provisional Government, May–July 1917; in Georgian Menshevik government, 1918; emigrated in 1919.

Tsiurupa, Aleksandr V. (1870–1928)—joined RSDLP in 1898; member of Bolshevik Central Committee from 1923; held important government posts from 1922.

Twentieth and Twenty-Second congresses of the CPSU—held respectively February 14–25, 1956, and October 17–31, 1961. These were the high points of "de-Stalinization" under Nikita Khrushchev, first secretary of the party. Khrushchev gave his famous "secret speech" denouncing some of Stalin's crimes at the Twentieth Congress. This was followed by a resolution condemning many of the repressive practices common in the Stalin era. At the Twenty-Second Congress speeches criticizing Stalin were made publicly, Stalin's body was removed from the Lenin mausoleum, and the congress was followed by a new series of investigations and revelations about the crimes of the Stalin era. After the ouster of Khrushchev in October 1964, de-Stalinization was greatly moderated and, under Brezhnev, materials once again praising Stalin have been allowed publication in the official Soviet press.

the 242 mandates—see Model Peasant Mandate on the Land.

Two Tactics, etc.—see Third Congress.

Ustrialov, N. V.—professor who held a leading post in one of the anti-Bolshevik governments during the 1918–1920 civil war; afterward an emigre and leading spokesman of the Changing Landmarks (Smena Vekh) group, which in 1921 and after urged Russian nationalists and intellectuals to work with the Soviet regime in the belief that it was evolving back toward capitalism and a conventional social order. Lenin said of Ustrialov, "Such candid enemies are useful." For Lenin's comments on Ustrialov and the trend he represented see CW, 33:285–87.

Verkhovsky, Aleksandr I. (1886–1938)—military commander of Moscow in August 1917; minister of war August–October 1917; after opposing the Soviet government, he joined the Red Army in 1919; held prominent posts in the Soviet military.

Verst—Russian unit of distance equivalent to 0.6629 miles.

Vesenkha—Supreme Council of the National Economy (acronym formed from the initials VSNKh; full Russian title, Vysshii Soviet Narodnogo Khoziaistva), established December 5, 1917, to organize the economy and finances and to direct the work of all economic agencies. Local *sovnarkhozy* (councils of the national economy; *soviety narodnogo khoziaistva*) were established to manage local economic affairs in coordination with the central Vesenkha.

Vinokurov, Aleksandr N. (1869–1944)—active in the Russian Social Democratic movement from 1893; commissar for social security, 1918–1921; president of Soviet Supreme Court, 1924–1938; then worked in public health.

Volga famine—a severe famine in 1921–1922 resulting from drought in 1920 and 1921 on top of civil war; affected some 35 million people in the Volga region and southern Ukraine. There were extensive international relief efforts; nevertheless an estimated 5 million died.

Volodarsky, V. (1891–1918)—active in the RSDLP, 1905–1913; internationalist during World War I and member of the Socialist Party in the United States; joined the Bolsheviks in 1917; one of the leading revolutionary orators in 1917–1918; a leader of the Petrograd Bolsheviks and commissar in the Soviet government; assassinated by SRs on June 20, 1918.

Volunteer Army—see Denikin.

VTsIK—abbreviation for All-Russia Central Executive Committee (Vserossiiskii Tsentralnyi Ispolnitelnyi Komitet) of the Soviets; also, TsIK, or Central Executive Committee, for short. In the midst of the mass demonstrations of February 1917, which brought the fall of the monarchy, a group of moderate socialist members of the Duma and other prominent socialist figures constituted themselves the Executive Committee of the Petrograd Soviet. The Petrograd Executive Committee, which included many of the national leaders of the Menshevik and SR parties and which had the prestige of the capital city's Soviet behind it, soon asserted nationwide authority. At an all-Russia conference of Soviets in March a dozen or so provincial members were added, and the Executive Committee's nationwide authority increased. These leaders were elected, along with many others, to become the first official VTsIK at the First All-Russia Congress of Soviets in June 1917. The VTsIK was dominated by the Mensheviks and SRs until October, when the Second All-Russia Congress of

Soviets elected a new VTsIK, with the Bolsheviks in the majority.
War communism—the policy followed by the Soviet government during the civil war, 1918–1920, notably a ban on private trade, forcible requisitioning of grain, and extreme centralization of economic institutions and activities.

Weitling, Wilhelm (1808–1871)—early leader of German workers; a tailor by trade; advocate of egalitarian communism; organized first German communist groups.

Weydemeyer, Joseph (1818–1866)—active in the German and American labor movements, took part in the 1848–49 revolution in Germany together with Marx and Engels; emigrated to the United States after its defeat; active with Sorge in the American labor movement.

Winter Palace—the tsar's official residence in Petrograd; Provisional Government established itself there in July 1917.

Witte cabinet—government formed in October 1905 by the tsarist official Count Sergei Yu. Witte (1849–1915), whose professed aim was a constitutional system; failed to obtain support from right or left; resigned as premier in May 1906; remained in the tsarist government as a member of the State Council.

Yakubovich, Mikhail P. (1891–)—Bolshevik before World War I, then a Menshevik; after the October revolution, favored collaboration with Bolsheviks; left Mensheviks in 1920; held responsible posts in Soviet government; arrested in 1930 and tried in 1931 on fabricated charges; survived Stalin's prisons and camps; released in 1953; partly rehabilitated in 1956; has written extensively since then about his experiences, but official Soviet press denies him publication; in 1968 Soviet security police confiscated a number of his manuscripts.

Yermolov, Aleksei P. (1772–1861)—Russian general prominent in the Napoleonic wars; from 1816 to 1827, in command of the Russian campaigns to subjugate the mountain tribes of the Caucasus.

Zhordania, Noah N. (1864–1953)—a leading Menshevik; defensist during World War I; head of the Menshevik government in Georgia, 1918–1920; emigrated to France, 1921.

Zinoviev, Grigory Ye. (1883–1936)—Bolshevik leader; member of the party's Central Committee, 1907–1927; Lenin's closest associate in exile, 1907–1917; returned to Russia with Lenin in April 1917; opposed Lenin's call for armed insurrection but took up leading work in the Soviet government after October; head of the party's Petrograd organization, 1918–1926; chairman of Communist International,

1919–1926; a leader of the United Left Opposition, 1926–1927; expelled from party but readmitted in 1928; expelled again in 1932; arrested in 1934; tried on fabricated charges in August 1936 in the first of Stalin's major show trials; executed.

Index